SOUTHAMPTON
MARITIME CITY
OCEAN LINERS TO CRUISE SHIPS

SOUTHAMPTON
MARITIME CITY
OCEAN LINERS TO CRUISE SHIPS
MIKE ROUSSEL

DB
PUBLISHING

First published in Great Britain in 2010 by The Derby Books Publishing Company Limited, 3 The Parker Centre, Derby, DE21 4SZ.

ISBN 978-1-85983-807-5
Printed and bound DZS Grafik, Slovenia.

CONTENTS

ACKNOWLEDGEMENTS

To complete this book I am indebted to all who gave me their support, advice and their time, often when under time pressures themselves to be interviewed and to share some of the experiences of their life, work and love of ships.

It has been a great privilege to meet and talk to those who are actively involved in the shipping world today. I am deeply indebted to Stephen Payne OBE, Senior Naval Architect for the Carnival Corporation and designer of *Queen Mary 2,* and to Commodore Ron Warwick OBE, who was the first master of *Queen Mary 2,* for their valuable advice and support of my project.

I am also especially grateful to Douglas Ward, author of the Berlitz *Complete Guide to Cruising and Cruise Ships,* whom I managed to interview in one of the short periods of time he spends ashore.

My sincere thanks go to ABP Southampton Port Director Doug Morrison and to Ron Hancock, Beth Evans and Lorraine Nottley for their support and contribution to this book.

My special thanks to Captain Panagiotis Skylogiannis, master of *Celebrity Eclipse,* whom I met and interviewed at the *Celebrity Eclipse* naming day in Southampton.

I am especially grateful to all who were interviewed and gave me permission to use some of their own material for my book. These include Bill O'Brien, Barbara Pedan, John Stamp, Gordon Brown, John Fahy, Geoffrey Le Marquand, David Main, Jean Edwards, Ann and Chris Wright, Roy White, Edwin Praine, Ann and Pat Royl, Jim Taylor, John Merry, Gus Shanahan, Harold Lloyd, Len Hillier, Leon Hanson-Vaux BEM, Sam Warwick, Cyril Duro, George Young, Roger Joyce, Mr MacPhial, Mr and Mrs Pegden and John Minto. Sadly John Minto passed away this year, and I feel very privileged to have met him and to have shared some of the many interesting moments from his experiences at sea, as well as his time as Mayor of Southampton.

My sincere thanks also to Bill Rife, who lives in Washington DC, for introducing me to George Young and to the story of Jimmy 'Bud' Thomas, an American serviceman who sailed from Scotland on the *Warwick Castle* as part of Operation Torch for the invasion of North Africa in 1942.

My special thanks go to all who have loaned me photographs from their collections. They include many of my close friends and colleagues, especially Richard de Jong, Mick Lindsay, Bert Moody, Jim Brown, John Humphreys, Nikki Goff, Graham Alton, Mary Parker and the 'Cooper Girls', Beryl Trewartha, Hazel Guy and Joan Turner, daughters of Roy Cooper.

I would like thank all whom I have met through our respective websites around the world, though not in person, and especial thanks to Michael Pocock, who lives in Dallas, Texas. Michael is a maritime historian and webmaster for www.maritimequest.com, a comprehensive research resource for those interested in ships and shipping, past and present. My own website www.PortsandShips.com has further information that links to the published books for readers to access.

My thanks also go to all those passengers who gave accounts of their experiences of voyages on the famous liners of the past and the cruise ships of today. They include Mavis Carter, Margaret and Dr John Dines, Christine Young, Jim and Marion Brown, John Harding, Ron and Beryl Williams, John and Fay Bratcher, Keith and Julie Mullard, and Anne Royl.

I am particularly indebted to maritime author Bert Moody for his encouragement and advice, and for checking the acuuracy of my work, and especially to author Jim Brown, who has consistently encouraged and supported my work. During a recent cruise on the *Queen Victoria* Jim talked to Amanda Reid, Entertainments Director, on my behalf.

Finally I am eternally grateful to my wife, Kay, for her constant encouragement, especially in the past months when her loving support and care has seen me through to the completion of this book.

FOREWORD

by Stephen M. Payne OBE RDI MNM HDSc FREng FRINA HFIED BSc(Eng)Hons CEng

Southampton is a true Maritime City. From its shores countless ships have arrived and departed. The *Mayflower* set sail from here in 1620 with the Pilgrim Fathers, stopping off en route at Plymouth. At the end of her career in 1856 Brunel's *Great Western*, the first of his mighty ships, languished in the port before being sold for demolition on the Thames. It was from Southampton that *Titanic* set sail on her maiden voyage on 10 April 1912 from the White Star Dock on her fateful appointment with destiny. In more recent times the port has hosted Cunard *Queens* and many other notable liners, many of which are sadly now just distant memories. Their place has been taken by the new breed of cruise ships – floating hotels with every convenience and fully optimised for the role of playgrounds for the maritime masses.

For his second book Mike Roussel reviews the history of Southampton and its maritime heritage. Notable shipping lines and their ships are described and placed in perspective with anecdotes and personal reminisces. The importance of the port in supporting oceanic transport in both ocean liner and the leisure cruising trades is fully explored.

Now pack your bags and head down to the Ocean Terminal! The whistle has sounded and your ship is about to leave port. Before you, a magnificent voyage beckons. As you'll need something to read as you lounge in a deck chair on the sun deck sipping an evening cocktail, why not take a companion with you? You could do no better than take a copy of Mike's book with you. Before long you'll drift back to the halcyon days of ocean travel. Let go forward and aft! We're off...

Stephen M. Payne
2 June 2010
Immediate Past President, The Royal Institution of Naval Architects
Designer, Cunard Line *Queen Mary 2*

INTRODUCTION

Migration to the New World

From the late 16th and into the 17th century migration to the New World had started, and it was in August 1620 that the Pilgrim Fathers left Southampton in the *Mayflower* and *Speedwell* to sail to New England. However, the *Speedwell* was leaking badly and they called in at Plymouth. It was just the *Mayflower* that finally set sail for New England, and when they eventually landed the Plymouth Colony was set up, known today as Plymouth, Massachusetts. Increasing numbers of Europeans started to emigrate to North America and Canada on sailing ships for long transatlantic voyages that were very crowded and uncomfortable.

Up until the early 19th century many immigrants would travel on the ocean-going sailing ships, but when the steamships started transatlantic crossings in the early 1830s there was a greater interest by the shipping lines in carrying mail and passengers because they could maintain a regular schedule and with a new 'steerage class' that increased profits.

There was a gradual changeover from sail to steam, but it was not the end of the sailing ships for carrying immigrants, especially when the gold rush started, first in California in 1849, then Australia in 1851 and South Africa in 1886. Some of the sailing ships that took the immigrants to the California gold rush had to go around Cape Horn and were thought to be the 'most worthless' vessels, purchased just to get to San Francisco harbour on a one-way trip. The ships were then abandoned because they would not survive a journey back to Europe.

As well as the passenger transatlantic crossings it is said that P&O 'invented cruising' when they offered their first pleasure cruise to the Mediterranean in 1844. By the 1850s and 1860s the shipping companies wanted to encourage more passengers, and to do that they started to look at better designs for a more luxurious environment, a sort of 'home from home'. This started to include more deck space for walking, deck games, various entertainment activities and even electric lights. Potential passengers were further encouraged by an article in the *British Medical Journal* of 1880 on the health benefits of cruising with the 'fresh sea air' as having 'curative qualities'.

Once the steamships started transporting immigrants, a 'steerage class' developed in which the passengers looked after themselves in the steerage area of the ship. However, the shipping companies gradually realised that the numbers of immigrants they carried were good for their profits and began providing food and better accommodation for them. Interestingly, the steerage class on the White Star 'Olympic Class' was thought to be as good as first class on some other ships.

It was at the end of the 19th and early 20th century that the liners became increasingly luxurious, with accommodation provided for the very wealthy seen as 'floating hotels' or 'floating palaces' in designs reminiscent of famous hotels, palaces and country houses. Once the Cunard Line's *Mauritania* and *Lusitania* arrived, the tradition of dressing for dinner was initiated and is still expected by many passengers today who sail on Cunard ships.

World War One was a disaster for the German shipping companies, which had taken the lead in ship design only to lose some of their famous liners to Britain and America in war reparations. The 1920s and 30s were the 'Golden Years' of sea travel, however, with the rich and famous, including Hollywood film stars, jazz groups and big bands, along with American tourists wanting to visit Europe for their vacations, making the ocean liners of the time so famous.

By the time World War Two came along the famous ocean liners were once more requisitioned for war service. After the war the European shipping lines transported war refugees to America and Canada and returned to Europe with tourists and business travellers. At that time America woke up to the fact that they were not gaining the profits of transatlantic travel and started building their own ocean liners. However, their first thoughts regarding design were for vessels that could be used as troop transporters in time of war.

It was the 1950s and 60s, along with the arrival of the jet airliner, that spelt disaster for ocean liner transatlantic passenger traffic. Though a number of shipping lines dropped out of the passenger business, others saw the opportunity to develop the cruise industry and cruises to the Greek Islands in the 1950s became popular. By the 1960s Ted Arison introduced cruises from Florida to the Caribbean that became very popular with the many wealthy Americans living in Florida.

The 1970s brought the era of the 'fun ships', with relaxing cruises and on-board entertainment. The popularity of the 1977 TV series *Love Boat* captured the interest of many people who had never sailed before and had thought that cruises were for the rich and famous. Offers of cheaper cruises encouraged many more people, including those that had watched *Love Boat*, to sample a cruise for themselves, rather than watching it on TV.

By 1999 the few mega-ships sailing at the time were just over 100,000 GT (Gross Tonnage), but the majority of cruise ships were still around 80,000 GT or even less.

Today there are mega-cruise ships everywhere and the vast size of them means that cruise passengers can spend almost a whole week exploring the ship, finding something new to do every day, and that is before exploring the ports of call; however, although there is a large uptake for the mega-cruise ships, there are still some people who prefer the smaller ships, and the choice is there.

Perhaps one of the most significant things about cruising in the 21st century is that it is a continual expansion of bigger and better offers and cruise choices. There has been a gradual change from the traditional two sittings for dinner, where passengers would sit at the same table, have the same waiters and same guests at their table, to the choice of eating wherever they want, at the time they want and with whom they want; however, there are still passengers who prefer to maintain the tradition of dressing for dinner and sitting at the same table with the same guests, and there are the famous traditional shipping lines, such as Cunard, who offer this facility.

There has also been a change over time in ships' entertainment. Once entertainment teams would provide all the entertainment, but today professional companies provide the shows, the musicians, variety performers and often a range of other activities, including creative pursuits, lectures and music concerts to delight the passengers.

There are also themed cruises for passengers who have a particular interest or hobby. One example is the Fred. Olsen Lines, whose Arts Club has activities that include painting, music, dance, photography, antiques and even gardening. They have a Civilization programme for cruises to historic locations and Flagship Golf, wherby golf enthusiasts have the opportunity to get advice from PGA professionals and to play on famous golf courses near the ports of call.

Some passengers prefer a quiet, refined type of holiday, while others prefer the 'Las Vegas glitzy-glamour' type of cruise. It is up to the shipping companies to plan, build, introduce and advertise ships that meet the needs of a wide range of passengers. The variety of choice today has encouraged more people to cruise now than at any time in the history of cruising. However, once you have paid for your cruise today there are always extras you will have to pay when on board. These can include a daily charge for tips for the crew taken from your credit card, medical expenses for treatment on board, charges for drinks and so on.

On board the cruise ships of today there are many more activities for families. For example, on the Royal Caribbean International mega-cruise ships there are rock-climbing walls, ice-skating rinks, golf areas, extensive pool sections, children's clubs, teens' clubs and even older teens' clubs. There are also cruise passengers who would prefer not to take part in the family-style cruises and opt for the 'Adult Only' cruise that is offered by some cruise lines, especially P&O Cruises.

This book looks first at the development of steamships from the early 19th century to the famous ocean liners of the Golden Years of the 1930s. It traces the start of World War Two, when passenger vessels were requisitioned for war service and many were sunk, causing replacement ships to be built after the war, and then examines in detail the decline in the use of the ocean liners through the introduction of jet air travel and the birth of the cruise 'fun ships' from the 1950s onwards. There are stories and anecdotes from by the crew and passengers who sailed on these ocean liners in the 1950s and 1960s. Moving into the 21st century, the book explores the cruise ships of today and their design and development. It features the life of the Port of Southampton and the cruise ships that visit the four cruise terminals. The final chapter looks at 2010, a year that will be memorable for the Port of Southampton, with the naming ceremonies of the new vessels P&O *Azura* and Celebrity Cruises' *Celebrity Eclipse* in April 2010, and of the new Cunard *Queen Elizabeth 2* in October 2010.

CHAPTER 1
STEAM POWER VERSUS WIND POWER

Setting the Scene

It was in the late 17th century and early 18th century that steam power began to be used as a method of pumping water from coal mines. It was not long before steam power was recognised as an alternative for wind power, and with it came the idea of using steam power to propel a boat. This was during the Georgian period, which ran from 1714–1830 and included the American War of Independence from 1757–83, the Industrial Revolution that began at the end of the 18th century and continued into the 19th century, and the Napoleonic Wars of 1803–15. The Regency period of 1811–20 saw the Prince of Wales became Prince Regent during the period of his father's insanity. On the death of George III on 29 January 1820 the Prince Regent became George IV, until his death in 1830. The Regency Period was notable for its elegance and achievements in the fine arts and architecture.

What was it like in Southampton during the Georgian and Regency Eras?

From the 16th century, trade with Italy had declined and died out, especially the wool trade, leaving most of the seagoing trade as largely coastal, bringing in cargoes such as coal and timber, which was then transported inland by cart. This continued until Southampton became more popular from 1750, when Frederick, Prince of Wales went bathing in the sea and returned again the following year because he thought the water was 'healthy and invigorating'. He died a year later, possibly as a result of a cricket ball hitting him during a game – not of bathing in the Southampton sea water!

From then on the town became a fashionable spa resort, although not as a recognised beach because it was very muddy. The Assembly Rooms were built and seawater baths constructed that filled with the tides, allowing frequent bathing during the daytime. A natural spring of chalybeate water had also been discovered north of the town walls and people, believing it could cure all ills, would visit it to 'take the waters'. The activities and amusement for people at that time were dining, dancing and theatre-going, and the town got its first theatre in French Street in 1766.

However, when the Prince of Wales, later to become the Prince Regent and then King George IV, visited Brighton in 1783 he preferred it to Southampton and from then on it became his first choice. All the royalty 'followers', the rich gentry, then also made Brighton their 'place' to visit. Southampton was no longer the number one seaside resort, and by 1820 sea bathing had died out.

Up until the 1790s the only communication with the east bank of the River Itchen was by fishing boats that ferried people across the river to the 'Itchen Ferry' village. Some famous names used the Itchen Ferry, including Samuel Pepys in 1662 and King Charles II in 1669. Jane Austen was known to have used the ferry on one of her visits to Southampton before moving to the town in 1806. One problem for the ferry passengers was the cold, and there is a story of a lady who died after she caught a chill while waiting for a ferry. This brought about the building of the Cross House for people to shelter in while waiting for the ferry.

One major improvement at the time was the building of the wooden Northam Bridge across the River Itchen by the Northam Bridge Company in 1799. With the completion of both the Northam Bridge and the Bursledon Bridge across the River Hamble there was a direct road link from Southampton to Portsmouth. During this period the vessels entering and leaving Southampton were sailing ships carrying bulky cargoes, such as coal, bound for Winchester along the River Itchen. The coal would be unloaded on the Northam Quay and then transported by barge to Winchester.

In the early 19th century Southampton was still surrounded by its mediaeval walls and there were areas outside the walls where people could walk along the water's edge. As the town was surrounded on three sides, to the west, the east and the south, there would have been plenty of fresh air blowing off the water and at times it could be quite rough when gales were blowing. This was well noted by the nicknames given to some of the towers in the west wall. At the corner of northern and western wall was the Arundel Tower, known as 'Windwhistle Tower' by the sentries who manned it because of the fresh breezes that came off West Bay. The next tower along the west wall was the Prince Edward Tower, which the sentries had called 'Catchcold Tower'.

Jane Austen in Southampton

Jane Austen lived with her parents in Bath, but when her father died the family and their companion, Martha Lloyd, moved to Southampton, where her brother Frank was a naval captain. However, the rent was expensive in their lodgings and after a few months they moved into a house in Castle Square. Today there is a plaque on the wall of the Bosun's Locker public house indicating where it is thought the house stood. The house suited them well as it was large and had a garden that spread down to the town walls. Jane would look over the waters of West Bay towards the trees of the New Forest.

While living in Southampton the family would travel by boat along the River Itchen and view the ships being built at Northam and also the ruins of Netley Abbey. They would have also sailed up the Beaulieu River to Beaulieu Abbey, passing the ships being built at Buckler's Hard.

During the spa period there were many visitors to the town and two coaching inns, the Dolphin and the Star, had approximately 10–12 coaches leaving Southampton for London each day. Jane Austen and her sister Cassandra attended dances in the Dolphin Hotel. In 1809 the family moved to live in a house on the Chawton Estate that belonged to her brother Edward. Jane lived there until she died in 1817.

Southampton was a major military port during the Napoleonic Wars (1803–15) when Jane and her family lived there. This was also the time of the Battle of Trafalgar in 1805, when Nelson was struck in the shoulder by a musket ball and died on the *Victory*. This period was not very helpful to the sea-going trade because of press-gangs that roamed the port looking for men aged between the ages of 15 and 55 who were experienced seamen to serve on the Royal Navy ships. This reduced the number of seamen available to sail on merchant vessels. The war did help the shipbuilding industry, however, which built ships for the Royal Navy. There were also large numbers of soldiers passing through Southampton who spent their money in the town prior to embarkation on ships. This was a welcome increase in business for the traders and inns.

The Wool House, built in the late 14th century as a wool store for the Cistercian Monks of Beaulieu Abbey, was used as a prison to house French prisoners of war during the Napoleonic War. The names of the inmates can be seen carved in the beams.

The Development of Steam Power to Propel a Boat

In the early 18th century Thomas Newcomen, who was a blacksmith, developed an effective steam pump system known as the 'Newcomen Engine', but it was James Watt who created the steam engine as we know it today. From then on various ideas and proposals for steam power to propel ships started to gather momentum, and later in the 18th century the first practical paddle steamer was invented by the Marquis Claude de Jouffroy. However, the first attempts in 1778 were not successful, but by persevering with his ideas his second boat design was more successful.

On the second boat an improved steam engine, possibly influenced by the improvements in steam engine design by James Watt, was used to drive two side-paddle wheels. This culminated in the first successful trials using steam propulsion on a ship. However, the Marquis was more successful with the *Pyroscaphe,* which was seen on 15 July 1783 'puffing' along the River Saône, France, despite its steam engine only being able to generate steam for 15 minutes of sailing. However, the fact that the vessel was sailing upstream made it the very first vessel to sail against a current under steam power.

Although France had produced the first steamboat, just two years later, in 1785, John Fitch had begun to design his first steamboat. On 22 August 1787 he trialled his 45ft (13.7m) steamship on the River Delaware, which was driven by side paddles. Two years later he built a 60ft (18.3m) steamship, and on 12 October 30 passengers and cargo were transported between Philadelphia and Burlington, New Jersey, a distance of 20 miles. A regular public service commenced for a time, with the steamboat being propelled by paddles at the stern of the vessel.

At that time there was battle between James Rumsey and John Fitch for the application to patent their different steam propulsion designs. John Fitch's steamboat propulsion was by paddles, but James Rumsey's invention focused on a water-jet steamboat, where the jet of water was pumped out at the stern of the vessel, thus propelling it forward along the River Potomac. In 1788 James Rumsey visited London and was responsible for building the *Columbian Maid,* which, during trials in 1792 at Greenwich, was noted as being propelled along 'against the tide'. Sadly James Rumsey died of a stroke in London on 21 December 1792, but it was not the end of the trials, which continued on the Thames in February 1793. It was again noted that the ship 'sailed against wind and tide at three miles per hour.'

In 1788, the same year that James Rumsey arrived in London, William Symington developed a marine steam engine that powered a 'pleasure boat' at five miles per hour on its first trial across a lake in Dalswinton, Dumfries, Scotland. Symington continued with another vessel, which in 1789 achieved a speed of seven miles per hour. In 1801 he built the first steam tugboat, the *Charlotte Dundas,* which in her trials in 1802 towed two barges along the Forth-Clyde Canal to Port Dundas, a distance of 19.5 miles in six hours. This was in spite of sailing against a strong headwind.

When John Fitch died in 1798 Robert Fulton came to prominence. He was a man who had a shrewd business sense and was able to sell the benefits of steam navigation, something that Fitch had been unable to do. Robert Fulton experimented with designing torpedoes and built the first submarine, *Nautilus,* which was launched in 1800 in Rouen. Little interest was shown in the submarine by France or Great Britain at the time, so he turned to designing and experimenting with steamboats. His first design for an experimental steam-driven boat sank after a storm, but his second attempt, using a stronger hull, was more successful and the vessel sailed up and down the River Seine in August 1803 at three miles per hour. In 7 August 1807 Robert Fulton built the *Clermont*, 150ft (46m) long, which was powered by a Boulton and Watt steam engine. The *Clermont* sailed from New York City to Albany, a journey of 150 miles, in 32 hours, averaging about five miles per hour. At this time the steamboat had not been thought of for sailing the oceans, and the intention had been for them to travel up and down rivers and canals. They were also to be used in helping ocean-going sailing ships to berth when there was little wind to bring them alongside a jetty.

The *Comet*, built by Henry Bell, was successfully used on the River Clyde in 1812, steaming from Greenock to Glasgow, a distance of 20 miles, in 3.5 hours. The *Comet* was the first regular steamboat service in Europe and signalled the start of passenger travel to ports around Great Britain. At this time the other European countries started to develop their own steamships.

By the early 19th century the Americans had regular sailing-packets of 300–500 tons, which were keeping a regular service between New York and Liverpool for passengers and cargo. The Black Ball Line had a scheduled service from 1817, which passengers wishing to cross the North Atlantic knew would sail on time and approximately 18–23 days later deliver them to their destination, depending on the weather conditions for the crossing. At the time, apart from the wealthier passengers, who could use a cabin or stateroom at the stern, passengers had to find their own space and own food. For many emigrants leaving Europe to sail to America to start a new life, conditions on board were often not very comfortable.

In 1829 the first steamship, a 22-ton paddle steamer named *Emerald*, was built by a Southampton shipbuilder, John Rubie, for the Southampton to Hythe service. In 1833, the same year as the Duchess of Kent and her daughter Princess Victoria opened the Royal Pier, the second paddle steamer, built by Alexander Cunningham, was aptly named *Princess Victoria*. The vessel was built for the Cowes Line, the forerunner of the Isle of Wight Royal Mail Steamships Company, to run the Southampton to Isle of Wight service.

The Beginning of Transatlantic Steamship Travel

The first steamship crossing of the Atlantic was undertaken by the *Savannah* in 1819. The *Savannah* sailed from Savannah, Georgia, for Liverpool on 24 May 1819, arriving on 20 June, but it was not entirely a complete steam engine crossing as it was also a fully-rigged sailing ship. The vessel had side-paddle wheels and the engines were used for just 85 hours along with the sails. At the time the ships were built for sail with the auxiliary engines. This was to eventually change to ships being built for the use of steam engines with an auxiliary sail.

In 1833 the Canadian steamship *Royal William* sailed the Atlantic from Quebec to London entirely under steam, using her steam engine for the whole crossing. However, her engines had to be shut down every fourth day for descaling, which took about 24 hours each time. Samuel Cunard, at the time a successful businessman in Nova Scotia, had shares in the *Royal William,* and he recognised the potential of steam navigation and became more involved in its future development.

The Peninsular & Oriental Steam Navigation Company

Brodie McGhie Willcox and Arthur Anderson are said to be the founders of P&O and had met early on in the 19th century, eventually becoming partners in 1822. They began with a small fleet of sailing ships for trade between England and Spain and Portugal. They worked hard to build the trade, but the return cargo was not easy to build at the time. In 1834 Willcox and Anderson issued a prospectus for a service to Spain and Portugal under the proposed company name of the Peninsular Steam Navigation Company, and they chartered their first steamship, the 206-ton paddle

Royal William (364 GT), built in Quebec and launched in 1831. She was wrecked off Long Island in 1821. (Mick Lindsay Collection)

William Fawcett (206 GT, 60 hp), built in 1828 to carry mail across the Irish Sea. She was broken up in 1845. (Mick Lindsay Collection)

steamer *William Fawcett,* from the Dublin & London Steam Packet Company. Captain Richard Bourne, a Dublin shipowner and the owner of the *William Fawcett,* joined them and in 1835 helped start a regular steamship service to the Iberian Peninsula.

During the next two years the service was not as regular as the founders had hoped, but by 1837 the company was advertising a fleet of seven ships, including the *Don Juan* and *Tagus,* which were specially designed and built with engines and auxiliary sail. This is accepted as the year that the Peninsular & Steam Navigation Company was founded. On 22 August 1837 the British government awarded them the contract to carry the mail to the Iberian Peninsula, sailing from Falmouth to the ports of Vigo, Oporto, Lisbon, Cadiz and Gibraltar. The 800-ton *Don Juan* was the first vessel to open the Iberian Peninsula service, but it was wrecked in thick fog just after it had left Gibraltar on the return journey.

In 1840 the company was awarded the mail contract for Britain's Empire in the East, and it was then that 'Oriental' was added to the company name to create the Peninsular & Oriental Steam Navigation Company, better known now as P&O. The service was extended from Gibraltar to Alexandria, and at that time an overland journey to Port Suez was necessary to continue on to India. The P&O ships would then leave Southampton for Alexandria, stopping only at Gibraltar and Valetta, Malta. The first vessel used on the new route was the aptly named 1,787-ton paddle steamer *Oriental*, reflecting the new service.

When travelling to India the quickest route was overland, with the passengers disembarking at Alexandria. There were two favourite routes that had been used since Biblical times and both went from Alexandria to Cairo. One route went across the desert to Suez and the other route went up the Nile, travelling in narrow-draught Egyptian Nile boats to Luxor and then across the desert to the Red Sea port of Kosseir. This was a distance of 250 miles from Suez and took 88 hours. The advantage of the Kosseir route was that passengers could see the pyramids at Giza on their journey up the Nile.

In 1844 the route was extended to Singapore and the Far East, and the 2,108-ton *Hindustan* was the first vessel to inaugurate the service. By 1851 P&O had started a Singapore to Australia mail service with the 699-ton iron screw steamer *Chusan*, which arrived in Sydney on 3 August 1852. In 1853 a service was inaugurated from Southampton to Capetown and then on to Australia.

With the completion of the Alexandria – Suez railway in December 1858, the route was changed. In 1869 the Suez Canal opened and shipping companies started to use the canal. At first the mail still continued to be carried across Egypt by land because this was in the terms of the contract, but by the middle 1880s the Suez Canal was the first choice.

By 1874 P&O had moved its home port from Southampton to London due the pressure of the shippers, who would not pay extra to move their goods by rail to Southampton. However, this was not the choice of the passengers, who preferred Southampton because it meant one day less at sea.

Hindustan (2,108 GT). She had a wooden construction, two funnels, three masts, which were also used for sails and side paddle wheels that gave a speed of 10 knots. (Mick Lindsay Collection)

Southampton Docks during the 1850s. The Outer Dock is in the foreground with the Inner Dock behind. (Bert Moody Collection)

The Victorian Era 1837–1901

William IV died on 24 May 1837, and so began the Victorian era. It was also in 1837 that Wheatstone and Cooke patented the first commercial telegraph, and Samuel Morse exhibited his electric telegraph and his Morse code in New York. The Victorian era was marked by a range of inventions and events, including the Great Exhibition of 1851, the first 'Penny Post' stamps in 1840 and the invention of the penny-farthing bicycle in 1872 (although it had no brakes). Alexander Bell invented the telephone in 1876, and Thomas Edison recited and recorded *Mary had a Little Lamb* on the first phonograph in 1878. By 1879 electric lighting had replaced the gas lamps in London. In 1885 Carl Benz built the first petrol-driven car, a three-wheeled vehicle powered by a one-cylinder engine, and John Boyd Dunlop invented the pneumatic tyre in 1890, making car journeys much smoother.

The Victorian era was a prosperous period for those involved in trade in the British Empire and a time when the middle class was developing. Working class life was very hard, but it was also a time when the upper class began to feel more responsible for the lower classes, and new laws were put in place for health and labour to help those in need. The new reform bills were aimed at giving better working and living conditions for the poor and also aspired to create a more equal society. However, although the sentiment was there, the new laws were not well thought out, and considerable hardship still remained for the working classes.

The rise in factory work in the towns meant that many of the home workers, such as women working with their spinning wheels, and the farm workers, who were attracted to the higher wages in the factories, moved to the larger towns and cities. However, many were living in slums and terraced housing in the overcrowded cities, rather than living in a healthier countryside environment. This resulted in the working class performing the physical labour, doing the dirtier work, while the developing middle classes did the 'white collar work' and the more mental work in offices, and in a cleaner environment. Finally there was the upper class that did not work but lived on inherited land or investments.

Southampton in the Victorian Era

Southampton was destined to become one of the most important maritime centres in the world. Until the early 19th century no real effort had been made in capitalising on the natural features of the area. The port had good access to the English Channel, North Sea and Atlantic Ocean and, importantly, it had direct sea links with Europe. There was also the advantage of the double tides, and the peninsula between the rivers Test and Itchen was a prime area for development. By 1840 the rail link from Southampton to London had opened and was much closer to London than Liverpool. It was the total of these factors that made Southampton attractive to the shipping companies.

The Royal Mail Steam Packet Company

It was in 1839, just at the time the docks at Southampton were being constructed, that the RMSP (Royal Mail Steam Packet Company) was awarded a mail contract to transport mail to the West Indies. They started a fortnightly service in 1841 from Falmouth with the *Thames* (1,889 GT) and *Tay* (1,858 GT). In 1842 the *Teviot* (1,744 GT) made her maiden voyage from Southampton to the West Indies, and a year later the paddle steamer *Severn* (1,886 GT) also made her maiden voyage to the same destination. By that time Southampton Docks had been established as the main port of departure instead of Falmouth.

By 1847 RMSP *Teviot* had started a transatlantic service from Southampton to New Orleans, via Bermuda, and in 1850 RMSP steamer *Esk* (232 GT) inaugurated a mail and passenger service to South America.

Due to the development of the docks and the position of the walled town any development in building houses could only be to the north as the town was bordered on three sides by water.

The Race for the First British Crossing of the North Atlantic

In 1838, the same year that the foundation stone was laid for the new docks at Southampton, the race to achieve the first British steamship crossing of the Atlantic commenced. It was between two British shipping companies, the Great Western Steamship Company and the British and American Steam Packet Company. The two vessels involved were *Great Western*, designed by Isambard Kingdom Brunel and the hull built by Paterson of Bristol in 1837, and the paddle steamer *Sirius*. The 700-ton *Sirius* was a wooden side-wheel paddler, also built in 1837 for the St George Steam Packet Company, operating the London to Cork route. The same year the vessel was chartered for two voyages by the British and American Steam Navigation Company for the opening of the transatlantic steam passenger service. It was the *Sirius* that arrived in New York first, just a few hours before the *Great Western*. However, the *Great Western* had made the transatlantic crossing in 15 days, having set off four days after the *Sirius*.

The problem with paddle ships was that in heavy seas the vessel could roll and one paddle wheel could lift out of the water and the ship could lose propulsion. The solution to gaining a more efficient propulsion through the

Great Western **(1,340 GT). She had a wooden construction with one funnel and four masts for sails. She was broken up in 1857. (Mick Lindsay Collection)**

British Queen (1,863 GT). She had a wooden hull and was built in 1838 by Curling & Young, London. (Mick Lindsay Collection)

water was found when Francis Pettit Smith patented the screw propeller in 1836, just before John Ericson, who had also been working on the development of the screw propeller at the same time.

The British & American Steam Navigation Company, the first North Atlantic steamship line to start a transatlantic service, was formed in 1838. The *British Queen*, a side-paddle steamship, was built in 1838 by Curling & Young, London, specifically for the British and American Steam Navigation Company for the transatlantic crossing. The *British Queen* was 1,863 GT, 275ft (83.8m) long and 64ft (19.5m) across the paddle boxes. She had a wooden hull and two 30-feet diameter paddle wheels which gave her a maximum speed of 10 knots. She was designed to carry 207 passengers. Her maiden voyage was on 2 July 1839 from Portsmouth to New York and took 15 days. Samuel Cunard was on board for this voyage. The company was short lived, however, and ceased trading in 1841, mainly due to the loss of its vessel, the 2,350-ton *President,* which had left New York in March 1841, but was lost in a gale along with 136 lives. When the company ceased trading that year the *British Queen* was sold to the Belgian government.

In 1838 the British government invited tenders for carrying mail from Liverpool to Halifax and Boston. Samuel Cunard, who was already interested in the future benefits of steam navigation, travelled to England to present his plans to the Admiralty. The Admiralty was so impressed with his plans that they awarded him the contract. Samuel Cunard formed the British & North American Royal Mail Steam Packet Company in 1839.

The contract stipulated that the ships built were required to be available, if necessary, in times of war to be able to carry troops and stores, and four steamers were ordered of similar design, the *Britannia, Acadia, Caledonia* and *Columbia*. The *Britannia* (1,135 GT) was 207ft (63.0) in length and had a beam of 34ft (10.4m). She had one funnel, three masts and was of wood construction. The vessel was built by Robert Duncan, Greenock, with engines by Robert Napier, Glasgow, propelling two side-paddle wheels at a service speed of 9 knots. When the *Britannia*, commanded by Capt Henry Woodruff, left Liverpool on 4 July 1840 for her maiden voyage, there were 63 passengers on board, including Samuel Cunard and his daughter. As 4 July was American Independence Day and also Samuel Cunard's birthday, it appeared to be a good omen for the future of the company. At a speed of 8.5–9 knots the crossing took 12 days, 10 hours to Halifax, and after a short stop there she proceeded to Boston, arriving on 17 July 1840.

The *Britannia* had four decks, with the lower deck taking the coal and other cargo holds. Some other cargo holds were on the next level with crew accommodation, including the 'glory hole', and other cabins for more senior members of the crew. On the third level were the passenger cabins, which at the time were thought to be luxurious but by today's standard would be judged as very cramped. On the top deck the Captain and Chief Officer had cabins either side of the wheelhouse.

The main saloon had room for two large dining tables with benches which the passengers would sit on for meals. The ship also carried a cow to provide fresh milk. At the start of the service the *Britannia* had the capacity for 115 first-class passengers; emigrants were still expected to sail on the sailing ships.

Britannia (1,135 GT). She was built by Robert Duncan, Greenock, in 1840. (Mick Lindsay Collection)

The *Britannia* was not without mishap during her service. In February 1844 she was trapped in ice in Boston harbour but was released when the townspeople cut a channel 7 miles long for her to escape from the ice.

Charles Dickens travelled with his wife and maid on the *Britannia* in 1842 but suffered seasickness quite badly. He was not very happy with the size of his cabin and referred to the vessel as 'a gigantic hearse with windows'. On his return trip he did not repeat his experience on the new steamship and travelled back on a sailing ship. Dickens was later to sail transatlantic again when he visited America for the second time. This time, however, he travelled on the 2,960-ton *Russia*, which made her maiden voyage in 1867. The *Russia* was propelled by a screw propeller and had a clipper bow. He was much happier on this ship and praised the size of his cabin and the comfort on board.

Another famous author, Samuel Clemens, better known as Mark Twain, also sailed on the steamships. He had trained as a steamboat pilot on the Mississippi river in 1859 and sailed transatlantic many times. In 1872 he sailed on Cunard's *Batavia* (2,553 GT) and later on the *Gallia* (4,809 GT.) Other shipping companies also carried Mark Twain, including the Inman Line on the *City of Chester* (4,770 GT) in 1873 and the North German Lloyd on the *Prinzessin Irene* (10,881 GT) on a voyage to Italy after a transatlantic crossing on the Cunarder *Lucania* (12,952 GT).

The North American Royal Mail Steam Packet Company sailed from Liverpool to New York and Boston, including for some years a stop in Halifax. Queenstown was also added to the route for the mail service and by 1847 the route extended to New York. By November 1848 the *Britannia* had made her last transatlantic voyage and in March 1849 she sailed from Liverpool to Bremen, where she was renamed the *Barbarossa* as part of the German navy. She was later used as a target ship and sunk in 1880.

As the competition between shipping companies became more intense, notably from the White Star Line, the name of the North American Royal Mail Steam Packet Company was changed to the Cunard Steamship Company Limited in 1878. This name was soon shortened to the well established Cunard Line of today. By the 1880s the voyage was taking less than six days on the faster ships from Liverpool to New York. Cunard also added routes to various other countries. They ran their mail vessels weekly, sailing on Saturdays, with other vessels sailing fortnightly on Tuesdays.

The aptly named 237-ton steamship *Archimedes* was used by Francis Pettit Smith to demonstrate the new screw propeller, and this ship was to influence Isambard Kingdom Brunel when it arrived in Bristol in May 1840 in changing from his planned side-paddle propulsion to screw propulsion for the *Great Britain*. This was the first iron-hulled ship to be built, and she was launched in 1843 and was used to take passengers to Australia. In fact, it was on the *Great Britain* that the English touring cricket team first travelled to Australia in 1861.

At about the same time the Royal Navy was engaged in considering the merits of paddle propulsion and screw propulsion. In 1845 the Royal Navy undertook tests to establish the best propulsion for their vessels and this was between HMS *Alecto* and HMS *Rattler*. HMS *Alecto* was powered by paddle wheels and HMS *Rattler* by screw propellers. In all the tests, which included distance runs at speed and a tug of war between both ships HMS *Rattler* won easily, and the decision taken by the Royal Navy was to concentrate on screw propulsion.

Adriatic (1) (3,888 GT). She was built by Harland &
Wolff, Belfast, and launched in 1871. (Mick Lindsay
Collection)

The first American steamship company to run a
regularly scheduled transatlantic service between New
York and Bremen was the Ocean Steam Navigation
Company, or Bremen Line. The company was formed by
the United States government's decision in 1845 to help
fund a steamship operation by offering mail contracts in
response to the support of the British government
awarding mail contracts to British shipping companies.

The first ship was the paddle ship *Washington*, 1,640 GT,
230ft (70.1m) long and with a beam of 38ft (11.6m). Her
paddle wheels were powered by twin side-lever steam engines at a service speed of 8 knots. The ship had the capacity for
300 passengers. The maiden voyage from New York in June 1847 found the *Washington* leaving the same day as the *Britannia*
left Boston. The *Britannia* arrived at Liverpool two days before the *Washington* arrived at Southampton. Despite this setback,
however, the *Washington* left Southampton to complete her journey to Bremerhaven, where she received a rapturous
welcome. This decision was very important for Southampton Docks as it established New York for the transatlantic mail
passenger route that served Southampton and Europe. It was also a fact that Southampton was closer to London than
Liverpool and had a mainline railway connection to London that had only opened seven years previously in 1840.

It was also in 1845 that the White Star Line of Boston Packets was founded in Liverpool by John Pilkington and Henry
Wilson, mainly to sail to Australia for the gold mine trade. The first ship purchased under the White Star Line name was the
879-ton clipper ship *Iowa*, of the barque class. They also chartered other ships, but the loss of the fully-rigged iron clipper
sailing ship *Tayleur* (1,750 GT) was a great burden to the company. They attempted to merge with other shipping companies,
such as the Black Ball and Eagle Lines, to form the Liverpool, Melbourne and Oriental Steam Navigation Company Limited.

White Star Line purchased its first steamship, the *Royal Standard*, but she was underpowered and only able to sail
between 6–8 knots, and was easily passed by the clipper ships under full sail. However, Thomas Ismay saw the failings of
the company and formed the Oceanic Steam Navigation Company to take over the company in 1869. The Oceanic Steam
Navigation Company from then on became better known as the White Star Line. New ships were built, including the
Oceanic, Atlantic, Baltic and *Republic*, to operate a transatlantic service between New York and Liverpool, with a call at
Queenstown, in 1871.

The *Adriatic (1)* was built by Harland & Wolff, Belfast, for the White Star Line and launched in 1871. It was 3,888 tons,
437.2ft (133m) in length, with a beam of 40.9ft (12.5m), and had one funnel, four masts that were rigged for sail, an iron
hull, single screw and a speed of 14 knots. Accommodation was for 166 first-class and 1,000 third-class passengers. The
Adriatic left Liverpool on her maiden voyage to New York, via Queenstown (Cobh), in April 1872. The vessel was scrapped
in 1899.

The Hamburg–America Line had been founded in 1847 and sailed from Hamburg, calling at Southampton and then on
to New York. The North German Lloyd Line (Norddeutsche Lloyd, or NDL) was founded in 1857 and sailed from Bremen
to New York. By the end of the century German shipping companies were building fast and comfortable ships and had
emerged as strong competitors to the two British companies, Cunard and White Star lines, based in Liverpool.

In 1848 Cunard was awarded a new contract by the Admiralty, due to the popularity of the mail service, to sail every
Saturday to either Halifax or Boston. However, the contract included a reference to possible wartime service by the four
new ships, the *America, Europa, Canada* and *Niagara*, in which they were required to have increased power and also able to
carry guns. Little was Samuel Cunard to know at the time that only a few years later his ships would be required by the
government for trooping in the Crimean War. This was a disaster for Cunard as 11 of their ships were requisitioned for war
service in 1854, leaving the American transatlantic services to prosper.

However, the Ocean Steam Navigation Company mail service was short lived and the mail contract was awarded to the
Collins Line in 1849, which intended to challenge Cunard's supremacy on the transatlantic service. They built four paddle
steamers of 3,000 tons that were much larger and faster than the Cunard ships. These ships were named the *Arctic, Baltic,
Atlantic* and the *Pacific*. The company had one big problem, however: in its aim to lessen the time taken for a transatlantic
crossing, they sacrificed safety for speed. In 1854 the *Arctic* was lost in a collision in fog with another ship off Cape Race,
Newfoundland, with the loss of many lives, and the *Pacific* disappeared at sea after leaving Liverpool in 1856, also with the
loss of many lives. The Collins Line was finally wound up in 1858.

The development in steam-powered ships really took off with the introduction of compound steam engines, patented
by Scottish engineer John Elder in 1854. The compound steam engine, which used steam twice in each engine cycle, cut
the fuel consumption and thus increased length of voyage that could be undertaken before refuelling.

Cunard was not to be beaten and launched its first iron ship, the 3,300-ton paddle steamer *Persia*, in 1855, becoming
the largest vessel afloat at the time. The *Persia* made its maiden voyage from Liverpool to New York on 26 January 1856 and

remained on this service until 1867. The *Scotia* was the last of the Cunard iron paddle steamers and made her maiden voyage from Liverpool to New York on 10 May 1862. She was in service until 1879 when she was sold. Both the *Persia* and the *Scotia* were holders of the Blue Riband and were very popular with all the passengers that sailed on them.

Cunard was late in joining in the emigrant trade and it was the 2,638-ton *China*, whose maiden voyage was in 1862, that had the first steerage accommodation. The *China* was also the first Cunard iron-screw steamer, but she was sold to Spain in 1880. Other Cunard ships were involved in the emigrant trade, including the *Parthia* (3,167 GT), which could carry over 1,000 third-class passengers, and the *Bothnia* (4,535 GT) and *Scythia* (4,557 GT), which could carry over 1,100 steerage passengers.

The last two Cunard steam ships to carry sails were the *Umbria* (1884) and the *Etruria* (1885). The *Umbria* (7,718 GT) was requisitioned as a troopship in 1885 and again in 1900 for both Boer Wars. However, the *Etruria* (7,718 GT) and the *Umbria*, held the Blue Riband westbound transatlantic records from 1885–1888.

Inman Line

It was in 1850 that the Inman Line was founded by William Inman, and it became one of the three largest British passenger shipping companies, along with the Cunard and White Star Line. They were forward thinking in replacing paddle wheels with the screw propeller for the transatlantic voyages. Their ships were all named after cities, including the *City of Berlin*, *City of Chicago*, *City of Chester*, *City of Richmond* and *City of Montreal*. However, the firm ran into financial difficulties and in 1886 was taken over by the owners of the Red Star Line and American Line and renamed the Inman and International Steamship Co.

The *City of New York* and the *City of Paris* were two Atlantic 'greyhounds' and both were a challenge to the Cunard express service, gaining the Blue Riband from them. The *City of Paris* gained both the westbound and eastbound record from the Cunard *Etruria* in 1889, and the *City of New York* took the eastbound record from the *City of Paris* in 1892, although it was lost to the Cunard *Campania* in 1893. The *City of Paris* lost the westbound record to the White Star *Majestic* and *Teutonic* in 1891, but regained it in 1892. She finally lost the Blue Riband to Cunard's *Campania*, which had regained both the eastbound record in May and the westbound record in June 1893.

The *City of New York* was 10,499 GT and 527.6ft (160.8m) in length, with a beam of 63.2ft (19.3m). She was built in steel and had three funnels. The engines were triple expansion steam engines, which powered two screws at a service speed of 20 knots. The *City of New York* was built by J.&G. Thomson, Glasgow, and was launched on 15 March 1888. She left on her maiden voyage from Liverpool to New York on 1 August 1888. Her accommodation was for 540 first-class, 200 second-class and 1,000 third-class passengers. In 1893 the *City of New York* was taken over by the American Line and renamed *New York*. Her accommodation was refitted to carry 290 first-class, 250 second-class, and 725 third-class passengers.

City of New York (10,499 GT). She was built by J.&G. Thomson, Glasgow, in 1888 and became *New York* in 1895. Between 1901 and 1903 she was rebuilt with two funnels. She was broken up in 1923. (Mick Lindsay Collection)

The *City of New York's* main dining salon. (Michael W. Pocock Collection)

The *City of Paris* was also built by J.&G. Thomson, Glasgow, and had the same statistics. She was launched on the 23 October 1888 and her maiden voyage was from Liverpool to New York, leaving on 3 April 1889. The capacity was for 540 first-class, 200 second-class and 1,000 third-class passengers (1,740 in total), with 362 officers and crew. In 1893 she was taken over by the American Line and renamed *Paris*. The ship was scrapped in Genoa in 1923.

Great Eastern

The largest ship to be built in the 19th century was Isambard Kingdom Brunel's *Great Eastern* (18,914 GT), launched in 1858. She was 689ft (210m) in length, 82ft (25m) beam, 120ft (36.6m) measuring over the paddle wheels and could carry 4,000 passengers. The *Great Eastern* was built with a double iron hull, had six masts for sails, which were named 'Monday' to 'Saturday', five funnels and separate engines to power the 56ft (17m) paddles and the propeller at a speed of 13.5 knots. There was a belief, though, that it was not safe to use the sails the same time as the engines because the hot exhaust from the funnels could cause them to catch fire. The *Great Eastern* was not very successful with the passenger trade, although she was used as a troopship and in 1863 had carried 1,114 passengers on a transatlantic crossing to New York, but the numbers of passengers became fewer and fewer. However, the *Great Eastern* came to prominence when she was the only ship big enough to carry the cable required to lay the first transatlantic cable. The vessel had been put up for sale, but as no purchaser was found, in 1864 the Telegraph Construction Company chartered her to undertake the laying of the transatlantic cable which was completed in 1886.

The introduction of steel hulls instead of iron hulls was significant because it made it possible to build much larger ships. In 1881 the Cunard two-funnel *Servia* (7,392 GT) was the first vessel to be constructed of steel, and with powerful compound engines she could make 16 knots. In 1884 she was able make the transatlantic crossing from New York to Queenstown in just seven days. The *Servia* was built by J.&G. Thomson for the Cunard Line and at 515ft (157m) in length and 52.1ft (15.9m) beam she was the second largest vessel, after the *Great Eastern,* in the world. The accommodation was of a very high standard and she was the very first ship to be fitted with electric lighting. From 1899 the *Servia* was used for trooping service in the Boer War, returning to its transatlantic service in 1900. She made her last voyage in September 1901 from Liverpool to New York before being scrapped in 1902.

In 1872 the American Steamship Company of Philadelphia commenced passenger and cargo services to Queenstown and Liverpool, mostly with chartered ships. One year later the Holland–America Line was founded in 1873 as the Dutch-America Steamship Company, a shipping and passenger line. Because its base was in Rotterdam, but it sailed to America, it became known as Holland–America Line (HAL).

The Canadian Pacific Railway Company was formed in 1881 and became involved in shipping. They formed the Canadian Pacific Line, mainly trading on the Great Lakes in North America. However, by 1903 they had commenced a transatlantic passenger service after the company had taken over the Beaver Line. Their transatlantic routes in the beginning were from Liverpool to Montreal, Quebec, in the summer and from Liverpool to St John and New Brunswick in the winter.

It was in 1884 that Charles Algernon Parsons invented the steam turbine and in 1897 the *Turbinia* was the first vessel driven by a turbine. The speed achieved in the trials was 34½ knots. This led to the building of steam turbine-driven ships on the transatlantic service.

In 1893 Cunard built their first twin-screw ships and these were built specifically for speed. They were the *Campania* (12,950 GT) and the *Lucania* (12,952 GT), which both had their maiden voyages in 1893. Both vessels gained the Blue Riband record, the *Lucania* on her maiden voyage. The *Campania* was noted as the first of the Cunarders to be fitted with the Marconi wireless telegraph. Luxury and comfort was the aim of the Cunard Line, and the first-class drawing rooms had wood panelling, velvet drapes, Persian carpets and all the luxuries that the first-class passengers would expect when at home. The *Lucania* was the first Cunard ship to have single berth cabins and stateroom suites.

White Star Line

The *Teutonic* (9,984 GT) was built for the White Star Line by Harland & Wolff, Belfast, and was launched in 1889. She was 582ft (177.4m) in length, with a beam of 57.7ft (17.6m). Her engines were triple expansion powering two screws at 2.5 knots. She could carry 300 first-class, 190 second-class and 1,000 third-class passengers. The maiden voyage left Liverpool on 7 August 1889 for New York, calling at Queenstown (now known as Cobh, ROI). In 1914 she was requisitioned for World War One and became the first AMC (Armed Merchant Cruiser).

In 1899 the White Star *Oceanic* (2) was built and launched by Harland & Wolff, Belfast. She was 17,274 GT, had two funnels, three masts and four decks, and was fitted with electric lights and refrigerating machinery. The *Oceanic* had twin screws powered by triple-expansion engines, giving a service speed of

The *Teutonic* (9,984 GT) had triple-expansion engines powering two screws at 20.5 knots. In No. 6 dry dock at Southampton. (Pamlin Prints postcard)

19.5 knots. At the time she was the largest and most luxurious liner in the world.

1899 was also the year when the Italian inventor Marconi put a radio receiver on board the American Line's *St Paul* while she was sailing from New York to Southampton. He was in contact with the Needles station when the *St Paul* was approximately 45 miles from the English coast. The news received from the Needles station was printed on the ship's printing press by Marconi in the newspaper he called *The Transatlantic Times*. In the same year the Royal Navy became interested in using radio on their vessels and fitted three warships with Marconi wireless sets in 1899. The Admiralty were so impressed that they ordered more sets for other warships.

Emigrant Trade

The emigrant trade from Europe in the 19th century was profitable for the shipping companies, with people wishing to travel to America and Canada to start a new life. Liverpool was the main port at the time as it had established transatlantic links with America and Canada. Up until 1870 many emigrants from north-western Europe would sail across the North Sea to Hull and then travel across country to pick up their ships in Liverpool. From 1846, due to the potato famine in Ireland, many Irish people also decided to travel across the Irish Sea to Liverpool and then to start a new life in North America. By the middle of the 19th century, although Liverpool was the main port for emigration to North America, to the gold rush in Australia and for emigrants sailing to New Zealand, other ports, including London, Southampton and Plymouth, began to get more involved.

With the number of emigrants arriving at the ports a decision was made to establish government-run depots that would look after them by providing food, accommodation and undertaking health checks before they sailed. This could be anything from a few days to a few weeks, but at least for many emigrants they had a roof over their head, warmth in winter and good food.

There was a Government Emigration Depot set up at Plymouth in 1847, at about the time of the Irish potato famine, and many Irish families travelled to Plymouth to sail to Australia or North America. By 1853 there were four depots, Plymouth, Birkenhead, Nine Elms and Southampton, which had replaced the Deptford depot.

Emigrants travelling from Germany were well looked after by the Hamburg–America Line, which made sure that they had free medical examinations and were housed in a 'village' until their time for sailing to America.

Norddeutscher Lloyd vessels also carried many emigrants from Bremen to New York, calling at Southampton.

CHAPTER 2
THE 20TH CENTURY BEGINS

The century began with the continuation of the Boer War, the first flight of the Zeppelin, the Boxer Rebellion in China and the formation of the Commonwealth of Australia. There was the first Davis Cup in tennis, W.G. Grace ended his cricket career, the Olympic Games took place in Paris, the first since the revival of the games in Greece in 1896, and the 'cake walk' became a popular dance.

After a century of steam development it was the beginning of a century of electricity and the first powered vacuum cleaner. Marconi wireless sets were also first used on passenger steamships when the German passenger steamer *Kaiser Wilhelm der Grosse* and the Belgian vessel *Princess Clementine* were the first ships to have Marconi wireless sets permanently onboard for commercial purposes.

Marconi travelled to Canada with his assistant and raised a high antenna, held aloft by balloons on Signal Hill, St John's, Newfoundland, and on 12 December 1901 he received the first transatlantic message by Morse code from the Poldhu station, Cornwall. Other events of the early 1900s were Wilbur and Orville Wright's first powered flight in 1903, the first Nobel Prize and the San Francisco earthquake in 1906.

The *Kaiser Wilhelm der Grosse's* smoking room. (Michael W. Pocock Collection)

Kaiser Wilhelm der Grosse (14,349 GT) was scuttled off Rio de Oro, West Africa, in 1914. (Mick Lindsay Collection)

Liner Services and Cruises

It has been said that 'P&O invented cruising' in 1844 when they started their Mediterranean and Black Sea cruises, sailing from Southampton. The Orient Line also started offering cruises in the 1880s and in 1904 P&O refitted the liner *Rome* (5,103 GT), a cruising yacht for first-class only, and renamed it *Vectis*. They teamed up with Thomas Cook, who arranged the shore trips. From the beginning of the 20th century regular cruises were also offered by the White Star Line, P&O and Hamburg–America Line.

Cruises were offered by the shipping companies that ran the transatlantic service for the winter season, as it was only the experienced passengers who braved the winter transatlantic crossing. The ships offering the cruises would be based in New York and cruise to the Bahamas and Caribbean.

Southampton Docks 'Gateway to the Empire'

From the formation of the Southampton Dock Company in 1836 there was a drive towards creating a port that would attract many of the shipping companies and increase trade links. With the rail link from London to Southampton opening in 1840 there were better transport links with Southampton and the docks. In May 1843 Southampton Docks was chosen by the government as a major port for the Royal Mail delivery to the British Empire and was designated a packet station. The prefix RMS (Royal Mail Ship) identified a sea-going vessel used to carry mail. By this time Southampton was established as the principal port for P&O, with sailings from Southampton to Australia, via Capetown, starting in 1853, and it was also the principal military embarkation port for the Crimean War of 1854–56.

However, a loss in trade when P&O transferred to London was a challenge to the Dock Company, and after a loan from the L&SWR (London & South Western Railway) the new Empress Dock was built and opened in 1890 by Queen Victoria. From then on Southampton Docks became more prominent and attractive to shipping companies in the late 19th century.

In 1894 Southampton Docks had been selected by the British government to be the principal base for the Indian and Colonial seasonal spring and summer trooping, and in 1899 the docks became the principal embarkation port for the Boer War. The importance of the docks in times of war was notable for the ease with which troops left and arrived at the port. This was helped by the rail connections from the army camps in Aldershot, where the troops could travel from their camp right up to the quayside and then board the ship.

With the advantage of double tides, enabling the largest ships to berth at any state of the tide, more shipping lines were attracted to the port. The American Line transferred its New York mail service from Liverpool to Southampton, with the liner *New York* commencing the service on 4 March 1893. The choice of Southampton was based on the opportunity to gain Continental traffic from ships calling at Cherbourg, the better connection for boat and train from London to Southampton, and the fact that the train journey was 100 miles shorter than a train journey from London to Liverpool.

At the beginning of the century Southampton business was booming, with new industries being attracted to the area due to the railway and the docks helping to make the town more prosperous. Each day a large number of trains would arrive at Southampton. There would be the trains with passengers bound for the ocean liners, trains bringing coal to fuel the ships, and export goods to be loaded on the ships to be taken around the world. The reverse happened with the trains leaving Southampton for London with passengers who had arrived on the ships and also taking freight that had arrived to every corner of the British Isles.

There was a good trade for the horse-drawn carts delivering goods to the shops and factories and for the hansom cabs waiting at the railway stations to convey passengers around the town.

In the early 1900s the Western Esplanade and area along by the Stella memorial had rows of cannons, and the water came right up to the quayside between the Town Quay and the Royal Pier, where sailing ships would tie up. The local residents and workers living and working nearby complained of the stench of the mud at low tide. The Stella memorial was erected to commemorate the heroism of a stewardess who gave her life to save another soul when the *Stella* sank off Guernsey in 1899.

Southampton Docks in World War One

The docks were again chosen by the government when World War One started and they became the number one military embarkation port. The traffic at that time was a reduced cross-channel service run by the L&SWR, and all commercial shipping services ceased to operate from the docks. From then on the only ships that operated from the port were those transporting troops, supplies and ammunition. It was not uncommon for anything up to 25–30 ships to leave the docks in one night.

Southampton Docks was known as a Railway Dock from 1892 when L&SWR took over the management, and this continued after 1923 when L&SWR became part of Southern Railway, which took over the management of the docks. During this time the docks were often fondly referred as the 'Railway Docks'.

Queen Victoria

Queen Victoria was 81 and in failing health when she travelled to Osborne House on the Isle of Wight for the Christmas of 1900. It was to be her last Christmas and she died there on 22 January 1901. The Queen was succeeded by Edward VII.

This was the start of the Edwardian era that broadly covered the years from 1901 up to 1910 (the reign of King Edward VII) and even extended into the sinking of the *Titanic* and through World War One, when the rigid class system became broken down through men of all classes fighting together in the trenches of France. They were not keen to return to the master/servant attitude of many households before the war.

It was also a period when rich Americans were keen to travel in outstanding luxury. The era was perhaps best captured by the grandness of the *Titanic*, with its first-class accommodation having ornamental decorations, wood panelling and furniture that was fit for a palace. In fact, it was a time when the ships were referred to as 'Floating Palaces'. The Edwardians were keen on leisure, sport and fitness, and to meet this interest the *Titanic* had a gymnasium, squash courts, Turkish bath and an indoor swimming pool. The designers also looked at the accommodation for the second and third-class passengers, and that was almost as good as the first class on other ships.

Some members of the royal family really liked to travel and their itineraries would include voyages to other countries around the world. In 1901 the Duke and Duchess of Cornwall & York (later to become King George V and Queen Mary) left Portsmouth on HMS *Ophir* for a Royal tour, during which they toured most of the British Empire, a tour that took approximately nine months, taking in Gibraltar, Malta, Egypt, Ceylon (now Sri Lanka), Singapore, Australia, New Zealand, Mauritius, South Africa and Canada. When the Duke and Duchess arrived back in England in November 1901 he was created Prince of Wales, and other tours followed. In 1904 the Prince and Princess of Wales went to Austria-Hungary and in 1905 to India then Spain and Norway for two royal weddings.

Emigrant Trade in the 20th Century

To attract more immigrants to the United States the steerage rates were cut to $10 in 1904. This was also the time when the Cunard Line launched the *Ivernia, Saxonia* and *Carpathia*. The *Ivernia* (14,058 GT) was built by Swan Hunter at Wallsend-on-Tyne and made her maiden voyage in 1900. She was the largest cargo ship of the day, but was also able to carry up to almost 2,000 passengers. However, she was requisitioned for war service in World War One and was sunk off Greece in 1916, with the loss of 36 lives.

The *Saxonia* (14,281 GT) was built by John Brown & Company, Clydebank, and also had her maiden voyage in 1900. She was a passenger ship that sailed from Liverpool to Boston, but after 1911 she transferred to carrying emigrants from Italy to New York. The *Saxonia* was eventually scrapped in 1925.

The *Carpathia* (13,555 GT) was built by Swan Hunter, Newcastle upon Tyne, and made her maiden voyage in 1903. She was an emigrant ship but was noted for her action in trying to save survivors from the *Titanic* in 1912. She also came to a sad end when she was struck by three torpedoes fired from *U-55* (Wilhelm Werner) on 17 July 1918. She was sunk off the coast of Ireland, approximately 170 miles from Bishop Rock, while sailing from Liverpool to Boston, with the loss of five lives.

The *Konig Albert* (10,643 GT) was built by A.G. Vulcan in 1899. She was seized by Italy in 1915 and renamed *Ferdinando Palasciano*. This picture shows the second-class dining room. (Michael W. Pocock Collection)

The *Konig Albert's* smoking cabin. (Michael W. Pocock Collection)

Also in the 1900s Cunard had contracted John Brown's, Clydebank, to build the *Caronia* (19,687 GT), launched on 13 July 1904, and the *Carmania* (19,524 GT), launched on 21 February 1905. These became the largest ships in the Cunard Line, that is until the *Lusitania* and *Mauretania* came along in 1907. Both vessels were 650.26ft (192.2m), with a beam of 72.1ft (22m). The difference was in the engines: Cunard was testing and comparing two engine systems. The *Caronia* had two sets of quadruple-expansion engines, which powered twin screws at a service speed of 20 knots, and the *Carmania* had three direct-acting steam turbines, which powered triple screws at a service speed of 20 knots. The *Carmania* was the first Cunard vessel to be fitted with steam turbines. Both undertook war service in World War One, and the *Caronia* was noted for inaugurating the London-Canada service and the *Carmania* for rescuing survivors from the emigrant ship *Volturno*, which caught fire in the Atlantic. The *Carmania* was scrapped in 1931 and the *Caronia* in 1933.

The Challenge of the German Ocean Liners

The *Bremen* was built for the NDL (Norddeutscher Lloyd) Line and commenced her maiden voyage on 5 June 1897 from Bremen, calling at Southampton and then New York. However, only a few years later, on 30 June 1900, she was badly damaged in a dockside fire at the NDL Line pier in Hoboken, New Jersey. Other NDL Line vessels were berthed nearby and were also damaged by the fire. They were the

The *König Albert's* staircase. (Michael W. Pocock
Collection)

The *König Albert's* promenade deck. (Michael W.
Pocock Collection)

Kaiser Wilhelm der Grosse, Saale and *Main,* with the *Saale*
sinking. After extensive repairs, during which the
Bremen's length was extended to 575ft (175.3m) and
her tonnage increased to 11,540 GT, she returned to
service in 1901. On 20 April 1912 the *Bremen* was
sailing from Bremen to New York when she passed
through all the wreckage from the *Titanic*. She did not
stop to pick up bodies from the water as the White Star
Line already had a ship engaged in that sad task.

It was the NDL *Kaiser Wilhelm der Grosse* (14,349
GT), which entered service in 1897, that took the Blue
Riband away from the Cunard *Lucania* in the same year.
Two other German ocean liners, the Hapag *Deutschland*
and *Kronprinz Wilhelm*, continued the German hold on
the Blue Riband.

Between 1899–1900 NDL introduced three new
ships, the 10,600-ton *König Albert* and *Prinzess Irene* for
the Far Eastern Service and the 12,500-ton *Grosser
Kurfürst* for the North Atlantic service. *Prinzess Irene's*
maiden voyage in 1900 was from Bremen to Japan via
Southampton and, and then in 1903 she travelled the
routes Bremen-Southampton-New York and New York

The *Grosser Kurfurst's* (12,500 GT) first-class dining
room. (Michael W. Pocock Collection)

to the Mediterranean. In 1917 she became the *Pocahontas* for the US government and in 1921 carried the US mail for the US Mail Steamship Company. From 1923 she returned to Bremen as the *Bremen* (3), sailing from Bremen to New York, and in 1928 she was renamed *Karlsruhe* (2) but was scrapped in 1932 in Germany.

The *König Albert's* first voyage was Bremen-Cherbourg-New York, but in 1915 she became the Italian hospital ship *Ferinando Palasciano*. She was scrapped in 1926.

Cunard plans to regain the Blue Riband

The superiority of the German ships and their hold on the Blue Riband caused Cunard to plan how they could regain the transatlantic record. It was in 1902 that negotiations began between Cunard and the government over the proposed plan to build two liners that would outclass the German vessels, both in speed and luxury. In 1903 the government made available the funds to build two ships. They were to be named the *Mauretania* and the *Lusitania* and were known affectionately during their service as the '*Maury*' and the '*Lucy*'. However, in accepting the funds Cunard would have to agree that both vessels could be armed and available for use if required for war service.

It was a challenge for Cunard to regain the Blue Riband from the German ocean liners as a matter of national pride. Both ships gained the Blue Riband in 1907, and the *Mauretania* was to hold it until 1929.

The *Grosser Kurfurst* forward passage. (Michael W. Pocock Collection)

The *Grosser Kurfurst's* ladies' cabin. (Michael W. Pocock Collection)

The *Grosser Kurfurst's* promenade deck. (Michael W. Pocock Collection)

The *Lusitania* (31,550 GT) was built by John Brown & Company, Clydebank. (Mick Lindsay Collection)

Lusitania

The maiden voyage of the *Lusitania* was in 1907, but due to rough seas she did not achieve the Blue Riband on her first voyage. However, on the second voyage she gained the westbound Blue Riband from the *Deutschland* in September 1907 in four days, 19 hours and 52 minutes, and the eastbound Blue Riband from the *KaiserWilhelm II* in October 1907 in four days, 22 hours and 53 minutes.

With the start of World War One the *Lusitania's* last voyage during peacetime found her arriving at Liverpool on 4 August 1914, the very day that war was declared. However, she was not requisitioned by the government and continued her transatlantic crossings to New York on a monthly basis.

There were some worrying incidents during this time as the seas around the British Isles were stalked by German U-boats. This became more worrying when the German Embassy in New York published warnings that passengers travelling transatlantic did so at their own risk. This was at the time when the *Lusitania* was boarding passengers for the homeward voyage to Liverpool. The *Lusitania* left Pier 54, New York on 1 May 1915 with 1,257 passengers and 702 crew members on board.

On 7 May she was approaching the Irish coast and fully prepared for emergencies. The *Lusitania* was seen 15 miles off the Old Head of Kinsale when the captain was informed that a torpedo had been seen approaching the ship. The torpedo had been fired by *U-20* (commanded by Walther Schweiger) and it struck the *Lusitania* on the starboard side. A second explosion was heard that at first was thought to be a second torpedo, but later, after the *U-20* commander had confirmed that they had only fired one torpedo, it was thought to be a boiler exploding. The *Lusitania* sank in just 18 minutes with a loss of 1,198 lives; although there were enough lifeboats the listing of the vessel prevented their launch on one side.

The German government claimed that the second explosion was caused because the *Lusitania* was carrying munitions, but the British government denied

The dining room of the *Lusitania*. (Bert Moody Collection)

this. There have been suggestions in the book *Lusitania*, by Colin Simpson (1973), that the *Lusitania* had been taken secretly into dry dock in 1913 to have her number one boiler room converted into a magazine, and the same with her mail room, including gun mounts for six-inch guns. It is true that the *Lusitania* had been fitted with gun mounts and she was listed as an AMC (Armed Merchant Cruiser), but the guns were not thought to have been fitted. The ship's manifest shows that she was also carrying a large consignment of rifle cartridges, including empty shell cases and non-explosive fuses, but Cunard did not classify that as ammunition.

The suggestion that she was carrying high explosives has not been proven, but the anger felt in Britain and America that an unarmed vessel had been attacked and sunk resulted in America joining the Allies in the war.

Mauretania (1)

The maiden voyage of the *Mauretania* was from Liverpool to New York on 16 November 1907, and despite rough weather she still arrived on 22 November. In 1908 the *Mauretania* damaged her propeller blades and after repairs and a refit she returned to the transatlantic service and broke both eastbound and westbound records in April 1909. She retained the Blue Riband for the next 20 years.

On 4 August 1914, when Britain declared war on Germany, the *Mauretania* was on her way to New York and was requisitioned for war service. It was only days later that both the *Mauretania* and *Lusitania* were released from those duties, with the *Mauretania* being laid up in Liverpool because of the reduced demand for transatlantic crossings. However, after the sinking of the *Lusitania* the *Mauretania* was recalled for troop transport to Gallipoli. The high speed of the *Mauretania* kept her free from torpedo attack, but she was later fitted out as a hospital ship to bring the wounded home.

The *Mauretania's* next tasks were to carry Canadian troops to the battlefields of France and later to carry American troops to Europe. At the end of the war she was used to take Canadian and American troops home. The trooping duties found the *Mauretania* sailing from Southampton and, following the final trooping to North America, the vessel returned to Southampton for refitting.

By September 1919 the *Mauretania* sailed from Southampton on its first commercial voyage since the war. Due to a fire on board in July 1921 while the vessel was docked at Southampton, and the subsequent repairs to the fire damage, the opportunity was taken to convert the vessel from coal to oil. After her overhaul in 1930 the *Mauretania* was used mainly for cruising, and after cruises to the West Indies in 1934 she returned to Southampton.

Bill O'Brien originally comes from Scotland, but the family moved to Southampton on 2 October 1932. When he was old enough to go to sea he joined the four-funnel *Mauretania* as a bellboy. He talks about some of his experiences on board the *Mauretania*: 'When I was a bellboy on the *Mauretania* on the West Indies cruises we would get paid $2 for two bellboys to have a boxing match on deck for some of the passengers. I was due to have a boxing match but got a temperature and was put into the ship's hospital. Another bellboy was told to take my place but wasn't happy to do so and started crying. The other bellboy didn't want to lose the money because $2 was worth quite a bit in those days and came down to plead with me to fight him. I agreed

The *Mauretania* (1) (31,938 GT) was built by Swan Hunter & Wigham Richardson, Wallsend-on-Tyne. (Mick Lindsay Collection)

to help him out and we had our three two-minute rounds and I went back to the hospital. The hospital doctor must have found out and the next morning the Captain's inspection was the ship's hospital. He must have told the Captain because when he saw me I expected to be told off, but he just smiled at me.'

Bill O'Brien also talks about the day the captain's morning inspection revealed some interesting 'finds' when he inspected the stewards' glory hole: 'The captain would do an inspection at 10.30 every morning and pick a section of the ship to inspect. One particular morning he chose the steward quarters for cleanliness. There was a glory hole steward who used to look after the steward quarters. He had a room where he used to do the ironing near the after deck. In that room was a door to another room that was always kept locked. The captain insisted on this door being unlocked, and when it was opened he found 10 stowaways inside. This was about the third or fourth trip the glory hole steward had made and it was thought he had taken stowaways on each trip and looked after them, feeding them each day with extra food he had collected from the galley saying it was for the crew.'

The steward was promptly arrested and when the vessel had returned to port he was prosecuted in the Southampton courts and sentenced to 28 days imprisonment. Bill O'Brien: 'Later, when I went to sign on a ship in the catering department in the Cunard-White Star and Union Castle Offices, there was a photograph of this man pinned up to remind the staff not to sign him on for any of their ships. He would find it difficult to get any work because of what he had been charged with.'

The *Mauretania* sailed out of Southampton for the last time to be scrapped at Rosyth in July 1935.

Cunard Starts Transatlantic Service to Canada

Prior to World War One Cunard was looking at the possibility of starting a transatlantic service to Canada, and this became possible in 1911 when they bought the *Gerona, Tortona* and *Cairnrona*. These ships were renamed by Cunard and became the *Ascania (Gerona), Ausonia (Tortona)* and *Albania (Cairnrona)*, the 'A' Class of 1911. There was a good reason for Cunard to start a transatlantic service to Canada. It made good economic sense, as the Canadian and French governments had signed a treaty that would allow goods to be shipped via Southampton with the same duty-free rebate as a French port.

Cunard's new route was inaugurated by the *Albania* on 2 May 1911, followed by the *Ausonia* on 16 May and the *Ascania* on 23 May 1911. This service was the first time that Cunard had vessels sailing up the St Lawrence River. During the winter months, when the St Lawrence River was closed by ice, the service called at Portland, Maine.

The *Albania* was originally built and launched on 3 February 1900 as the *Consuelo* for Thomas Wilson & Sons of Hull. She was bought by Thomson Line in April 1908, renamed the *Cairnrona* and bought by Cunard in 1911, who renamed her *Albania*. She was not up to Cunard's standards and in 1912 was sold to the Bank Line and renamed *Poleric*. The vessel was broken up in Japan in 1929.

The *Ascania* (1) (9,111 GT) was launched on 3 March 1911. She was wrecked off Cape Ray, Newfoundland, on 13 June 1918. (*John Humphreys Collection*)

The *Ausonia* was also originally built for the Thomson Line and launched on 18 August 1909 as the *Tortona*. At the start of World War One the *Ausonia* continued with crossing the North Atlantic from August 1914 to July 1915, but at the time she was under charter with the Anchor-Donaldson Line, sailing from Glasgow to Moville and New York. From 1915 the *Ausonia* became a troopship in the Mediterranean and also sailed to Indian ports before returning to Cunard in 1916. Similar to the *Ascania,* she carried Canadian troops to the battlefields in France.

The *Ausonia* was torpedoed twice by German U-boats. On 11 June 1917 she was torpedoed by *U-55* (commanded by Wilhelm Werner) off the coast of Ireland on her transatlantic voyage from Montreal to Avonmouth, but was able to make it to Queenstown. The vessel was repaired and went back into service, but on 30 May 1918 she was torpedoed by *U-62* (commanded by Ernst Hashagen) approximately 620 miles south-west of Fastnet. The submarine surfaced and shelled the ship, causing it to sink. There were no passengers on board, but 44 members of the crew lost their lives. The remainder of the crew abandoned ship and travelled 900 miles in lifeboats until 8 June, when they were picked up by HMS *Zennia* and an American destroyer.

The *Ascania* was originally laid down as the SS *Gerona* for the Thomson Line, but in 1911, before the vessel was completed, she was taken over by the Cunard Line and renamed *Ascania*. With a steel hull the *Ascania* had a shelter deck, with the upper and main decks below, and midship there was a promenade and the boat decks, with a verandah café situated on the promenade deck. She could carry 200 second-class and 1,500 third-class passengers. The second-class cabins and public rooms were amidships and the cabins fitted with electric radiators. The smoke room was fitted with rectangular windows with furniture and panelling in oak.

The *Ascania* made her maiden voyage from London-Southampton-Quebec-Montreal on 23 May 1911. The cargo was loaded at Tilbury Docks, London, and the passengers embarked in Southampton. From then on Cunard provided a fortnightly service to Quebec and Montreal.

During the 1914–18 war, the *Ascania* was used as an AMC (Armed Merchant Cruiser) sailing across the North Atlantic, but on the eastbound voyages all the third class was occupied by Canadian troops on their way to the battlefront in France.

On the night of 13–14 June 1918 the *Ascania* (1) was wrecked off Cape Ray, Newfoundland. There were no casualties, but the vessel had broken its back and was declared a total loss.

Cunard's Purpose-Built Ships for the Canadian Service

After the Canadian service had been inaugurated in 1911 Cunard decided to obtain their own purpose-built ships for the route. Three vessels, the *Andania, Alaunia* and *Aurania*, were ordered and all were almost identical in construction. The first two, the *Andania* and the *Alaunia*, were ordered from Scotts Shipbuilding & Engineering Company Ltd, Greenock, early in 1912.

There were improvements and additions to the passenger accommodation, especially the third class, where four and six-berth cabins replaced the old-style dormitories. The second class now had a writing room, lounge, library and smoking room on the promenade deck.

The first vessel to be launched was the *Andania* on 13 March 1913, followed by the *Alaunia* on the 9 June 1913. *Andania* left Liverpool on 14 July 1913 for her maiden voyage, calling at Southampton, Quebec and Montreal. Among the guests on board were representatives from the Canadian government. For the second voyage the *Andania* sailed from London, but because she was the largest ship to have entered the Thames the approach channels had to be dredged for the occasion. She was requisitioned as a troopship, but was hit by a torpedo fired by *U-46* (commanded by Leo Hillebrand) on 27 January 1918 and sunk off Rathlin Light, Ireland, with the loss of seven lives.

The *Alaunia* made her maiden voyage from Liverpool to Portland, Maine, calling at Queenstown. In August 1914 she was requisitioned as a troopship and at first was used to carry Canadian troops, but by the summer of 1915 she was involved in the Gallipoli campaign. Later the same year she carried troops to Bombay. During 1916 the *Alaunia* returned to the North Atlantic and carried troops from Canada and America. On 19 October 1916 the *Alaunia* struck a mine in the English Channel and sank.

Aurania (2) was the third of the three purpose-built ships and was ordered by Cunard in December 1913, but due to the outbreak of World War One the build was delayed and finally completed in 1916. The accommodation was similar to the other two vessels, but the *Aurania* (2) was fitted out as a troopship and hired to the government. She made her maiden voyage from the Tyne to New York on 28 March 1917, returning to Liverpool. Although the *Aurania* (2) was used on the transatlantic service, she only made seven round trips before being torpedoed and wrecked in February 1918. She had left Liverpool on 3 February for New York but had to follow a route around the coast of Northern Ireland where, on 4 February, about 15 miles north west of Inistrahull, off the coast of Donegal, she was hit by a torpedo from *U-67* (commanded by Gerard Schulz). Nine of the crew were killed in the explosion. A trawler started to tow the ship, but the *Aurania* (2) became stranded at Caliach Point, near Tobermory, on the Isle of Mull. It did not take long for rough seas to break the ship up and she was declared a total loss.

White Star Line Terminal Transfers to Southampton

The White Star Line Terminal was transferred to Southampton in 1907 and on 22 May 1907 the *Adriatic* (2) left New York for Southampton, calling at Plymouth and Cherbourg, arriving in Southampton Docks on 29 May with 996 passengers on board.

The *Olympic* (45,342 GT) passing Hythe Pier. It was broken up in 1936–37. (Nikki Goff Collection)

From 5 June 1907 the *Adriatic* commenced the Southampton-Cherbourg-Cobh-New York sailings.

The maiden voyage of the *Adriatic* (2) left Liverpool for New York on 8 May 1907. After the White Star Line and the Cunard Line merged to become the Cunard-White Star Line the *Adriatic* was used for cruising before being scrapped in Osaka, Japan, between 1934 and 1935.

The Olympic Trio and the White Star Dock

The White Star Dock was built in Southampton Docks especially for their Olympic Class liners, *Olympic, Titanic* and *Britannic,* and opened in 1911. With the success of the Cunard's *Lusitania* and *Mauretania* in 1907 the White Star Line decided that they would need to create three new liners to maintain a weekly service between New York and Southampton. However, they were not interested in challenging the Blue Riband held by the *Mauretania,* but instead wanted to offer the travelling public ships that were superior in luxury to Cunard's ocean liners. The original aim was to name vessels *Olympic, Titanic* and *Gigantic,* and the first ship to be launched was to be the *Olympic.* After the sinking of the *Titanic* it was decided not to name the third ship *Gigantic,* and the name was changed to the *Britannic.*

The *Olympic* was the first of the Olympic Class liners, built by Harland & Wolff, Belfast, and launched on 20 October 1910. In their publicity White Star boasted the first indoor swimming pool on an ocean liner and cabins whose décor was aimed to be at the highest level of luxury. At first there were 1,054 berths in the first-class cabins and only 510 berths in the second class. However, because of the profits that could be made from emigrants on the westbound voyages the company made available 1,030 third-class berths.

The *Olympic's* first-class dining room. (Bert Moody Collection)

The *Olympic's* smoking room. (Michael W. Pocock Collection)

The maiden voyage was from Southampton to New York on 14 June 1911, but later that year, on 20 September, she was in collision with the cruiser HMS *Hawke* in the Solent. After temporary repairs in Southampton the *Olympic* sailed for Belfast and had more permanent repairs done over a period of six weeks.

In 1912 there was the sinking of the *Titanic*, and as a result of the public enquiry White Star decided to make some safety improvements to the *Olympic*. The vessel was in dry dock in Belfast for six months to have the double bottom further extended up the sides to the waterline and the bulkheads fitted to the full height. Additional lifeboats were fitted – one of the problems on the *Titanic* was not enough lifeboats. This increased the ship's tonnage to 46,359 GT. The *Olympic's* transatlantic service from Southampton to New York restarted on 2 April 1913. During the time the *Olympic* was in the dry dock the transatlantic service was still operated by the *Oceanic* and *Majestic*.

During World War One the *Olympic* was at first 'dazzle-painted' for camouflage while trooping, but on 12 May 1918 she was attacked by *U-103* (commanded by Claus Rücker). The *Olympic* retaliated and rammed the submarine, sinking her.

The *Olympic* was converted from coal to oil firing in 1919 and during the 1920s she was very popular with Hollywood film stars on their transatlantic travels.

With the declining sales during the Great Depression the *Olympic* started to cruise, but in 1935 she was laid up in Southampton and eventually sold, first to Sir John Jarvis and then again to T. W. Ward, with the proviso that the vessel was broken up at Jarrow to alleviate the unemployment in the North East. The *Olympic* sailed from Southampton for Jarrow in October 1935 and in 1937 the remains of the hull were towed to Inverkeithing.

The *Olympic* was in fact the only vessel of the Olympic trio that completed the transatlantic crossing from Southampton to New York.

The *Olympic's* **first-class cabin, which is in a French Empire style. (Michael W. Pocock Collection)**

The *Olympic's* **grand staircase. (Michael W. Pocock Collection)**

The *Olympic* in New York. She was known as 'Old Reliable'. (Nikki Goff Collection)

The *Titanic's* grand staircase. (Michael W. Pocock Collection)

The *Titanic*

The *Titanic* was launched on 31 May 1911 and her maiden voyage began on 10 April 1912 from Southampton. After she had left Ocean Dock she proceeded at approximately 6 knots and approached the American Line *New York*, who was tied up alongside the White Star *Oceanic*. Neither vessel had steam up because of a coal strike. The suction of the *Titanic* as she passed started to pull the *New York* and the lines to the *Oceanic* snapped. However, due to the quick thinking of Captain Gale on the tug *Vulcan* and the swift action of Captain Smith on the *Titanic*, a disaster was avoided. The tug *Vulcan* got a line to the *New York* and pulled her away, allowing the *Titanic* to sail down Southampton Water and continue with what was to be her fateful voyage.

The *Titanic* sailed across to Cherbourg and picked up more mail and passengers. However, because the vessel was too large to dock, the passengers came out to the ship by tender. The *Titanic* left Cherbourg for Queenstown, where many Irish emigrants boarded her. When the *Titanic* collided with an iceberg just before midnight on 14 April, six compartments were ripped open below the waterline. On board, the two Marconi operators, Jack Phillips and Harold Bride, sent their first distress message out at 00.05hrs on 15 April, approximately 25 minutes after the ship had struck the iceberg. They continued on with their emergency signals until the power to the radio equipment was lost. At that point they abandoned ship, just before the *Titanic* sank at 02.20 hours, but the operator Jack Phillips was lost. However, the *Carpathia* came to the rescue and Harold Bride was saved. Once on board he continued work as an assistant operator on the *Carpathia*.

After the *Carpathia* had docked in New York on 18 April Marconi came on board to visit the operators, who were exhausted from the hours they had worked. Marconi had initially planned to sail on the *Titanic* but had at the last minute decided to sail on the *Lusitania*.

The *Aquitania* (45,647 GT) was built by John Brown & Co., Clydebank, and left Liverpool on 30 May 1914 on her maiden voyage to New York. The passenger capacity was for 618 first-class, 614 second-class and 1,998 third-class passengers. She was requisitioned for war service and carried troops to the Dardanelles in 1915 and was converted to a hospital ship.

In 1919 Cunard transferred their Express North Atlantic Service from Liverpool to Southampton, and after being converted from coal to oil fuel, the *Aquitania* returned to her transatlantic service in 1920, becoming popular with the Hollywood film stars. In 1926 the *Aquitania* had a major overhaul and the passenger accommodation was changed to 610 first-class, 950 second-class and 640 tourist-class passengers. Her voyages also included Mediterranean cruises. During a further refit new propellers were fitted and her speed was increased to 24 knots.

The *Titanic* had sailed with 1,316 passengers, of whom 825 were lost. Of the 885 crew, 673 were lost.

The *Britannic* (48,158 GT). She was built by Harland & Wolff, Belfast, in 1914 but never entered service for White Star Line due to World War One. (Mick Lindsay Collection)

Britannic

As a result of the Titanic inquiry the *Britannic* had changes made to her construction as a requirement for better safety at sea. These improvements consisted of a double hull along the engine and boiler rooms and raising the height of watertight doors. Further improvements included extra lifeboats and providing davits that enabled all lifeboats to be launched on either side of the ship, even if the ship was listing. The problem had been that once a vessel started to list to one side the lifeboats on the opposite side could not be launched.

As soon as the *Britannic* had been launched work started on fitting her out as a luxurious transatlantic passenger ship, but before she could start her transatlantic service from Southampton to New York, the invasion of Belgium by the Germans caused Britain to declare war on 4 August 1914.

The *Aquitania* as a hospital ship. (Mick Lindsay Collection)

The *Aquitania's* cabin-class palladian lounge. (Bert Moody Collection)

The *Aquitania's* second-class lounge. (Bert Moody Collection)

The *Aquitania's* cabin-class dining room. (Bert Moody Collection)

The *Aquitania's* third-class lounge. (Bert Moody Collection)

The *Aquitania's* first-class smoking room. (Bert Moody Collection)

The *Aquitania* (45,647 GT) on a C.R. Hoffmann postcard. (Bert Moody Collection)

The *Imperator's* (52,117 GT) eagle sculpture. The inscription reads 'Mein Feld ist die Welt'. (Mick Lindsay Collection)

At first the War Office only requisitioned the smaller ships as armed merchant cruisers or for troop transport. With the danger at sea the White Star Line withdrew the *Olympic* from service and she returned to Belfast on 3 November 1914. Just one year later, on 13 November 1915, the *Britannic* was requisitioned as a hospital ship. She returned to the fitting-out basin and was repainted white with large red crosses and a horizontal green stripe along the hull. She was renamed HMHS (Her Majesty's Hospital Ship) *Britannic*, and was under the command of Captain Charles Bartlett.

On 12 November 1916, almost one year from the day she was requisitioned, HMHS *Britannic* left Southampton for Lemnos, but while sailing near the Greek Island of Kea on 21 November 1916 there was a large explosion at 08.20 hours.

The *Imperator's* Winter Gardens leading into the Ritz-Carlton restaurant. (Bert Moody Collection)

A postcard sent from the *Imperator* dated 9 July 1914. (Bert Moody Collection)

It was not at first certain if the ship had hit a mine or been struck by a torpedo. It has been reported that the *Britannic* had hit a mine, but in fact she was torpedoed by the German submarine *U-73* (commanded by Gustav Sieß). Captain Bartlett, realising that the ship was sinking, gave the order to abandon ship at 08.25 hours. By 09.07 hours the *Britannic* had disappeared below the waves. The *Britannic* was the largest ship to be sunk in World War One.

Who has the Longest Ship?

The German shipping companies were challenged by the new ships coming on line and wanted to build the largest ships in the world. However, in their ambition to build the largest ship they were concerned about the British claim that the *Aquitania* was to be the largest and longest ship. To make the *Imperator* longer than the *Aquitania* they had a sculpture of a large bronze eagle, created by Professor Bruno Kruse of Berlin, attached to the bow. This sculpture had the words 'Mein Feld ist die Welt', which in English is 'My field is the world', in gold leaf. However, the stormy Atlantic weather was not very kind to the sculpture, which by 1914 had lost its wings in heavy seas and was eventually removed.

The *Imperator* left Cuxhaven for her maiden voyage on 10 June 1913 and anchored in Cowes Roads while she was served by tender from Southampton Docks before her transatlantic run to New York. The accommodation on the ship was very luxurious: the first-class saloon had a glass dome and was able to seat 700. The design of the ship, although containing outstanding luxury for the first class, also looked into improving the facilities and the comfort of the steerage passengers.

The *Vaterland* left Cuxhaven on her maiden voyage on 14 May 1914, but on her fourth transatlantic voyage she arrived in New York as World War One started and was seized when America entered the war.

However, World War One also ended German importance in transatlantic travel. Both these ships were taken as war reparations after the war. The *Vaterland* became the United States Line *Leviathan*, and another German ship, the *Bismarck* (56,551 GT), built in 1914, became the White Star Line *Majestic*, which was often fondly referred to as the *Magic Stick*.

A view from the chimney of the *Imperator's* smoking saloon. (Bert Moody Collection)

The *Imperator's* promenade deck. (Bert Moody Collection)

The *Imperator* was purchased by Cunard and renamed RMS *Berengaria* in April 1921, sailing from Southampton to New York. In October 1921 she had a six-month refit and her accommodation then became 972 first-class, 630 second-class and 515 tourist-class passengers with her gross tonnage increased to 52,226.

The *Berengaria's* catering department crew. (Mary Parker Collection)

The *Berengaria* (previously the *Imperator)* in Southampton Docks. (Mick Lindsay Collection)

The *Berengaria's* **Palm Court. (Bert Moody Collection)**

France

The French Line *France* left Le Havre for her maiden voyage to New York on 20 April 1912. In World War One she transported troops and was also a hospital ship. After the war she was used to transport troops back to New York. She resumed her commercial transatlantic service in 1923, when the vessel was taken into dry dock for an extensive refit and was also changed from coal to oil fuel. After this she had a period of cruising to the West Indies, Norwegian fjords and the Mediterranean until 1932, when she was laid up in Le Havre, before finally being scrapped in Dunkirk in 1935.

RMSP Company Cruising Ships *Arcadian* and *Atlantis*

The Royal Mail Steam Packet Company began cruising from the beginning of the 20th century and the two vessels at the forefront of this venture were the *Arcadian* and the *Atlantis (previously Andes)*.

The *Berengaria's* **swimming pool. (Bert Moody Collection)**

The *Ortona* (7,950 GT) was built for the Pacific Steam Navigation Company by Vickers, Sons & Maxim and launched in 1899. She was a two-funnel steamship and 500ft (152.4m) in length. The ship could carry 130 first, 162 second and 300 third-class passengers, and was used for taking passengers to Australia. In 1906 RMSPC Ltd took over the *Ortona* and she was used for the Liverpool to Australia service sailing under the joint Orient-Pacific Line. However, in 1910 the *Ortona* was rebuilt and converted to an 8,950-ton cruise ship for 320 first-class passengers and renamed *Arcadian*. The RMSPC advertised the vessel as an ocean-cruising yacht. It was while sailing to New York in January 1912 on board the *Arcadian* (1) that the founder of the Boy Scouts, Sir Robert Baden-Powell, met his future wife, Olave St Claire Soames.

The *Arcadian* was requisitioned by the government during World War One and converted for troop transport. On 15 April 1917 the ship was in the southern Aegean, 26 miles north-east of Milo, and sailing from Salonika to Alexandria when she was torpedoed by the German submarine *UC-74* (commanded by Wilhelm Marschall). At the time the torpedo struck the troops had just completed a boat drill. The *Arcadian* was so badly damaged that she sank in just six minutes, with a loss of 277 out of a total of 1,335 passengers and crew on board.

Asturias (1) and *Arcadian* (2)

The *Asturias* (1) left London on her maiden voyage on 24 January 1908 bound for Australia via the Suez Canal. The vessel was requisitioned on 1 August 1914 and converted into a naval hospital ship, leaving Southampton on 5 August to join the Grand Fleet at Scapa Flow. However, she returned to

The *Arcadian* (1) was named the *Ortona* prior to 1912. She was 7,950 GT in 1891 but later work increased her weight to 8,950 GT. She was torpedoed and sunk on 15 April 1917 while she was commissioned as a troopship. (Author's Collection)

The *Arcadian* (2) (12,105 GT), formerly the *Asturias,* at Bergen. She was rebuilt as a cruise ship. (Beryl Trewartha Collection)

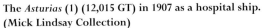

The *Asturias* (1) (12,015 GT) in 1907 as a hospital ship. (Mick Lindsay Collection)

Southampton on 23 August to become an army hospital ship and was refitted to carry 1,700 wounded. The wounded were brought from Le Havre to the Royal Victoria Military Hospital at Netley, Southampton, for treatment.

Due to the Dardanelles campaign the *Asturias* was sent to the Mediterranean and she transported the wounded between the Dardanelles, Salonika, Egypt and the UK, but on 1 February 1915 she was attacked by a submarine off the French coast, near Le Havre. This time she was lucky because the torpedo missed.

However, the *Asturias* was torpedoed again off Start Point on the night of 20 March 1917 with the loss of 35 lives. Although the vessel was declared a total loss by the underwriters the government purchased the ship and she was salvaged, becoming a floating ammunition hulk at Plymouth.

The RMSPC repurchased the ship in 1919 and she was towed to Belfast where she was rebuilt as a cruise ship and renamed the *Arcadian* (2) in 1923. From then on the *Arcadian* cruised to Scandinavia, the West Indies and Mediterranean and was also used for for some of the New York to Bermuda services. By the early 1930s, however, the luxury cruises were not very successful and by October 1930 the *Arcadian* (2) was laid up at Southampton, where she stayed until February 1933, when she was eventually sold to Japanese ship breakers.

Andes-Atlantis

The *Andes* was built by Harland & Wolff, Belfast, and launched on 8 May 1913. Along with the *Arlanza, Alcantara* and *Almanzora*, she operated the service from Southampton to the River Plate, South America.

The maiden voyage of the *Andes* left Liverpool on 26 September 1913, when she sailed from Liverpool to Valparaiso, Chile. For the maiden voyage the *Andes* was sailing under the Pacific Steam Navigation Company flag. Although the company had been taken over in 1910 by the RMPSC, the Pacific Steam Navigation Company still operated separately within the RMSPC group, but ships were often shared between companies. The *Andes* work was between Southampton and Buenos Aires, with ports of call at Lisbon, Rio de Janeiro and Montevideo.

From 1915 the *Andes* was used as an AMC on convoy escort work, but after the war she resumed the South American River Plate services. In 1929 she was refitted as a cruise ship for 450 first-class passengers, converted from coal to oil firing, her hull was painted white and she was renamed *Atlantis*.

During World War Two the *Atlantis* became a hospital ship and put into Southampton many times after the Normandy Landings in 1944. In 1946 she was released from war service and refitted to carry emigrants from the UK to Australia and New Zealand from 1948–52, when she was laid up and finally scrapped that year.

Roy Boulter Levi Cooper was born in 1910, the eldest of six children. At the age of 13 he left home and became a bellboy for the White Star Line. He gradually worked his way up to be a steward and eventually sailed on the *Arcadian* and the *Atlantis*. He used to tell his family that the worst thing was that when the ship ran into a raging storm and the waves were washing over the deck he still had to work, carrying a tray on the flat of his hand at shoulder height, but he was proud that he was never seasick. However, Roy was always pleased to come home to have some good home cooking!

The *Andes* (15,620 GT) was built by Harland & Wolff, Belfast, in 1913. She was renamed *Atlantis* in 1929 or 1930. (Bert Moody Collection)

The *Atlantis* (15,620 GT), formerly *Andes* (1), was refitted as a cruise ship in 1929. She was scrapped in 1952. The picture shows a postcard by C. R. Hoffmann. (Bert Moody Collection)

ROYAL MAIL LINE

GOOD MORNING

R.M.S.Y. "ATLANTIS"

Breakfast.

Chilled Grape Fruit

Apples   Oranges   Tangerines

Compote of Prunes

Rolled Oats   Cream of Wheat   Kellogg's Bran
Shredded Wheat   Post Toasties   Puffed Wheat
Grape Nuts   Force   Puffed Rice   Corn Flakes

Kippered Herrings
Fillet of Hake, Italienne

Hashed Mutton with Gherkins
Mashed and French Fried Potatoes

TO ORDER:

Eggs:—Boiled, Fried, Turned, Poached, Scrambled,
Shirred or en Cocotte

Omelettes:—Plain, Tomato, Savoury, Ham, Sweet, Paysanne,
Parmentier, Asparagus Tips, Artichoke, Lyonnaise

FROM THE GRILL (10-15 Minutes)

Wiltshire Bacon   Tomatoes   Grilled Gammon
Small Steak   Fried Sheep's Liver

COLD BUFFET:

Roast Ribs of Beef   Roast Leg of Mutton
Chicken Galantine   Breakfast Sausage   York Ham

Digestive Scones   Vienna & Wheatmeal Bread   Toast   Hot Rolls
Sultana Scones   Graham Rolls   Grissini Bread   Corn Cakes

Preserves   Maple & Golden Syrup   Honey

Teas:—China, Blended, Ceylon
Coffee   Chocolate, Menier   Instant Postum   Cocoa

Beef Tea and Ice Cream will be served on Deck at 11 a.m.

Thursday September 22, 1932

The abstract of the log for the Mediterranean cruise on the *Atlantis* for 9 September 1932–1 October 1932. (Beryl Trewartha Collection)

ROYAL MAIL
"ATLANTIS"
ABSTRACT OF LOG

The breakfast menu on the *Atlantis* on 22 September 1932. (Beryl Trewartha Collection)

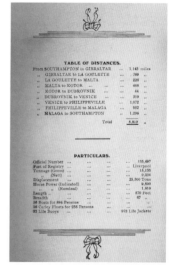

TABLE OF DISTANCES.

From SOUTHAMPTON to GIBRALTAR	...	1,143 miles
„ GIBRALTAR to LA GOULETTE	...	789 „
„ LA GOULETTE to MALTA	...	220 „
„ MALTA to KOTOR	...	468 „
„ KOTOR to DUBROVNIK	...	44 „
„ DUBROVNIK to VENICE	...	319 „
„ VENICE to PHILIPPEVILLE	...	1,072 „
„ PHILIPPEVILLE to MALAGA	...	952 „
„ MALAGA to SOUTHAMPTON	...	1,206 „
Total		5,819 „

PARTICULARS.

Official Number	...	...	135,497
Port of Registry	...	...	Liverpool
Tonnage (Gross)	...	...	15,135
(Nett)	...	...	9,334
Displacement	...	...	23,300 Tons
Horse Power (Indicated)	...	...	9,500
„ „ (Nominal)	...	...	1,610
Length	...	...	570 Feet
Breadth	...	...	67 „
16 Boats for 894 Persons			
16 Carley Floats for 256 Persons			
22 Life Buoys	...	...	975 Life Jackets

A table of distances for the *Atlantis's* Mediterranean cruise. (Beryl Trewartha Collection)

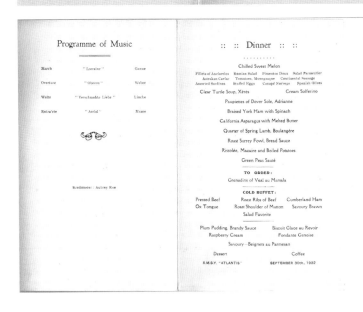

The abstract of the log for the *Atlantis's* Mediterranean cruise from 9–26 September,1932. (Beryl Trewartha Collection)

The abstract of the log for the *Atlantis's* Mediterranean cruise from 27 September–1 October 1932. (Beryl Trewartha Collection)

Below: The cover for the *Atlantis's* farewell dinner on 30 September 1932. (Beryl Trewartha Collection)

Bottom left: The menu for the farewell dinner on the *Atlantis* on 30 September 1932. (Beryl Trewartha Collection)

The *Almanzora* (15,551 GT) was refitted as passenger ship in 1919 after her war service. (Bert Moody Collection)

Almanzora

The *Almanzora* (16,034 GT) was the last of a class of ships built by Harland & Wolff, Belfast, for the Royal Mail Line's South American service and was launched 19 November 1914. In 1915 she joined her sister ship, *Andes*, as an armed merchant cruiser.

After World War One the *Almanzora* made her maiden voyage as a passenger liner on 9 January 1920 on the South American service. This service continued until 1939 when she was requisitioned as a troopship in World War Two. The *Almanzora* took Russian troops home in 1945 and John Minto remembers his time on the ship after he had left the Royal Navy: 'I was a first-class assistant steward in the dining-room sailing in the Mediterranean. I was also personal assistant steward to the captain's tiger.'

The *Almanzora* was taken out of service and in 1948 lay in Southampton Water for some time, but she was scrapped in 1948.

CHAPTER 3
THE GOLDEN YEARS

At the end of World War One returning soldiers were disillusioned with the world, but in North America there was a new-found wealth with the increasing wages offered through working in certain industries, such as the Henry Ford mass-produced Model T car industry.

There was an increasing prosperity and for many Americans that period became known as the 'Roaring Twenties', but in Europe it was known as the 'Golden Twenties'. For many it was a period of great social, artistic and cultural change. There was the introduction of radio broadcasting in Britain with the opening of the Marconi station 2MT at Writtle, Essex, and an increase in crystal sets ('Cat's Whisker') in the listeners' homes. In 1922 the BBC's first station, 2LO, opened. In 1925 John Logie Baird invented the television, and the movies were becoming very popular. It was also the time of the jazz age, the music of the Duke Ellington Band and George Gershwin. There were the great entertainers, Al Jolson and Charlie Chaplin, the 'flappers' and dancing the Charleston. It was also the time of the Art Deco period of art and design that influenced architecture, interior design, fashion and painting.

From the use and development of aircraft in World War One came the transportation of freight and mail, and Charles Lindbergh became the first aviator to cross the Atlantic in May 1927. Just one year later Amelia Earhart became the first woman to fly the Atlantic. Because she had no experience in flying the tri-motor Fokker 'Friendship' or of instrument flying, the aircraft was actually flown by Wilmer Stultz and Louis Gordon, with Amelia acting as 'Commander'. The flight took off from Newfoundland on 17 June 1928 and 20 hours 40 minutes later landed at Burry Point, Wales. After staying the night in a hotel Earhart flew on to Southampton, landing at Woolston to be welcomed by the Mayor of Southampton, Mrs Foster Welch, and had the experience of crossing the River Itchen on the floating bridge. Her journey continued on to London to a hero's welcome.

The era ended with the Wall Street Crash and the beginning of the Great Depression, a time of great hardship. In America there was the period of Prohibition in the 1930s; however, just a few miles out at sea, the ships were able to sell alcohol and this was the start of the 'booze cruises' that left New York for weekends afloat. The shipping companies saw this as a way of making profits and they started to compete to provide the best in luxury and comfort for their passengers.

It was the ocean liner that was the popular way to cross the Atlantic Ocean in the 1920s. This was important for the businessmen travelling to conduct their business overseas. There were travelling film stars and stage entertainers and music groups, including jazz musicians and big bands, visiting Europe. It was also in 1925 that P&O returned to Southampton as their home port after an absence of 44 years.

During the 1920s and 1930s cruising in Britain was mainly for the rich due to the economic climate after World War One and the 1929 Wall Street Crash. The ordinary British citizen could not afford a cruise and went to the seaside, which was very popular for families who could not afford holidays. At that time, travelling by train was probably the most popular means of transport for the average British family, but for those who could afford their own car the Austin 7 was the most desirable car of the 1920s.

Replacing Ships of the P&O Fleet after World War One

From World War One to the end of World War Two P&O had acquired other shipping companies, including the British India Steam Navigation Company, the New Zealand Shipping Company, Federal Steam, Orient Line and General Steam. However, a significant number of the P&O fleet were lost during World War One and there was a need to replace those lost. P&O placed an order for both the RMS *Mooltan* and her sister ship, the RMS *Maloja*, on 29 November 1918.

Mooltan was built for the P&O Line by Harland & Wolff, Belfast, with accommodation for 327 first-class and 329 second-class passengers. She was launched on 15 February 1923 and sailed from London on her maiden voyage to Australia on 21 December 1923. As well as carrying first-class passengers she carried many thousands of emigrants to a new life in Australia.

In 1929 the *Mooltan* had alterations made to her engines, and along with her quadruple-expansion engines, low-pressure turbines were added that increased her service speed to 17 knots.

At the start of World War Two in 1939 she became an AMC, serving in the South Atlantic and based in Freetown, Sierra Leone. By 1941 she was refitted as a troopship but kept her second funnel, and she took part in Operation Torch and the North African landings at Oran.

In 1947 the *Mooltan* was returned to P&O and refitted in 1948 with accommodation for 1,030 tourist-class passengers before returning to the Australia emigration trade. In January 1954 the *Mooltan* was sold and scrapped at Faslane.

The *Mooltan* (20,847 GT) was built for P&O (SNC) by Harland & Wolff, Belfast. She was broken up in 1954. (Mick Lindsay Collection)

Competition Between the White Star Line and the Cunard Line

Prior to World War One Norddeutscher Lloyd planned to build two sister ships of 34,000 GT, and they were to be called the *Columbus* and *Hindenburg*, with the *Columbus* launched first on 17 December 1913. However, with the war starting in 1914, work on the *Columbus* and *Hindenburg* was stopped. It was not until the end of the war that war reparations were discussed and in 1919 Britain was allotted the *Columbus*. Work commenced on completing the ship and in June 1920 she was purchased by the White Star Line from the British government and joined the *Olympic* and *Majestic* on the transatlantic service. The *Columbus* was renamed *Homeric* in keeping with the White Star Line, ending their vessels' names with '-ic'.

The *Homeric* sailed into Southampton on 21 January 1922 and left on her maiden voyage to New York on 15 February 1922. One of the *Homeric's* qualities was that she was one of the steadiest ships afloat in rough weather and passengers often chose the ship because of this. She became affectionately known as 'Old Reliable'.

With the completion of the White Star Line trio *Olympic*, *Majestic* and *Homeric* there was now direct competition in place with Cunard's *Berengaria*, *Aquitania* and *Mauretania*.

Cunard Replaces Ships Lost in World War One

The *Scythia*, *Samaria* and *Laconia* were the first vessels that Cunard built to replace those lost in World War One for the passenger and cargo transatlantic service and also for cruising.

Scythia (2)

The *Scythia* (2) made her maiden voyage from Liverpool to New York in August 1921. The *Scythia* and her sister ships were very popular with passengers for their comfort and reliability, but the *Scythia* did have some mishaps. One was on 30

The *Homeric* (34,351 GT) shown on a C.R. Hoffmann postcard. She was built for Norddeutscher Lloyd as *Columbus* before being bought by White Star Line in 1920. She was broken up in 1936. (Bert Moody Collection)

The Ocean Dock in 1922. The *Homeric* and *Olympic* can be seen sailing and the *Berengaria* and *Aquitania* are also visible. The picture was taken by F.G.O Stuart, the official War Office photographer for the docks. (Edwin Praine Collection)

September 1923 when she was outward bound to Boston but was making for Queenstown. She was in dense fog in the Irish Sea when she ran into the White Star liner *Cedric*, which was leaving the harbour. Neither vessel was seriously damaged, but the *Scythia* returned to Liverpool to be repaired.

During the period before World War Two the *Scythia* was engaged in transatlantic crossing and cruising, but when she left for New York in August 1939 she was packed full with mainly American passengers wanting to get home before the war started in Europe. From 1939 she became a troopship and returned to service in 1945. The *Scythia* was finally broken up at Inverkeithing in 1958.

Samaria

The *Samaria* was the sister ship to the *Scythia*, and she made her maiden voyage from Liverpool to Boston on 19 April 1922. By November of that year she was also calling at New York.

World cruises followed in 1923, which became so popular that they were repeated for their interested passengers. By August 1939 she made her final transatlantic crossing before World War Two started on 3 September 1939. The *Samaria* was converted to troop transport and in 1948 returned to service, but she was broken up at Inverkeithing in 1956.

Laconia

The maiden voyage of the *Laconia* left Southampton on 25 May 1922 for New York, calling at Queenstown. The accommodation was for 350 first-class, 350 second-class and 1,500 third-class passengers. After sailing from Liverpool to New York in June 1922 she transferred to sail from Hamburg to New York, calling at Southampton and Cherbourg for four

The *Scythia* (2) (19,730 GT) was built by Vickers-Armstrong, Barrow-in-Furness. She was broken up in 1958. (Mick Lindsay Collection)

The *Ascania* (2) (14,013 GT) was broken up in 1957. (Mick Lindsay Collection)

voyages, and in January 1923 she undertook the first world cruise before returning to the Liverpool to New York service. In 1928 the *Laconia* was refitted for cabin, tourist and third-class passengers, but in 1934 she was involved in a collision in thick fog with the freighter *Pan Royal* off the coast of the United States. Both vessels were seriously damaged but able to continue under their own steam. The *Laconia* returned to New York for repairs and in 1935 was back in service. She was converted to an AMC in 1939 and was a troopship in 1940. She was torpedoed in the South Atlantic in 1942 and sank.

Ascania (2)

After the *Scythia, Samaria* and *Laconia* there was the *Aurania* (3), whose maiden voyage was in 1924, and the *Ascania* (2) and *Alaunia* (2), with maiden voyages in 1925. They were to be used on the Canadian service.

The *Ascania* (2) was built in 1923 by Armstrong Whitworth & Co. yard, Newcastle upon Tyne, and launched on 20 December 1923. She sailed on her maiden voyage on 22 May 1925 from Southampton to Cherbourg, Queenstown, Quebec and Montreal. She was designed for the Canada trade, carrying migrants in 1927 in cabin, tourist and third class, but then in 1939 changed to cabin and third class.

During the summer the *Ascania* would sail from London, calling at Southampton and on to Quebec and Montreal, but in the winter when the St Lawrence River was frozen she would sail to Halifax and New York.

There were also some mishaps when *Ascania* collided with the Canadian Pacific *Beaverbrae* at Quebec in 1934, and in 1938 she hit a rock while sailing down the St Lawrence River, causing damage to the propeller and flooding some holds. However, within a short time the vessel had been repaired and was back in service.

In the first week of October 1934 the *Ascania* was involved in answering a distress call from a British cargo vessel, the 4,213-ton *Millpool*, which was seriously taking on water. The *Millpool*, with a crew of 25, was taking a cargo of grain from Montreal to Danzig, but despite an extensive search by the *Ascania* and the cargo ship *Beaverhill* no wreckage or survivors could be found and the search was called off. It was thought the *Millpool* had sunk approximately 700 miles from Labrador. However, in December 1934 the *Ascania* did rescue nine crew members from the freighter *Usworth*, which was sinking in the Atlantic. The *Ascania's* master, Captain Bisset, had experience of other famous disasters at sea; as Second Officer on the *Carpathia* he had been involved in the rescue of many of the *Titanic's* survivors. During World War Two he was master of the *Queen Mary* from 1942 and after the war Commodore Sir James Bisset took command of the *Queen Elizabeth*.

Royal Mail Lines
Asturias (2)

In 1924 two Royal Mail liners were ordered and built by Harland & Wolff, Belfast. They were the *Asturias* (2) and the *Alcantara* (2), the largest in the Royal Mail Fleet, and the largest diesel-powered ships in the world.

The *Georgic* (26,943 GT) was the last ship built for the White Star Line. She was broken up in 1956. (Mick Lindsay Collection)

The *Asturias* was the second Royal Mail Line ship with that name and was built and launched on 7 July 1925. At the time she was the largest motor ship in the world and also the first Royal Mail passenger ship to have a cruiser stern. Her forward funnel was a dummy. The *Asturias's* maiden voyage left Southampton on 26 February 1926 with Captain E.W.E. Morrison in command, heading for La Plata (River Plate), Argentina, but suffered with poor speed and bad vibration.

In 1934 she was converted to geared turbine propulsion, and new propellors by Harland & Wolff gave a service speed of 18–19 knots. A new bow was fitted that had been reshaped and lengthened a further 10ft (3.05m), making the length 665ft (202.7m). In addition the funnels were made taller. Passenger accommodation was altered to 330 first-class, 220 second-class and 768 third-class passengers. She carried a crew of 425. The same alterations were made to the *Alcantara* (2).

In 1935 the *Asturias* took part in the Silver Jubilee Spithead Review in 1935 for George V and Queen Mary, representing Royal Mail.

White Star Line *Britannic* & *Georgic*

The *Britannic* and the *Georgic* were the last two White Star Line ships built. The maiden voyage of the *Britannic* was on 28 June 1930 and the maiden voyage of the *Georgic* was on 25 June 1932. However, in the early 1930s both the White Star Line and the Cunard Line were in financial difficulties and a decision was made to merge both companies. This was completed on 10 May 1934 and from then on the newly merged companies became known as Cunard-White Star Line. Both the *Britannic* and the *Georgic* were able to keep the White Star colours when the companies merged.

Both ships had two funnels, but the forward funnel on each ship was a dummy. On board the *Georgic* the space inside the funnel was used as the engineers' smoking room and the wireless room.

Canadian Pacific *Empress of Britain*

The *Empress of Britain* was launched by HRH the Prince of Wales, later to be Edward VIII, on 11 June 1930. She left Southampton on her maiden voyage to Quebec on 27 May 1931, and at the same time set a westbound Canadian transatlantic record.

The *Empress of Britain* started her first world cruise on 3 December 1931. As speed was not important on the cruises, two of the ship's turbines were shut down and the two outer propellers were removed to help reduce fuel costs, although this did not happen on all the world cruises, when all four propellers were in use. On these cruises the *Empress of Britain* left New York, crossed the Atlantic to the Mediterranean sea, through the Suez Canal to India, Java, Bali, and then on to China and Japan. From Japan she crossed the Pacific to the west coast of America, through the Panama Canal, returning to New York.

In June 1939 King George VI and Queen Elizabeth sailed home on the *Empress of Britain* after their Canadian tour. By September 1939 World War Two had started and the *Empress of Britain* then became a troopship. On 26 October 1940 the

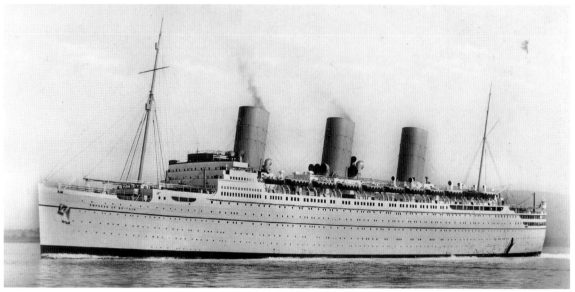

The *Empress of Britain* (42,348 GT) shown on a C.R. Hoffmann postcard. She was built in 1931 by John Brown & Company, Clydebank. (Bert Moody Collection)

Empress of Britain was attacked by a German plane off the coast of Ireland and set on fire. Although she was taken in tow, after many of the passengers and crew were saved, the *U-32* (commanded by Hans Jenisch) sank her two days later with two torpedoes.

The *Empress of Britain* (42,348 GT) was the largest British liner sunk during World War Two. However, the Italian liners *Rex* (51,062 GT) and *Conte di Savoia* (48,502 GT) were larger and both were destroyed by Allied attacks. The *Rex* was thought to have been anchored near Trieste when she was attacked in September 1940 and she rolled over on her port side after she was set on fire, but no attempt was made to salvage her. The *Conte di Savoia* was laid up near Venice when she was bombed by Allied aircraft, set on fire and sunk in September 1943.

A first-hand account of the attack and sinking of the *Empress of Britain* can be read in *The Story of Southampton Docks* by Mike Roussel.

Italian Line
Rex and *Conti de Savoia*
The *Rex* left Genoa on 27 September 1932 for her maiden voyage to New York, calling at Naples and Gibraltar. The *Conti di Savoia* was more luxurious than on the *Rex*, and her maiden voyage left Genoa on 30 November 1932 for New York, calling at Villefranche.

Interestingly, the *Conti di Savoia* had a unique gyroscope stabilising system and appears to be the only vessel to have been fitted with it. The design of the gyroscope system was to limit the roll to three degrees in rough seas and was popular with passengers. However, the fin system of stabilisers was the chosen system for the other shipping lines, partly due to the cost, efficiency and the external use, the fins extending out from the ship's hull. In addition, the amount of space and weight (each gyro weighed 100 tons) that the gyros took up within the vessel may have limited its value, and the fin system was thus more attractive.

P&O
The 'Straths'
Between 1930 and 1938 P&O changed their livery from the previous black hulls and stone-coloured superstructure to white hulls and buff funnels. Five ships were built and became known as the 'White Sisters'. They were the *Strathnaver* (22,547 GT), *Strathaird* (22,568 GT), *Strathmore* (24,428 GT), *Stratheden* (23,722 GT) and *Strathallan* (23,722 GT), collectively known as the 'Straths'.

The *Strathnaver* and *Strathaird* were built for the P&O fleet in 1930 and were the first major P&O passenger ships to have the all-white hulls and buff funnels that were to become the P&O livery that we see on their cruises today. They had three funnels, but the first and third funnels were dummies. P&O *Strathnavar* was to be on the run from London through the Suez Canal and on to Bombay (now Mumbai) and then to Australia. She left London on her maiden voyage on 1 October 1931 for the Australian mail service to Sydney, via Marseilles, Suez, Bombay and Colombo. By 1938 the *Strathnaver* was fitted out with refrigeration equipment to carry beef. P&O *Strathaird's* maiden voyage to Sydney left on 12 February 1932, and from then on the two White Sisters took part in a regular cruise programmes in between their Australian runs.

The *Strathnaver* (22,547 GT) before World War Two with three funnels. She was built in 1931 by Vickers-Armstrong, Barrow-in-Furness, but was rebuilt in 1949 with one funnel. She was broken up in Hong Kong in 1962. (Mick Lindsay Collection)

P&O *Strathmore* was the third of the 'Strath' series and her maiden voyage was a cruise to the Canary Islands, leaving Tilbury on 27 September 1935. P&O *Stratheden* also sailed from Tilbury to Australia on her maiden voyage, on 24 December 1935, calling at Freemantle, Melbourne and Sydney. P&O *Strathallan* entered service in 1938, but was sunk by *U-562* (commanded by Horst Hamm) on 21 December 1942, approximately 40 miles north of Oran, while part of Operation Torch.

By 1938 P&O had continued their pre-war builds with the launch of the P&O *Canton*, which joined the P&O *Corfu* and P&O *Carthage*, built in 1931 on the Far East service. P&O *Canton* made her maiden voyage from Tilbury on 8 October 1938, calling at Bombay, Singapore, Hong Kong and Yokohama.

The *Strathnaver*, post-war, with one funnel. (Mick Lindsay Collection)

THE FLAGSHIP—ILE de FRANCE

French Line

The *Ile de France* (43,153 GT) was completed in 1927 for the French Line (CGT). (Bert Moody Collection)

The *Ile de France* in 1948. She was rebuilt in 1947 with two funnels, having had her dummy third funnel removed. She was sunk for the making of the film *The Last Voyage* in 1960. (Bert Moody Collection)

The first-class boat deck on the *Ile de France*. (Bert Moody Collection)

Ile de France

Ile de France sailed on her maiden voyage from Le Havre to New York on 22 June 1927, calling at Plymouth. At first she was fitted with a catapult in her stern for a seaplane to take off and this was used on 13 August 1928 when a seaplane was launched while still 200 miles off New York. This aimed to speed the delivery of mail. However, it was not very successful and the catapult was removed in 1930.

Further accommodation work was carried out in 1932 when the accommodation was increased for 670 first-class, 408 cabin-class and 508 third-class passengers.

The service from Le Havre-Southampton-New York started on 9 January 1935, but the accommodation was changed to cabin, tourist and third class. Southampton was used as a port of call instead of Plymouth, although Plymouth was still used at times.

Normandie

The aim of the French Line was to build the world's largest liner and to create a luxurious environment that would attract passengers. On her maiden voyage in May 1935 she captured the Blue Riband from the Italian liner *Rex*.

With the pending launch of the *Queen Mary*, which would be larger than the *Normandie*, plans were made to increase her size to meet the challenge. When she went for her

The *Ile de France's* grand dining salon. (Bert Moody Collection)

winter overhaul her size was increased by building a large deckhouse, which made her tonnage 82,799 GT and finally 83,423 GT, thus beating *Queen Mary's* 80,774 GT. However, the *Queen Mary* was launched and still won the Blue Riband in

The *Normandie* (79,280 GT) was completed in 1935 by Penhoet St Nazaire. She caught fire in February 1942 and was burnt out. She was broken up in 1946. (Bert Moody Collection)

The *Normandie's* first-class dining saloon. (Bert Moody Collection)

The *Normandie's* Escalator of Honour. (Bert Moody Collection)

1936 with a speed of 30.1 knots. The *Normandie* was not going to give in and regained the Blue Riband in 1937 at a speed of 30.9 knots and improved again in August 1937 with a speed of 31.2 knots.

One year later, in August 1938, *Queen Mary* regained the Blue Riband at a speed of 31.6 knots, holding it until 1952 when the *United States* took it away.

Queen Mary

A new liner was planned as a replacement for the *Mauretania* and in 1930 Cunard announced that the vessel was to be built by John Brown & Company. The keel of job number 534 was laid down on 31 January 1931. The construction of 534 continued through the year, with a

A theatre presentation on board the *Normandie*. (Bert Moody Collection)

launch date set for May 1932. However, in December 1931 the work was suspended due to the economic depression, with the John Brown workforce laid off.

The *Queen Mary* (80,773 GT) in Southampton Docks. (Nikki Goff Collection)

An illustration of the third-class lounge on the _Queen Mary_. (Courtesy of Edwin Praine)

The _Queen Mary's_ tourist-class swimming pool. (Courtesy of Edwin Praine)

The _Queen Mary's_ main hall and shopping centre, located on the prom deck. (Courtesy of Edwin Praine)

An illustration of the third-class lounge on the _Queen Mary_. (Courtesy of Edwin Praine)

It was the government that came to the rescue with loans, providing the two rival shipping companies Cunard and White Star amalgamated to become Cunard-White Star Ltd. The loan enabled the work on Job No. 534 to continue and in April 1934 work recommenced. She was launched and named _Queen Mary_ on 26 September 1934 by Her Majesty Queen Mary, accompanied by His Majesty King George V. This was also the first time that an event such as this was broadcast live to the whole nation by the BBC.

The _Queen Mary_ was finally completed in March 1936, but due to the death of King George V on 20 January 1936 it was his eldest son, now Edward VIII, who visited the newly completed _Queen Mary_ on 5 March 1936.

After completing the initial trials off Arran the _Queen Mary_ then set sail for Southampton, arriving on 27 March and sailing down Southampton Water to the King George V dry dock (No. 7 dry dock) to be painted. After receiving three coats of paint the _Queen Mary_ then set sail again on 15 April to undertake speed trials at the Admiralty Measured Mile off the Isle of Arran. The _Queen Mary_ was designed with a cruising speed of 28½ knots, but although no official figure was given it is thought that she achieved speeds of over 32.84 knots. The _Queen Mary_ then returned to Southampton on 20 April to take on stores and take part in her shake-down cruise. She was handed over to Cunard on 11 May 1936 and the Cunard flag was flown from the mainmast and the White Star flag flown below it. The _Queen Mary_ moved into Ocean Dock to prepare for her maiden voyage.

Accommodation On Board

The accommodation on the new _Queen Mary_ was for 749 cabin-class, 760 tourist-class and 579 third-class passengers. The two top decks, which included the sports deck and sun decks, were used exclusively by the cabin class. The passengers could play squash, deck tennis and other deck games or visit the Verandah Grill, which was also on the sun deck and was a place where many famous celebrities were seen eating. It also gave a good view aft of the ship and sea.

The public rooms were aimed to reflect all that was best in modern living afloat in the 1930s. The magnificent first-class main lounge was one of the largest rooms afloat, and libraries, swimming pools, cinemas, gymnasiums, garden lounges and ballrooms show some of the diversity of the public rooms.

Most of the cabin-class public rooms were situated on the promenade deck and included the main foyer, which was the main shopping centre, leading to the lounge and gallery. Further aft was the ballroom and smoking room, and still further aft on the promenade deck was the tourist-class promenade and smoking room. Moving forward on the promenade deck was the cabin-class library, drawing room, and the observation and cocktail lounges.

The _Queen Mary's_ tourist-class lounge on the main deck. (Courtesy of Edwin Praine)

The main deck was below the promenade deck and forward was the third-class garden lounge, situated directly below the observation lounge. To the aft was the tourist-class public room that included the lounge and cocktail bar, library and writing room and also a children's playroom.

The cabin-class cabins were all amidships, with the tourist class aft and third class towards the bows, ensuring that the most comfortable sailing positions were in order of class. It was possibly better when the ship was pitching, but there would have been little difference when she was rolling!

Beneath the main deck were A to H decks. On A deck was the third-class smoking room and on B deck the third-class lounge. On B, C and E decks forward were the cabins for crew. Other crew cabins, including the stewards, were aft on C, D and E decks.

The Galley was on C deck, with the cabin, tourist and third-class dining saloons all on the same deck. The cabin-class swimming pool was on E deck and the tourist-class on F deck.

Cargo or cars were carried on G deck forward, and below on H deck was the baggage and/or cars. In order there was the No. 1 boiler room, No. 2 boiler room, forward turbo generator room, No. 3 boiler room, No. 4 boiler room, aft turbo generator room, No. 5 boiler room, forward engine room and aft engine room.

The Inaugural Cruise and Maiden Voyage

The *Queen Mary* left on her inaugural cruise from Southampton on Thursday 14 May and returned on Friday 15 May. On 24 May, three days before she left on her maiden voyage, she was visited by Queen Mary, the Queen Mother, accompanied by the new monarch, King Edward VIII, the Duke and Duchess of York and their children, Princess Elizabeth and Princess Margaret.

On 27 May 1936 the *Queen Mary* left Southampton at 4.33pm for her maiden voyage, arriving at Cherbourg at 8:47pm and departing again at 12:39am on 28 May. There was the expectation that with her power and speed she would break the Blue Riband record on her maiden voyage, but she was held up when she ran into thick fog and had to reduce speed. She arrived at Pier 90, New York, at 4.20pm on 1 June 1936.

Bandleader Henry Hall, who was the conductor of the BBC Dance Orchestra, was asked by Cunard to conduct the *Queen Mary*'s band on her maiden voyage. He wrote *Somewhere at Sea* as a special tribute for the occasion. It was sung by Dan Donavan when it was recorded on 6 May in advance of the maiden voyage. On board for the maiden voyage there were broadcasts from the ship, and guests artists included Larry Adler on the harmonica and Frances Day, who sang *Somewhere at Sea*.

Edwin Praine was a crew member on the *Queen Mary* for her maiden voyage and remembers the bands playing on the quayside as they left Southampton. During the maiden voyage across the North Atlantic Edwin Praine was given a souvenir booklet of the maiden voyage by two passengers. They told him, 'We have two booklets so you can have one of them.' The welcome in New York was a sight to be seen with many sailing craft on the Hudson sailing alongside the *Queen Mary* and the quayside so crowded that it was difficult to disembark.

Another famous name who had sailed as a passenger on the *Queen Mary* was R.J. Mitchell, the designer of many of the Supermarine aircraft, including the aircraft that won the Schneider Trophy for Britain, but perhaps was most well-known for the famous Spitfire of World War Two. He was on deck and saw a member of the crew taking photographs of an aircraft flying over the *Queen Mary*, and he asked the photographer if he could see the photographs when they were developed. He was not well-known to the crew and was asked if he was interested in aviation. R.J. Mitchell said he was and added, 'As a matter of fact, I designed that plane.'

The aim to win the Blue Riband for the fastest transatlantic crossing was achieved by the *Queen Mary* on her westbound voyage from 20–24 August and eastbound from 26–30 August 1936, when she took away the record from the French Line *Normandie*. However, the *Normandie* claimed the Blue Riband back for the westbound crossing in March 1937 and the eastbound in August 1937. The *Queen Mary*, not to be beaten, regained both the westbound and eastbound transatlantic crossings in August 1938 and held the record for 14 years until it was broken by the *United States* in July 1952.

Bill O'Brien sailed on the *Queen Mary* one year after she had made her maiden voyage: 'I sailed on the *Queen Mary* as a commis waiter and was then aged 16 in 1937. I started serving in the main saloon and then went down to the third-class saloon. There I had my own table and also served some of the crew, including the master at arms, the masseur, and then the passengers.'

Cruises for German Workers in the 1930s

Wilhelm Gustloff (25,484 GT) was built as a cruise ship and was the first of Hitler's KdF (Kraft durch Freude, meaning 'Strength through Joy') vessels, which enabled the German workers to take part in cruises.

The overall aim was to give the workers cheap holiday activities and pleasure cruises so that they would focus more on their jobs and increase productivity. *Wilhelm Gustloff* was launched in 1937 in the presence of Adolf Hitler. She later became a hospital ship during the war and was also used to accommodate U-boat trainees. In 1945 *Wilhelm Gustloff* was used to evacuate over 6,000 refugees, prisoners and the wounded from Gotenhafen, Germany (now Gdynia, Poland), when she was torpedoed by a Russian submarine with a great loss of life.

The Build-up to World War Two

Mauretania (2)

The *Mauretania* (2) was built by Cammell Laird of Birkenhead and was the first new ship delivered to the merged Cunard-White Star Line. She was launched on 28 July 1938.

The *Mauretania* (2) (35,738 GT) was launched in 1938 and completed by Cammell Laird, Birkenhead, in 1939. She was broken up in 1965. (Mick Lindsay Collection)

On her first transatlantic crossing the *Mauretania* sailed from Liverpool, although the Cunard terminal was in Southampton. After that the sailings were from London-Southampton-Le Havre-New York, working alongside the *Georgic* and *Britannic*. At the time she was claimed to be the largest vessel to enter London Docks. However, this service did not last long because the ship was laid up in New York in December 1939 and later converted to a troopship.

The Royal Mail Line *Andes* (2) was launched on 7 March 1939 by Viscountess Craigavon, the wife of the Prime Minister of Northern Ireland, at the Harland & Wolff yard in Belfast. It was the Royal Mail Line's largest passenger ship ever to be built. However, she arrived just as World War Two started and was still in the fitting-out dock when war was declared on 3 September 1939. Her maiden voyage, planned for later in September, was cancelled and she was painted in grey wartime colours.

Last Peacetime Transatlantic Crossings

Just before war was declared there was a rush to leave England for the United States, and one of those departing ships was the *Samaria* (2), which left Liverpool on 26 August 1939 and arrived in New York on 3 September 1939, the day that war with Germany was declared.

Just four days later, on 30 August 1939, the *Queen Mary* made her last peacetime transatlantic crossing from Southampton to New York and was then berthed there at the start of World War Two. When she left Southampton she was carrying 2,552 passengers, including Bob and Dolores Hope, who were returning to New York after a holiday in Europe, a journey Bob mentions in his autobiography, *Don't Shoot, It's Only Me*. It was the largest number of passengers the *Queen Mary* had carried to date. The ship also had gold bullion on board during this voyage, and she remained in New York until the end of the year while a decision was made about what role she would play in World War Two.

The *Queen Mary* had left Southampton on 30 August 1939, and on the day war was declared the captain received a message from the Admiralty instructing him to be on 'Full War Alert' and to look out for aircraft and submarines. The captain ordered the *Queen Mary* to full power and assumed a zigzag pattern, arriving at New York on 4 September 1939.

Bob Hope found out that war had been declared from his wife Dolores, who had just returned from Mass: 'When she came back, she said to me, "We are at war". That woke me up. It was better than a cold shower.

'I went up to the saloon. It was jammed. The ship was overloaded with passengers, many of whom slept on deck. They had paid any price to get aboard what they felt might be the last boat to freedom. Everyone was crying. It was one of the saddest moments I can remember.'

The captain announced that the *Queen Mary* would run without lights at night, and as an extra precaution the crew had to black out the ship's portholes. Bob Hope: 'There were German submarines in those waters. I did a show for the passengers that evening to cheer them up and prove we weren't frightened, but it was tough dancing wearing a life preserver!'

The *Queen Mary* was joined in New York by the newly built *Queen Elizabeth*, which sailed secretly to confuse the Germans. Bill O'Brien remembers this clearly: 'The *Queen Elizabeth* liner was built on Clydebank and was known as the "Pride of the Clyde". She was finished and was due to sail down to Southampton, and all the riggers were waiting on 43 Berth for her arrival. The *Queen Elizabeth* didn't arrive but sailed directly to America instead to mislead the Germans, and the crew were paid a bonus of £30 to sail over with her!'

Both the *Mauretania* and *Normandie* were also berthed in New York. The *Normandie* was laid up on 28 August 1939, just before war was declared on 3 September 1939, and was never to leave New York. Five days after Pearl Harbour the United States government seized the *Normandie* and she was renamed USS *Lafayette*. The vessel was being fitted out as a troop ship, but caught fire, capsized and was lost. She was eventually scrapped.

On 1 September 1939 the *Ile de France* sailed from Le Havre to New York, but once she had arrived in New York the French Line decided that it would be better for her to remain in New York than be lost if she returned to the war in Europe. On 1 May 1940 the *Ile de France* sailed to Marseilles and then eventually on to Singapore where, with the fall of France, the Royal Navy seized her. The ship was requisitioned, converted for trooping and sailed from Singapore to Sydney while operating with French crew under Cunard-White Star management for the remainder of the war.

The 'Phoney War'

The 'Phoney War' has been described as a period when Britain was waiting for something to happen after war was declared on 3 September 1939, as nothing much happened until April 1940. However, that was not the case at sea, where the *Athenia* was sunk on the very day war was declared. The *Athenia* was the first civilian ship sunk by a U-boat without warning in World War Two. She had left Glasgow on 1 September 1939, calling at Liverpool and Belfast before sailing out into the North Atlantic. Two days later Britain declared war on Germany. The German *U-30* had been at sea since leaving Wilhelmshaven on 22 August 1939, under strict orders to avoid contact or be seen but to keep a look out for armed merchant cruisers. The U-boat commanders had been issued with orders to stop merchant ships and search them. If they were carrying enemy cargo they could then sink the ship. The *U-30* (commanded by Fritz-Julius Lemp) had known about this and also received a message on 3 September 1939 that Germany was now at war with Britain. The commander acted against his orders and attacked the *Athenia* because he assumed she was an armed merchant cruiser as she was sailing without lights and zigzagging.

The attack was carried out approximately 250 miles west of Inishtrahull, Ireland. The *U-30* fired a torpedo at 19.39 hours on 3 September 1939, which struck the port side of the engine room. The *Athenia*, under the command of James Cook, sunk at 10.00 hours on 4 September with the loss of 118 lives, including 28 American passengers.

On land for the British civilians nothing seemed to happen, especially as they had been expecting a similar attack to the one the Germans had made on Poland in 1939. Winston Churchill had referred to this period of time as the 'Twilight War'.

Information on U-boats has been obtained from www.uboat.net.

CHAPTER 4
WORLD WAR TWO 1939-45

Southampton in the War Years

With the threat of war looming in the late 1930s it became clear that if there was a war Southampton would be a high-priority target for the German Luftwaffe because Southampton Docks was the number one military port, a major commercial port with ship building and ship repair facilities. It was also where the Vickers Supermarine Factory was based for building the Spitfire. The authorities prepared well with advanced air raid precautions, including blackout rehearsals and bomb shelters identified for the public.

In total there were 57 air raids on Southampton, but on 24 September 1940 the Supermarine works at Woolston was hit by German bombs and 100 workers were killed. There was little damage to the works, but just two days after there was another air raid on the factory when 30 more workers were killed. This time the factory was badly damaged and the Minister for Aircraft Production, Lord Beaverbrook, ordered production to be spread along the south coast away from Southampton. However, the Spitfire production in Southampton did continue, but in various buildings, including bus stations, laundries and garages that were dotted around the local area.

This was the start of Southampton's Blitz and in the last weeks of November, especially 30 November and 1 December, the town centre was almost destroyed and the other bomb sites spread around the town and suburbs. The docks were also badly hit, with many of the sheds bombed, including the International Cold Store, causing the many tons of butter to burn for days.

In total there were 630 civilians killed, 898 seriously wounded and many more that had less serious wounds. However, one of the most tragic stories was the 500lb-bomb direct hit on the School of Art in the Civic Centre. This was on the afternoon of 6 November 1940 when 12 bombs were dropped on Southampton. In total 30 people were killed by the bomb on the Civic Centre. Although all children went to the air-raid shelter in the basement it made very little difference as 14 children were killed, including their teacher and many other adults. Only one child in the air-raid shelter survived.

Colin Hall remembers he was with his school friends watching an aircraft battle in the sky when a German Messerschmitt shot down a British Hurricane fighter. The British pilot bailed out, but the German pilot followed, shooting at him all the way down.

Another incident was when they were on their way to school and a low flying Messerschmitt machined-gunned them as they were walking along the road. As they dived over the garden fences to avoid being hit they could see the pilot very clearly as he was flying so low. The road was splattered with bullets.

Sailing on the *Queen Mary* to America in World War Two

By August 1942 the *Queen Mary* was making fast eastbound crossings, carrying up to 15,000 US troops on each crossing. When she sailed back she would be carrying German and Italian POWs to work on farms in America and Canada. Other passengers sailing on the *Queen Mary* included RAF trainee pilots who were going to America and Canada for flight training.

RAF Trainee Pilots Undertake Flying Training in North America

In the 1930s the RAF started to replace their older aircraft with the newer, well-designed, high-performance single-wing aircraft, but realised they did not have enough fully trained pilots to fly them. The Germans, on the other hand, had already built up an Air Force of fast aircraft and experienced pilots, but with the closeness of Germany to Britain they would not hesitate to attack and shoot down the inexperienced trainee pilots. There was also the threat of airfields being bombed by German bombers.

Britain had a desperate need to find somewhere that was further away from Germany and less likely to be attacked, and after successful negotiations with America, RAF trainee pilots were sent over for flight training as part of the Arnold Flight Training Scheme. The scheme was set up in June 1941 and lasted until March 1943 and consisted of three flying stages, with training taking place at separate primary, basic and advanced flying schools. The primary courses took place at flying schools in South Carolina, Georgia, Florida and Alabama.

After the attack on Pearl Harbour in December 1941 America came into the war, and in August 1942 John Dines joined the *Queen Mary* to sail across the Atlantic to Halifax, Nova Scotia, as an RAF cadet for flight training after first receiving some flight training on Tiger Moths in England. The *Queen Mary* was packed to the gunwales but they had very good food and slept in hammocks. John Dines did not enjoy the voyage at all as it was a very uncomfortable journey, but some didn't like having to sleep in hammocks at night, as well as being seasick!

On the crossing there was an escort of destroyers and if they heard five blasts on the ship's horn then all was well and they were still being accompanied by destroyers. However, if they heard six blasts then that was the signal to abandon ship, which fortunately did not happen – the speed of the *Queen Mary* did not give the submarines much chance to line up their torpedoes on the ship.

Once the *Queen Mary* had berthed in Halifax the pilot cadets travelled by train to Toronto and then on to Tuscaloosa, Alabama, for their pilot training. After the flight training John Dines travelled back from Tuscaloosa to Halifax, Nova Scotia, in late February or early March 1943, and sailed on a zig-zag route to avoid torpedoes via Gibraltar to England.

John Dines was flying again in England on 3 June 1943, and was then transferred to Burma where he flew Dakotas, dropping supplies to the troops on the ground.

After the war the RAF gave their pilots the opportunity to study for a career of their choice, as many had joined before the war as young men having not long left school. John Dines went to the Middlesex Hospital and took up medical studies. After he had completed his studies he returned to flying Dakotas for a time and then left the RAF to become a medical doctor. Later Dr John Dines went to the United States to work for the American Space Agency, experimenting in the medical effects of space on astronauts.

Queen Mary Returns to Commercial Service

At the end of the war the *Queen Mary* began transporting over 22,000 war brides and their children, (known as the 'Bride and Baby Voyages') from the UK to America and Canada.

During the course of World War Two the *Queen Mary* carried 765,429 passengers and steamed 569,943 miles. On 27 September 1946 the *Queen Mary* was decommissioned and returned to the Cunard Line. She underwent a refit, spending approximately 10 months in the King George V (No. 7) Dry Dock in Southampton. The first commercial post-war sailing was in 1947.

The Bravery of the Merchant Navy Seamen Supported by the Royal Navy

At the start of World War Two the shipping lines had many of their vessels requisitioned for war service, and with them went some of their peacetime crew. However, there were some crew who were called up and others who volunteered for the Royal Navy and were involved in escorting the wartime convoys. During the course of the war a large number of requisitioned vessels were sunk or badly damaged, and many of their crew and troops on board were lost while engaged in carrying servicemen to and from the battlefields. Being part of convoys was at times a frightening experience, with torpedoes being fired from U-boats or dropped by aircraft as well as the bombing attacks.

There were many ships requisitioned by the government for war service, including Cunard-White Star's 'Queens' *Aquitania, Ascania, Scythia, Britannic, Georgic* and *Laconia,* Union-Castle's *Windsor Castle, Warwick Castle, Durban Castle, Langibby Castle* and *Arundel Castle,* Canadian Pacific Empress ships and P&O vessels. P&O *Strathmore* was requisitioned for war service

The *Stratheden* (23,722 GT) was built by by Vickers-Armstrong, Barrow-in-Furness, and launched in 1937. She was sold to the Greek shipowner John S. Latsis and later broken up in 1969. (Courtesy of Alan MacKenzie)

P. & O. 'STRATHEDEN'

in March 1940 for trooping, as was the *Stratheden*, serving until 1946 when she returned to commercial service. During her war service the *Stratheden* also took part in the North African landings where her sister ship, the *Strathallan*, was sunk. Following this she took part in trooping with transatlantic crossings to Canada.

Sailing on P&O *Stratheden* to Canada for RAF Flight Training

Len Hillier also remembers his wartime voyage across the North Atlantic to Canada to take part in flying training: 'It was during the night that my group boarded the P&O *Stratheden* at Liverpool to sail across the North Atlantic to Canada.' The P&O *Stratheden* sailed as part of a convoy from Liverpool and Len remembers seeing the destroyer escort: 'As we sailed near Iceland I noticed we had a sizable destroyer escort, but soon they left us and we sailed without escort until we were close to Halifax, Nova Scotia. A Canadian escort joined us and accompanied us into Halifax, arriving in the daylight.'

Len recounts what life was like on board the ship: 'While on board the servicemen were in groups of approximately a dozen sitting on forms at the dining table. At mealtimes one of the group would go to the kitchen to pick up the food for the group, but at night we slept on blankets using the tables and forms. Some of the servicemen slept like sailors in hammocks hanging from the beams.'

After disembarking the servicemen were soon on a train heading west: 'It was to be a 2–3 day journey, but at Winnipeg when we were on the platform we were showered with all kinds of chocolates and fruit, and then it was back on the train.'

They were heading for a very small town called Swift Current, where a Flying School had been established. The British Commonwealth Air Training Plan (BCATP), also known as the Empire Training Plan, was established during World War Two to support the training of air and ground crews far away from the air battlefields of Europe. One of the training aircraft was the Tiger Moth, built in Canada especially for use in the BCATP. The 39th Service Flying Training School (SFTS) at Swift Current, Saskatchewan, operated from 15 December 1941– 24 March 1944. Len Hillier: 'Our training aircraft was to be a Tiger Moth and within 10 hours you went solo. One day I was flying solo when I stalled and crashed. As I realised I was spinning down, the only thing in my mind was that I had failed the cadre!' For that he was taken off the pilot's course and went on a navigator's course, training on Catalina flying boats at a US Naval Air Station at Pensacola, Florida.

Len Hillier: 'I was there for four months and flew in Catalinas on section searches across the Gulf of Mexico. The Catalina flying boat was used for long sea surveys and in our case for about four to five-hour flights. There would be three or four students; one would be helping navigation and the others on observation. In April 1941 we left Pensacola after we had finished the course to return to the UK.'

After returning to Halifax they boarded a ship to return to England: 'It was in the middle of the night when we boarded and we were one of many ships closely guarded by destroyers. Every night depth charges were being dropped against submarines, and although we were in cramped conditions we were all quite calm. One night we had a particular scare and that was because a destroyer had dropped a depth charge on a submarine very near us. We were shocked because the explosion seemed too near and many rushed to get up the stairs!

The ship was divided into compartments and each compartment was closed for the night as this was the most dangerous time. I was always so glad when daylight came. It was a great relief to arrive back on Merseyside. From there we boarded awaiting trains to take us to Bournemouth. This was a sorting-out station for all crew. It was from there, with others, that I started night flying exercises. After so many hours night flying I was presented with my Navigator's Wings, and from then on I was flying in Wellingtons. I was stationed at Lossiemouth, mainly flying at night searching for submarines.'

Samaria (2)

In 1940 *Samaria* was used to transport children as evacuees to America and took part in other trooping duties to the Mediterranean. In 1942 she was part of the North African landings, codenamed Operation Torch. Mr MacPhail was just 19 years old and a support group machine gunner attached to Middlesex Regiment when he boarded the *Samaria* to sail to North Africa: 'We sailed on the Cunard *Samaria* from Greenock in a convoy of 200 ships to Algiers. It took 10 days, but while in the North Atlantic there were packs of submarines all around us. We were down in the holds sleeping in hammocks that were squashed close to each other, but that was not the best place to be because we were about two decks down below the waterline. We could hear from where we were down in the holds a 'thunk' as a dud torpedo hit the ship. The ship's crew would say "We've been hit by a dud"! I don't think that Jerry was putting the fuses in properly. That pack of submarines must have been in the middle of the convoy.

'The conditions on board were pretty good but crowded…the decks were full of hammocks and everything. For our food we used to go to one deck where they used to cook just for us. There were, I think, up to 3,000 troops on board.

'We were being violently tossed about in the Bay of Biscay. I well remember going through the Bay of Biscay. There was a terrible storm and we were up on deck and had food in our hands, but we were getting sick everywhere. I was prostrate with seasickness!

'When we were in Algiers we were swimming alongside the ship and I dived off the deck, not realising just how high it was, hit my head and nearly knocked myself out. I remember I kept going down, down, down deeper until I eventually started to come up to the surface. I saw light ahead of me, but I was nearly out of breath and gasped as I reached the surface. I can't remember anything else and must have passed out when I reached the surface. Someone must have rescued me and took me back on board because that is where I remember waking up.

'We first went into action in North Africa, bypassing the Germans towards Egypt. We left Bone, North Africa, for the Sicily invasion in LCTs (Landing Craft Tank), but the sea was so rough while we were in the landing craft that many of us got seasick. While we were along the coast at Taranto as part of Operation Slapstick on 9 September 1943 we saw all the Italian ships lying on their sides where they had been attacked and sunk. At the same time from the landing craft we saw an air raid going on in Malta. The trouble was we lost all our motorbikes on the way across. It was the British 1st Airborne Division that landed from the ships at Taranto and captured the airfield at Foggia. I was hoping they would capture the bakeries at Foggia because we could smell the bread, but no such luck.

'Our vehicles were in a very bad condition and we needed new vehicles, but the convoy bringing replacement equipment and all our new lorries had 15–16 ships blown up, so we had to make do again.

'When we had landed we found a big black grape farm and tucked into them, but afterwards I had a really bad stomach ache for two nights.

'Another of my memories was while we were going through Sicily I remember a volcano blowing up.

'I am 87 now, but then I was 19. The best of it was when the war ended, because I was a volunteer. On the day the war ended you were sent home.'

The 'Laconia' Order

The *Laconia* (19,680 tons) was one of the Armed Merchant Cruisers in the British 3rd Battle Group in Halifax but became a troopship in 1941. She was en route from Suez to Canada when she was hit by two torpedoes fired by *U-156* (commanded by Werner Hartenstein) at 22.07 hours on 12 September 1942 and sank just over an hour later. At the time the *Laconia* was unescorted, and of the 2,741 on board, the ship's master, Captain Sharp, 97 crew members, 133 passengers, 33 Polish guards and 1,394 Italian prisoners were lost. There were 1,083 survivors.

When the captain of *U-156* realised who the passengers were he ordered immediate rescue operations and raised the Red Cross flag to indicate that they had survivors from the sinking on board. However, a US Army B24 Liberator bomber arrived from its base on Ascension Island and flew overhead the *U-156*, which was surfaced with its deck crowded with survivors. The bomber pilot radioed its base for orders and was told to attack the U-boat. *U-156* was forced to submerge and leave the survivors in the water, and it was left to the Vichy French warships to eventually arrive and rescue those still in the water.

This incident led to what became known as the '*Laconia* Order' by Admiral Dönitz, which stated that U-boat captains were no longer to rescue survivors from torpedoed ships.

Union-Castle Line *Warwick Castle*

In September 1939 the *Warwick Castle* was requisitioned by the government for trooping duties. In November 1942 she was part of the KMF 1 (UK–Mediterranean Fast) assault force for Operation Torch, the North African landings.

The *Warwick Castle* left the Clyde on 1 June 1942 with convoy WS 19P to Freetown, then with the same convoy to Durban. From Durban the *Warwick Castle* joined the WS 19L convoy to Capetown and then on to Aden. From Aden she went independently to Mombasa, arriving on 14 July 1942. The *Warwick Castle* left Mombasa on her return voyage on 19 July to Capetown and then back to the Clyde, arriving on 19 August 1942.

After that voyage Cyril Duro had some leave and then went back to Scotland to rejoin the *Warwick Castle*. He was on board as part of the KMF 1 convoy, consisting of 40 merchant ships and 36 escort ships, which left the Clyde on 26 October 1942, arriving at Oran on the North African coast on 8 November 1942: 'I think we landed about 3,500 American troops when we went to North Africa the first time. You never saw the protection you had; they were often out of sight over the horizon, and they never lost a ship when we landed in North Africa.'

Jimmy 'Bud' Thomas, One of the American Serviceman On Board the *Warwick Castle*

Jimmy 'Bud' Thomas joined the US Army in February 1942 and did his basic training at Camp Robinson, Arkansas. In August 1942 the 1st US Amphibian Brigade left America for Britain and was attached to Maritime Command, a naval administrative unit, and units were spread throughout the country. Jimmy's unit, the 531st Engineer Shore Regiment, sailed from Staten Island to Belfast and then on to Londonderry by train where they took part in further training. The unit transferred to Rosineath, Scotland, which was being taken over as an American naval base by the Maritime Command, and the British Amphibious Training Centre at Inverary on Loch Fyne, Scotland. On 23 September the battalion moved to Toward Castle, Scotland, for training with British Amphibious troops. They practiced beach landings, carrying logs in four-man teams, and climbed rope ladders with full 60lb packs, while losing some of the less coordinated troopers during the exercises.

The Third Battalion of the 531st was then attached to the First Infantry Division. As part of the Western Task Force it sailed out of Scotland in the largest convoy ever assembled up to that point (Operation Torch) to invade North Africa.

Jimmy spent 30 days at sea on the *Warwick Castle*, passing up the tripe and savouring only the mackerel and freshly baked bread from the bare-bones Royal Navy rations. He had won $900 in poker games on the way over and became the key man in negotiations for the powerful rum the British sailors were allowed.

Cyril Duro: 'We landed the troops at Arzew, which was about 2 miles off Oran and was held by the Vichy French. At that time we were fighting the Vichy French. I can remember the last lot of French planes took off from the land and they actually machine-gunned the boats as they went across and landed in the south of France. I can also remember the battleships HMS *Nelson* and HMS *Rodney* were laid off and they were shelling, and the shells were flying overhead. As well as the shells from the naval vessels the shoreline was bombarded by the rocket ships while the American troops were in the landing craft on the way to the beach landing. The troops could see people patrolling up and down the beach, but when the rocket ships laid everything down on the shore, and barbed wire, everything disappeared. Afterwards you couldn't see any people around.'

When the *Warwick Castle* arrived on the North African coast on 8 November 1942 Jimmy 'Bud' Thomas's unit landed at Arzew, Algeria (near Oran), under enemy shell fire. The battle of Arzew ended in two days, but the greatest threat to the unit had been friendly fire, which claimed two of Jimmy's friends.

As well as the North African Landings Jimmy took part in the landings in Sicily in July 1943 and Salerno, Italy, in September. He was also on the D-Day landings in Normandy in June 1944 and continued the invasion into France, crossing the Rhine and into central Germany in 1945.

Despite being in a unit that was always first ashore, clearing beaches and sweeping mines, preparing the way for the invasion troops to land while under intense fire, Jimmy survived the war but lost a lot of his friends on the beaches. Jimmy passed away in 2007 at the age of 92.

Sinking of the *Warwick Castle*.

The *Warwick Castle* had been in convoy KMF 1 for Operation Torch and landed her troops at Arzew, Algeria, near Oran on 10 November 1942.

The *Warwick Castle* left Gibraltar as part of the convoy MKF 1X on 12 November, bound for the Clyde, but a westerly gale forced the liners to reduce speed to allow the escort destroyers to keep to their stations. This continued for some time until 08.44 on 14 November when she was hit by one of two torpedoes from *U-143* (commanded by Gustav Poel), hitting below the bridge, which flooded the cargo holds and engine room. The second torpedo hit the ship at 08.57, causing the vessel to sink in just over an hour. Destroyers made for the sinking ship in the heavy seas, and it was HMS *Achates* that came close and saved many from the lifeboats and rafts. The position of the *Warwick Castle* was approximately 200 miles NW of Cape Espichel, Portugal, 39.12N, 13.25W.

The casualties included the master, Captain Richard Leepman-Shaw, 61 members of the crew and 34 service personnel, a total of 96 lost. The survivors included 201 crew members, 29 gunners, five naval personnel and 131 service personnel out of a total complement of 462. The survivors were rescued by escort vessels and the British motor vessel *Leinster*.

An Account of the Sinking of the *Warwick Castle*

Cyril Duro was a member of the crew when the *Warwick Castle* was attacked and sunk. He gives an account of his experiences after they had taken part in the Allied Landings on the North African coast and their return voyage when the ship was torpedoed.

The MKF 1X convoy left Gibraltar on the 12 November for the Clyde. Cyril Duro: 'The convoy was about 30 hours out of Gibraltar when we were torpedoed. I had just come off the watch on the *Warwick Castle* at 8am that morning. I had the four to eight watch, and as I had a cold coming on I decided that I didn't want any breakfast, so I turned in at about 8.20am. At about 8.30 or so there was this big, big bang, and I didn't know what it was. I woke up and got out of the cabin and walked down the alleyway to the number two hatch. All I could smell was the cordite. I ran back and said, "I think we been torpedoed." We all went to our stations.

'The crew on combined operations had taken the lifeboats out of the davits and put landing craft in their place, so when the ship sailed from port there were landing craft in place for the troops who were to land on the beaches instead of lifeboats. There were one and two boats either side of for'ard, and one and two were accident boats. They were what they called "barmaid" boats because to propel them you had handles and you pulled them back just like barmaids at the bar did when pulling a pint. One and two boats were intact and 16 and 18 were intact. The job then was to get the boats away with as many people as we could. Of course, when we came back after the landings a lot of these landing craft were left ashore. The idea was if you could get them head up then the tide would come and you could float them off again. Once the American troops were landed then the landing craft were left ashore. Then you were left with a few landing craft that we pulled up on board and carried those.

'However, I did see a tragic thing. Number 16 boat was down in the water with a full complement on. A landing craft dropped in front of them, came astern and stove in the bow, and they were on their own, and had to find other means to save themselves. That's when the Carley floats came in. You lay on them and hung on for grim death. That's all we had to do really.

'Our skipper, Captain Shaw, he was a Navy man, RNVR (Royal Navy Voluntary Reserve). A good man, he was blowing his whistle and shouting out to the men, "Keep your spirits up."

'My mate Bill Shuckford and a few of us were left on board by then, and all we were doing was trying to get as many people off as possible. Bill was the man at the wheel at the time, the quartermaster, and he stayed at the wheel until Captain Shaw said to the station quartermaster, "Abandon ship, you've done your duty." The *Warwick Castle* was sinking and Bill couldn't swim!

'Bill said he could always remember that for'ard there was the paint shop. The explosion had blown a lot of the paint all across the deck, and he said he could remember picking his way across the deck so he didn't get any paint on his shoes!

'Bill went up to the forecastle head, but by that time the *Warwick Castle* was fairly well down in the water. What happened if you'd gone up to a station which was one of the barmaid boats, you stood by, put the boat over the side so that people could get in. Once they were all in you would pick up one of the lifelines and pull one of the centre lifelines out and loop around the hand rail so that the boat could be lowered down. Once the boat was down in the water you would swing out on that line and lower yourself down in into the boat and then take over the boat. That was your job.

'However, Bill said everything was done accurately, to plan, and he lowered the boat into the water. All he remembers was suddenly a cook, (he knew it was a cook because he had check trousers and a white jacket on), ran up, grabbed the line, swung out and dropped down into the boat. The boat was by this time moving towards the bow. Bill was then forced to drop down into the water, even though he couldn't swim and the boat picked him up. He then took over the boat, and for that action he got a medal. I think it was the BEM (British Empire Medal).'

Most of the passengers and crew had gone by the time Cyril Duro and a few others started to evacuate: 'What happened was we started to get down to the Carley float we had thrown over the side. We went down on the scrambling nets on the side of the vessel into the Carley float. There was another AB Seaman (Able Seaman) beside myself and a purser's assistant, one of the crew, but he died because he couldn't let go the Carley float when we got alongside rescue vessel that had a scrambling net over the side. We were picked up by a British and Irish Steam Packet Company ship called the *Leinster*. It was very bad and you had to climb up the nets. Two of us made it, and we really tried to get the crew member to let go, but he wouldn't and he died. It was very sad.

'When we were picked up one of the crew that saved us said that it was bad weather when we got torpedoed. At that time we were supposed to be zig-zagging, but there were several ships in the convoy who didn't have the speed to zig-zag and some were keeping straight. We tried to zig-zag, but had no steerage way. You had to be at a certain speed to be able to zig-zag and keep your station. We couldn't all do that.

'Some of the men who were picked up by a destroyer told us later that Captain Shaw had hit his head on the side of the destroyer and died and was buried at sea from the destroyer.

'When we got back on the *Leinster* after being torpedoed we landed at Gourock, and they really thought we were prisoners of war. The crew of the *Leinster* had given their very last shirts, trousers and clothes away. We didn't have anything when we came out of the water, because after being in water for a number of hours all your clothes come off as they never seem to hang on to your body, and you finish up naked. They gave us everything they had and we still looked a very scruffy bunch.

'In the end we went to the Seamen's Mission where we met up with some of the crew we didn't know had survived, which was a wonderful thing because we didn't really expect to see them again. Then we were fitted out with some utility suits which were made in wartime, but they were pretty rough. All I had was a little cardboard box with a few bits and pieces in.

'When we went from Gourock to Glasgow to get the train the lads said, "There are no officers with us," and they asked me to go and see the station master because the crew were all shaken up and traumatised. I went and saw the station master at Glasgow Central and said, "Well, I know there is a fast train that leaves at 5.10pm and it gets to Euston in the morning about 6.30am. If we could get that, our people could get across from Euston to Waterloo and then down to Southampton." He said, "I can't do that, but there's a train at 9.38pm, a slow train and I'll make sure you're all right on that train." The station master kept to his word and gave us a whole carriage to ourselves. That station master was tops and a wonderful gesture he made to us by giving us a carriage to ourselves.

'I got off the train at Kensington and walked along to the Piccadilly Line and went to see Peggy (Cyril's future wife), who lived in north London. When I arrived in their street they walked slowly down the street, but didn't know what had happened. I said, "We had had a bit of an accident and we lost a ship." I was just 20 years old at that time.

'My mum was a post woman and used listen to Lord Haw-Haw on the radio, and, of course, they were told not to take any notice of him, but he put out that the *Warwick Castle* had been sunk. My grandfather was the pier manager for the Red Funnel Line and said to my mum, "I think Cyril will come home as a distressed seaman."

'When I got home after the sinking of the *Warwick Castle* I couldn't sleep. My mum said "You had better go and see the doctor around the corner." When I saw the doctor I said, "My mum sent me around, there's nothing wrong with me." The doctor said, "Let me be the judge of that, you haven't been sleeping." He gave me some medicine that made me sleep at night.

'If nothing had happened to the *Warwick Castle* I would probably have stayed with the Union-Castle Line. That was what it was like in those days; you would have loyalty to your company. If you joined Cunard, White Star, P&O or any other company you tended to stay with the company. It was because I had lost my ship that I then joined other ships, and my next ship was to be a tanker crossing the Atlantic from the Clyde to New York.'

Wartime Convoys

During the war years there was rationing in Britain and anyone living at that time will remember the ration book. This was presented to the shopkeeper for the food you were allowed. Petrol was also rationed and to avoid people selling it on the black market the fuel was coloured. There was a black market on which people could buy extra things, but if those selling the black market goods were caught then they would be in very serious trouble with the police.

There were special allowances made for farmers and firms that produced food and machinery for the war effort, but much of Britain's oil and food had to be brought in by merchant ships that had been requisitioned for the Ministry of War Transport. The officers and crew of the merchant ships showed great resolve, determination and bravery in attempting to get their cargoes safely to the British ports, despite the German submarines and surface vessels, including fighters and bombers, intent on sinking as many ships as they could in the convoys.

The protection of the convoys was undertaken by the Royal Navy and other Allied vessels, which, despite many losses, fought bravely to get the convoys through. In the Mediterranean, the island of Malta was desperate for supplies and convoys were having great difficulty getting through. Leon Hanson-Vaux gives an account of his experiences in the war, especially taking part in Operation Pedestal for the relief of Malta.

HMS *Kenya* and HMS *Kimberley*

Leon Hanson-Vaux joined the Royal Navy in June 1939 when he was just 16 and trained on HMS *Ganges* until 1940. After he had passed out he went to Devonport: 'No sooner had I got there then I was put on a train to Glasgow where I was met by a naval rating. I was to join a brand new ship that had just been built in Glasgow. She was HMS *Kenya*, a cruiser, and we sailed to Scapa Flow to undertake a training routine for a new ship. It was then my war started and I went all around the world on that ship until 1943.'

In 1940 HMS *Kenya* began patrols around Iceland and also in Russian convoys: 'When on the Russian convoys we picked up a number of survivors but had to be very quick because of the freezing cold sea.'

Further service was undertaken on the Norway invasion in 1941: 'We went right up in the fjords and stayed there all day. Shells were fired at us, but they missed because we were on the move all the time.'

HMS *Kenya*'s Russian convoys in icy conditions. (Leon Hanson-Vaux Collection)

HMS *Kenya*'s Russian convoys in rough sea. (Leon Hanson-Vaux Collection)

Operation Pedestal for the relief of Malta. The bombs miss their targets. (Leon Hanson-Vaux Collection)

Operation Pedestal

HMS *Kenya* had returned to Scapa Flow by July 1942, but at the end of July she sailed to Greenock and took on fuel, ammunition and stores. Convoy WS21S was formed of 14 fast, modern merchant ships, including *Rochester Castle, Clan Ferguson, Empire Hope* and just one oil tanker, the *Ohio*, owned by Texaco and on charter to the Ministry of War Transport. HMS *Kenya* was going to be part of the protective screen for this convoy.

The aim of this convoy, code-named 'Operation Pedestal', was to sail to Malta to relieve the island's desperate situation for supplies. Leaving on 2 August the convoy sailed to the Mediterranean, but it was a very dangerous passage with German U-boats, E-boats, Italian submarines and sustained air attacks from their bombers. However, there was a large Royal Navy presence to provide anti-submarine cover and air cover, including Spitfires and Bristol Beaufighters from Malta.

It was not long before the German and Italian attacks started to reduce the Royal Navy vessels and merchant ships in the convoy. The tanker *Ohio* was hit by torpedoes and set on fire, and HMS *Kenya* was hit in the bows by the Italian submarine *Alagi*. However, the *Ohio* was able to continue, despite being bombed again, and HMS *Kenya* was still seaworthy and resumed her station.

MV *Rochester Castle*, although torpedoed, kept going and entered Grand Harbour, Valletta, on 13 August along with MV *Port Chalmers* and MV *Melbourne Star*. MV *Brisbane Star*, also damaged, arrived on 14 August and the tanker *Ohio* managed to make it to Grand Harbour, even though she was seriously damaged.

Out of the convoy of 14 merchant ships only five got through, but because of the sacrifice of the merchant and naval sailors Malta was saved. HMS *Kenya* first sailed back to Gibraltar, then back to South Shields for repairs, and later sailed for the Far East.

The torpedo damage on the HMS *Kenya*. (Leon Hanson-Vaux Collection)

Operation Pedestal. The *Ohio* was hit by the bombs and set on fire. (Leon Hanson-Vaux Collection)

Leon Hanson-Vaux: 'When we were in the Far East I was put into hospital in Ceylon with appendicitis. When I got well HMS *Kenya* had gone and so I was sent to the north of the country and by train all the way to Bombay. It was a three-day journey, but I can't complain because one half of the carriage was a sitting room and the other half had bunk beds.'

When he arrived in Bombay Leon Hanson-Vaux joined the destroyer HMS *Kimberley*, one of the famous Lord Louis Mountbatten ships: 'From there I went back to the Mediterranean and back to war.'

HMS *Kimberley* was a K Class Destroyer, built by John I. Thornycroft at Woolston, Southampton, and launched on 1 June 1939. On 12 January 1942 HMS *Kimberley* was hit by a torpedo from *U-77* (commanded by Heinrich Schonder) off Tobruk, which caused major damage to the stern. The destroyer was disabled and taken in tow, first to Alexandria and then to HM Dockyard, Bombay. It was not until January 1944 that HMS *Kimberley* was recommissioned and left for service in the Mediterranean.

Operation Dragoon – Allied Invasion of Southern France, August 1944

HMS *Kimberley* took part in Operation Dragoon on Special Duties. The Commander in Chief (C in C) for the Mediterranean, Admiral John Cunningham, Royal Navy, embarked to observe the assault convoys through the Straight of Bonificio. The C in C gave the order to commence Operation Dragoon while he was on board HMS *Kimberley* on 14 August 1944. The Prime Minister, Winston Churchill, boarded HMS *Kimberley* on 15 August and toured the landing beaches on 16 August with the C in C and Military Commander, General Maitland-Wilson.

Leon Hanson-Vaux: 'I was a messenger for the C in C, who was very amiable and always listened.' Once HMS *Kimberley* was released from Special Duties she took up patrolling the Adriatic: 'When we were in the Mediterranean we were on the invasion of Italy, going right up the east coast. However, we ran out of ammunition and had to return to Malta.'

At the end of the war they sailed back to England and arrived in Dartmouth, where Leon Hanson-Vaux went back to Devonport Barracks: 'By that time I was a Leading Seaman and became a Navy policeman. I was sent to an air station in the north of Scotland that was being run down and was a bit of a dumping ground for aircraft. I did quite a bit of flying there as a passenger and also learned to fly an aircraft. After being promoted to Petty Officer I decided I was better off on a ship than on an air station and joined HMS *Illustrious*, an aircraft carrier.

'After that I returned to Devonport and got married and then I was sent to Portsmouth, to HMS Collingwood, a training centre. After being there for five years I retired from the Royal Navy in 1963. However, just before I left I was summoned by the captain, who told me that I had been awarded the BEM.'

Leon Hanson-Vaux BEM now lives in Southampton.

Chapter 5
POST-WAR LIFE

Holiday Camps for Family Holidays

In 1931 the first holiday camp was set up by Warner's at Hayling Island and was followed by the first Butlins camps in 1936 in Skegness and Clacton. Although Billy Butlin had bought the land for the Filey camp in 1939, it was not until 1945 that the camp opened. These camps were taken over as military bases in World War Two.

Bert Moody remembers the Filey camp in the war because it was in use as a training camp: 'When I was in the RAF during the war I spent several weeks there in November 1943 in "summer chalets" with no heating. We were supplied with extra blankets to keep warm'.

After World War Two the average British public could not afford to undertake cruises and tended to go for seaside holidays, and it was the holiday camps that became a popular venue for family holidays. In 1946 Pontin's opened their first camp at a disused camp site at Brean Sands, which had been a US Army base in the war.

From 1946 the holiday camps became very popular for family holidays because they could get their accommodation, food and entertainment for the cost of a week's wages. However, the 'campers' had to be happy with the regimented style of life that the holiday camps portrayed. The TV sitcom *Hi-de-Hi* showed vividly an idea of what life was like in a holiday camp. The entertainment staff in the series were called 'Yellow Coats', but many will remember the Butlins 'Red Coats', the Pontin's 'Blue Coats' and maybe the Warner's 'Green Coats'. Many famous entertainers made their start in the holiday camps, including Butlins Red Coats Dave Allen, Charlie Drake, Jimmy Tarbuck, Roy Hudd and Moira Anderson. Pontin's Blue Coats included Shane Ritchie and Brian Conley, and Warner's 'Green Coats included ventriloquist Roger De Courcey and Nookie Bear, and comedian Joe Pasquale. The holiday camps were also the starting point for many of the entertainment staff who eventually worked on the cruise ships.

Holiday camps could be compared to a small town or even a cruise ship, with shops, sports facilities and on-site entertainment. In 1949 Pontin's redesigned their main entertainment building to represent an ocean liner and called it SS *Berengaria*. When the Cunard *Berengaria* was scrapped in 1938 some of the items auctioned were bought and eventually displayed in the Pontin's entertainment building. Interestingly, in 2005 Butlins built their first hotel and decorated it in Art Deco style. Their Shoreline Hotel is shaped like an ocean liner and even has telescopes for the 'passengers' to look out to sea.

With air travel to holiday destinations for foreign holidays there was increasing interest by the British public to take advantage of the new, cheap package holidays. This impacted upon the holiday camps and there was a decline in holidaymakers using them. However, the holiday camps are still a popular venue for those who prefer to take their holidays in the British Isles because it is still cheaper than going abroad.

Memories of the 1950–60s

Between 1950–53 the Korean War took place and many young men were called up for National Service and travelled on troopships to the war zone. 1953 was the Coronation year, with Queen Elizabeth II being crowned in Westminster Abbey. It was also the year that Edmund Hillary and Sherpa Tensing were the first to climb to the summit of Mount Everest.

With the end of petrol rationing more people started to buy cars and this led to a need to build new roads, which became known as 'motorways'. Television sets started to appear and for children there was an end to sweets rationing! In 1954 medical student Roger Bannister, at the age of 25, became the first man to run a mile in less than four minutes, and in October 1957 the Soviet Union blasted Sputnik I into space.

By 1961 the Berlin Wall was erected. The Beatles became popular in the United States in 1964, and Neil Armstrong became the first man to step on the moon on 20 July 1969.

On a sad note, in 1967 the RMS *Queen Mary* left Southampton for the last time and the RMS *Queen Elizabeth* a year later.

Hard Hat and Scuba Diving in Southampton Docks

On 11 November 2008 the *Queen Elizabeth 2* arrived in Southampton Docks for her last day before sailing out that evening on her final voyage to Dubai. As she sailed early in the morning towards Southampton Water the weather was very poor, with Force 7 winds causing her to go aground on the Bramble Bank in the Solent. After the tugs had helped her off the bank the *QE2* arrived at her berth alongside the Queen Elizabeth II terminal, and two scuba divers were tasked to go down to check her hull for damage. These divers would have been able to swim freely along the hull without much restriction, making it quite an easy task to undertake. However, in the 1950s the British Transport Commission (BTC) 'hard hat' divers would have been responsible for this type of work and would have been more restricted, as the following story illustrates.

One of the problems for ships arriving or leaving Southampton Docks was that they could have their propellers fouled by debris in the water, or the vessel might have a vibration that required an inspection to see whether the ship needed to go into dry dock for further detailed inspection. There would also be times when a ship would run aground on the Bramble Bank in the Solent, and that would need an underwater inspection to assess any damage, and there would be occasions when passengers' luggage and equipment would fall into the water from the cranes. In the early 20th century underwater work was carried out by hard hat divers working on the river bed from their launch.

George Holmes was one of the hard hat divers who worked in Southampton Docks until the 1960s, and his work was limited at times because of the tide height, when he would find difficulty in reaching the hulls of vessels from the river bed. It was also very difficult because of the mud and George Holmes, through a long experience of diving, had developed an uncanny skill of being able to identify objects through touch because of the nil visibility he worked under at times.

Development of the Hard Hat Divers

By the early 18th century there was a system whereby air was pumped from the surface using a form of bellows, which kept the diver supplied with a constant flow of air, and by the 19th century the metal helmet was being used. However, although the air was pumped from the surface into the helmet, which was sealed to the collar of a waist-length jacket, the air would have to escape from the bottom of the jacket. By the middle of the 19th century the sealed air-tight suit had been developed.

It was in the 20th century that further development occurred, with the mixed breathing gases of helium and oxygen allowing divers to go to a greater depth, but although the diver's time below the surface could be extended by using the hard hat diving suit there was less mobility for some jobs. This was overcome by self-contained underwater breathing apparatus (scuba) diving.

The standard hard hat diving dress has a metal helmet, an airline to the surface where air is pumped to the diver, a sealed canvas suit, a diver's knife and weights on the chest, back and boots to keep the diver on the sea bed.

Working in Southampton Docks after World War Two

George Holmes worked as a hard hat diver at Southampton Docks after World War Two. He had joined the Royal Navy in August 1914, aged 14, and during his time there he had learned to dive. He served on board HMS *Prince of Wales* and saw the landing of the Dardanelles Expeditionary Force in 1915. Later he was transferred to the torpedo destroyer HMS *Lysander* and was on board when they picked up the survivors of the Destroyer HMS *Contest* (975 GT) that had been torpedoed in the Western Approaches while helping the damaged steamer *City of Lincoln* (5,867 GT), sailing from Holland and bound for New York. It was on 18 September 1917 that *U-106* (commanded by Hans Hufnagel) had torpedoed and damaged the *City of Lincoln* and the same day sank the destroyer HMS *Contest*. George Holmes was later involved in minelaying around Heligoland, and, as fate would have it, *U-106* was lost with all hands after hitting a mine in a new minefield in Heligoland on 7 October 1917.

After he left the Royal Navy George Holmes took part in diving recovery work in North Wales before joining the Southern Railway Docks' Engineers Department. Much of the work in Southampton Docks was at depths up to 60ft (18.3m), but the underwater visibility at those depths can be very poor and walking around on the river bed in weighted boots would stir up the mud and George would not be able to see anything. He would have to work with his hands, feeling around, and in March 1953 an unexploded wartime bomb was found while he was looking for tools on the river bed that workmen had lost. He came across a shape and spent about 40 minutes feeling around it, and he decided that it was a bomb. Army and Navy bomb disposal arrived and dealt with it.

The hard hat diver has to work with a team and has to maintain contact with the linesman, who in turn communicates with the boat crew undertaking the pumping operations. There are certain signals that the diver will have with his linesman, and tugging the line four times means 'I am coming up'. Resurfacing is undertaken in stages because to rise to the surface too quickly would give the diver the 'bends'.

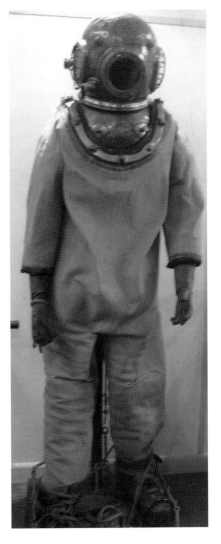

A hard hat diving suit worn by George Holmes. It is currently located in Southampton Maritime Museum. (Author's Collection)

Getting ready to dive. (Nancy Pegden Collection)

Emergencies come at any hour and the diver is on call. George Holmes's daughter, Nancy Pegden, remembers the call on her father's time: 'We used to go to Falmouth every year for our holidays because we had free rail passes. As we didn't have a telephone the Engineers Department used to come and get him out of hours. They were often standing by our gate when we arrived back from Falmouth because they had an urgent job to do.'

At one time it was necessary to cut one of the *Aquitania's* propellers away, and this job took 21 hours with both George Holmes and his assistant diver working in turns, but the ship was able to get away on time.

Nancy Pegden: 'My father's favourite liner was the *Queen Mary*. He loved her and got on well with the captain. It was invariably ropes around the propellers which he had to release. For every job he had to write a report and hand it in. My father didn't mince his words if he didn't approve of anything.'

One of George's last jobs on the *Canberra* was on 30 May 1961 at 106 Berth, where he had to remove electric anodes which were screwed in underneath the hull. In his report George Holmes wrote, 'I could not see the ship's hull, let alone touch it, and came up and told them it would be a waste of time and money to carry on.' As he had weighted boots on and the tide was high he couldn't reach the hull, but P&O was unhappy because he couldn't complete the job. He had a similar job to do in similar conditions for the *Queen Elizabeth*, but they provided a powerful magnet to pull him up to the hull and he could then finish the task. One job he didn't like was bringing up dead bodies of people that had fallen over the side of a ship.

Once George had to lash up a loose propeller on the *Mauretania* and the ship was then brought into dry dock for repairs. Other work included the examination of the port propeller for the SS *Washington*, recovering a case of gin and a lost gangway for the *Ile de France*, plugging a discharge in the port side in the SS *Washington* and examining the port side propeller of the *Atlantic* after collision with a French tug at Le Havre, which sank.

In 1956 the *Queen Mary* hit an underwater obstruction off the Isle of Wight. After the ship's arrival the diver went down to inspect the propellers but found nothing wrong and the ship sailed on time. Another job for the diver was in February 1960, when the Dutch liner

British Transport Commission (BTC) divers' launch. (Nancy Pegden Collection)

Maasdam lost luggage that was being unloaded at Berth 107, Western Docks. Baggage had been dropped between the ship and the quayside. George Holmes was called to dive, but not many cases were recovered.

Nancy Pegden: 'The water was so cold at times that my father got frostbite. Because of his job he couldn't work with gloves on. Anyway, you could never get gloves to fit him because his hands were so large. My father's hands were enormous and swelled up because of the cold water.'

When George was working in the culverts that connect Southampton Docks with the Southampton Power Station, a distance of 1½ miles, his light attracted hundreds of fish that followed him. At one time a conger eel was attracted and he stuck his knife into it, but the eel swam away. His employers were not happy to have to provide him with another knife!

The hard hat team with a diver going down the ladder. There were three men in the support team, Tom Pearce, Jack Le Page and Eric Fry. (Nancy Pegden Collection)

A scuba diver and team working in 2009 near *Norwegian Jade*. **(Keith Mullard Collection)**

Nancy Pegden: 'Another dangerous time for him was when somebody opened the wrong valve and my father was trapped for a time in the culverts. There were panic stations!

'One of his jobs was featured in the national newspapers when a Lady Diane Colville was travelling back to South Africa from Southampton in a flying boat after a holiday. As she was walking up a gangway, swinging her jewel case, which was not locked, the jewel case opened, allowing all the jewels to fall into the water. My father went down and managed to find a substantial amount of the jewellery in the mud. He recovered jewellery worth £800 that included diamond earrings, an emerald and diamond ring, a sapphire and diamond brooch, a gold brooch, a lucky charm bracelet, a diamond star, a jade necklace, a gold cufflink, one earring and a gold chain. This was in 60ft (18.3m) of water with mud and silt on the river bed. He could only feel for the jewellery because he couldn't see in the muddy water.'

There is quite a difference between the hard hat diver, who has quite a weight to carry, and the scuba diver. For example, when the diver is fully dressed he will weigh about 3cwts. The helmet weighs 39lb, the diver suit 15lb, corselet 40lb, breast and back weights 40lb each and the boots 18lb.

In Southampton Docks today it is the scuba diving teams that inspect the hulls of the ships if they have any cause for concern. It is much easier for them because they have the freedom to swim along the hull and undertake any inspection or work on the hull. The hard hat diver was more restricted and had to rely on tide height to work on the hull, and would then only be working in limited visibility.

Post-War Life as a Merchant Seaman
After World War Two many of the merchant seamen who had survived the war after serving on the wartime requisitioned liners just wanted to return to their families, and a new generation of young merchant seamen started to join the ships. There were always the 'Old Hands', for whom the sea was their life, who stayed in the merchant navy and were able to train the new generation of seamen. However, many of the stories told by the post-war merchant seamen are about their experiences when the ships were being returned to commercial service.

First-Class Waiters in First-Class Hotels
Many of the merchant sailors interviewed had first lived in different parts of Britain and moved to the Southampton area due to their sailing from Southampton. Some of the seamen had their wives and children move to the area, mainly because their visit to the port was so short that they could at least spend some time with their families without having to travel to other parts of the country. What is striking is that the majority that were interviewed have made very good careers for themselves, and some made sure they had a healthy bank balance by saving the large tips that they received while working in the first-class restaurants on the ocean liners. However, their success after leaving the sea may reflect on the discipline and hard work that they had to undergo as crew on the passenger ships, and also the 'cunning' of some of these 'special characters' who tell their stories.

From Newcastle, England to Washington DC

'Geordie' George Young used his skills as a first-class waiter on the ocean liners to work in some of the best hotels in America and is now retired in Washington DC. One of his American friends, Bill Rife, who meets him weekly for drinks says: 'George Young is 80-ish, a true Newcastle Geordie, who, even after many years as a Washington DC resident, hasn't lost the "burr" and is totally incomprehensible after a few pints at our local!'

George Young lived in the north of England and remembers barrage balloons, searchlights, ack-ack guns, fighters and the bombing in the war. After some time working in the coal mines he did not like the work and decided to go to sea: 'I was under 18 and I took off and worked my way down to Tilbury, and then I joined the *Ormonde* on 14 December 1948 when we sailed from Tilbury to Ellesmere Port.'

In 1949 George Young joined a series of ships, including the *Edinburgh Castle* for two trips, *Athlone Castle* and then the *Warwick Castle* from August until October 1949, when he joined the *Asturias* to sail to Australia. In February 1950 he joined the *Alcantara* and by April he was back on the *Warwick Castle*.

George Young: 'We were young fellows in the cabin and had lots of fun. There was never a dull moment, even though we worked hard for 11 hours a day, seven days a week. The glory hole steward used to come around six in the morning to give us a wake-up call. Then it was scrub out, take a shower, get changed and then go to serve two sittings. After that we did the floor and cleaned the silver. Everything had to be immaculate. Then it was lunch and afternoon teas. Dinner started at six for two sittings and then we went to the Pig and Whistle, where we bought a beer for just 10 cents.'

While sailing in those days there was an opportunity to buy food that they couldn't get in England. George Young: 'We used to get food and send it to Britain because there was still a shortage of food after the war from the food rationing.'

George's experience continued as he worked for a while on the cross-channel steamers from Southampton to Jersey and Guernsey, and across to France: 'This was an overnight trip leaving Southampton at 9pm.' After this George decided to return to Union-Castle and sailed on the *Caernarvon Castle* in October 1950.

George Young joined the *Ocean Monarch* on the New York run: 'I enjoyed the *Ocean Monarch* the best. Charlie Chuckles was the captain of the ship and he knew every sandbank around Bermuda. It was good when we were in Nassau Bay looking at all the stingrays and the sharks that had been attracted by the light. From Bermuda to New York was just a 34-hour trip and we would do a quick turnaround, and often the ship was filled with women.

'In New York the Market Diner was the place where all the guys used to meet. In those days we all wore suits and ties and we were well dressed.'

From there he joined the *Queen of Bermuda* in 1952, where he stayed until deciding to end his seagoing career in April 1953. George Young: 'With my experience as a first-class waiter I decided to come ashore in America, where I worked as a waiter in hotels in New York and Miami, where there were quite a number of new hotels around Miami Beach. I ended up in Palm Beach, which was the greatest place and where I worked in the Everglades Club. That was where the richest people in the world went, and it was nothing to handle $50 bills, which in those days were quite uncommon. I spent two years there, just at the time of the invasion of the Bay of Pigs in Cuba during the early 1960s. From there I went to work two or three seasons in Atlantic City and then to Washington DC, where I still am 40 years later'.

Requisitioned Ships for War Service Returned to the Shipping Companies
Post-War P&O

During World War Two P&O had a number of their passenger ships sunk and those requisitioned ships that were returned to the shipping line were refurbished prior to returning to commercial passenger services.

After all the *Strathnavar* had been through during the war, she collided with the small cargo ship *Fluor*, which sank at Berth 103 in Southampton Docks in October 1946. In November 1948 she went to Harland & Wolff Ltd, Belfast, to be refitted to carry 573 first-class and 496 tourist-class passengers. She also lost her two dummy funnels before returning to her commercial passenger service to Australia. However, on 16 June 1953 she was chartered by the government to take government guests to the Coronation Review at Spithead.

Both *Strathnavar* and *Strathaird* were converted to one-class ships in June 1954 with accommodation provided for 1,250 tourist-class passengers.

In 1946 P&O *Canton* was released from her war duties and was refurbished in Scotland for a return to her commercial passenger service. The *Canton* was then able to carry 296 first-class and 244 tourist-class passengers. From 1947 she initiated a service to the Far East, culminating in China, but by August 1962 P&O *Canton* was taken out of service and sold for scrap to ship breakers in Hong Kong.

The *Strathmore* was returned to P&O in May 1948, and reconditioned for her return to commercial service. Her first voyage was from Tilbury to Australia, calling at Bombay. However, there were some mishaps and in October 1956 she collided with the Norwegian cargo ship *Baalbek* off Gravesend.

In 1950 the *Stratheden* was chartered to make four voyages from Southampton to New York. However, she was sold along with the *Strathmore* to a Greek shipping company and renamed *Henrietta Latsi* in 1964. She was used as a pilgrim vessel and hotel ship at Jeddah in Saudi Arabia. There was confusion about the *Strathmore* and *Stratheden* being called the *Henrietta Latsi* and *Marianna Latsi* because the names were interchanged between the vessels. Both the *Strathmore* and the *Stratheden* were scrapped at La Spezia, Italy.

The *Himalaya* (27,955 GT) was completed in 1949 by Vickers-Armstrong, Barrow-in-Furness. She was broken up in 1975 at Kaohsiung, Taiwan. (Mick Lindsay Collection)

After the war P&O decided that there was a need to replace the passenger ships lost and placed an order for the *Himalaya* (27,955 GT) and shortly after for the *Chusan* (24,215 GT). The *Himalaya* left Tilbury on her maiden voyage on 6 October 1949 and sailed to Sydney, calling at Bombay, Colombo, Fremantle and Melbourne. She was the first ship to sail the P&O trans-Pacific service in 1958, travelling from Sydney up to the west coast of North America and continuing through the Panama Canal back to the UK.

The *Chusan* (24,215 GT) was completed in 1950 by Vickers-Armstrong, Barrow-in-Furness. She was broken up in 1973 at Kaohsiung, Taiwan. (Mick Lindsay Collection)

A first-class single cabin on the *Strathnavar*. (Bert Moody Collection)

The need for full air conditioning found the *Himalaya* being fitted with it in the Netherlands during the winter of 1959–60. She was also the first ship to have her own water distilling systems. In 1969 she moved from Tilbury to Southampton, the last P&O ship to do so, and went into cruising. In January 1975 she was scrapped in Taiwan.

It was on 1 July 1950 that P&O *Chusan* sailed on her first commercial voyage, and that was from Southampton to Madeira and Lisbon on a nine-day cruise. P&O *Chusan* was built for the Indian and Far East service and continued on these routes until 1959, when she was refitted to take 464 first-class passengers and 541 tourist-class passengers. However, in 1953 she was in collision with the cargo ship *Prospector* while outward bound and had to return to Tilbury for repairs to the hull. In April 1954 the *Chusan* left on the first P&O world cruise, and in 1959 she was fitted with air conditioning, which would have made conditions a lot more pleasant for passengers when sailing in hotter parts of the world. She was later to have a new funnel top fitted at Thornycrofts, Southampton, because of the smoke and fumes on the upper deck bothering the passengers.

The *Strathnaver's* first-class sports deck. (Bert Moody Collection)

With the jet airliners increasingly attracting passengers in the early 1960s further adjustments to the passenger capacity came, with 455 first-class and 517 tourist-class passengers. P&O *Chusan* was transferred from the Far East service to a new service between Australia and Japan, calling at Hong Kong. It was on 26 March 1973 that the *Chusan* returned to Southampton on her final voyage before being scrapped in Taiwan later in 1973.

In 1960 the Orient Line and P&O Line merged and the *Strathnavar* was taken over by the P&O-Orient Lines. By then the emigrant trade had diminished and P&O decided to retire both the *Strathnavar* and *Strathaird*, leaving the emigrant trade to the newer *Strathmore*. The *Strathnavar* was taken out of service and scrapped in Hong Kong in 1962.

Both the P&O *Arcadia* and *Iberia* were ordered in 1951. The *Arcadia* was built on the Clyde and the *Iberia* was built by Harland & Wolff of Belfast in 1954. P&O *Arcadia* left on her maiden voyage in February 1954 for Sydney. It was easy to distinguish between them because of their funnel tops, with the *Arcadia* having a black smoke deflector at the top of her funnel.

P&O *Iberia* operated on the UK–Australia passenger service and received full air-conditioning on a refit in Southampton in 1961, after which she undertook more and more cruises. *Iberia* was not a very lucky ship and had been in a number of collisions with other ships. She was withdrawn from service in 1972 and scrapped in Taiwan.

Post-War Cunarders

At the end of the war the *Aquitania* took American and Canadian troops back from Europe, and was also used to carry the war brides of Canadian servicemen over to Canada. Harold Lloyd remembers these voyages: 'The accommodation for the mothers and babies was four sharing a cabin, and once they had arrived in Canada and had disembarked they were all put on trains to go to their final destinations to start their new lives.' For the return voyage the ship had to be altered to take the German POWs back to Southampton. It was on that voyage that Harold Lloyd got to know one of the German submarine commanders: 'I used to talk to the Germans and there was one U-boat Commander who said to me, "Do you know, we had this ship lined up to fire a torpedo at many times, but couldn't get her because she was too fast."' The *Aquitania* was withdrawn from service on 1 December 1949 and left Southampton for Faslane to be scrapped.

It was in 1947 that the *Mauretania* (2) started her commercial sailings again with the first voyage from Southampton to New York via Le Havre and Cobh. Gus Shanahan joined the *Mauretania* in October 1955 and sailed with her for five years on the

The *Aquitania* (45,647 GT), still in her wartime colours but with Cunard funnel colours. (Courtesy of Harold Lloyd)

North Atlantic service in the summer from Southampton to New York and then cruising in the West Indies in the winter. By 1957 she was fully air conditioned, but the advent of air travel began to affect the numbers of passengers using the service.

Gus Shanahan: 'I was often backwards and forwards to the States, but when I was on the *Mauretania* we used to do a lot of West Indies cruises, which started at Christmas time. It was on the *Mauretania* when I saw the film star Alan Ladd, who was sailing back to America for Christmas. Alan Ladd was surprised that we were not going home for Christmas as it was very important to him to be at home for Christmas each year.

'We used to leave Southampton just before Christmas and when we arrived in New York that would be our base for the cruise season. We would do a fortnightly cruise to Barbados, Trinidad and Jamaica and used to go to Cuba quite a lot until Castro took over in 1959. Then it was back to New York, and after two nights in New York we would do another cruise. After eight cruises we would return to Southampton in the April and start the North Atlantic run. We would sail from Southampton to Cherbourg, Cobh, and then over to New York and return to Southampton. We did about nine trips, and in November to December we would go into dry dock, and after that back to the cruises again. I did five years of that.'

However, Gus Shanahan was on the *Mauretania*, anchored in the Havana harbour, when Fidel Castro invaded on 2 January 1959. Gus Shanahan: 'We used to arrive in Havana at 7am and anchor in the harbour and leave at 7am the next morning. The passengers would go ashore and have plenty of time to look around Havana, watch the Mardi Gras and horse racing before returning to the ship for the next morning's sailing.

'This day was going to be different because Fidel Castro invaded Havana and there were his people driving around with flags waving and firing guns.' A decision was made to leave at 2pm and as the *Mauretania* went through the breakwater, vehicles were driving alongside with guns firing. 'We pulled up the anchors and left the harbour. I could see all the cars with flags waving and a body lying on the ground, a victim of the shooting.'

In 1963 the *Mauretania* started a Mediterranean service between Naples and Gibraltar via Genoa and Cannes, and transatlantic to New York. However, the cruises started to take over, and these left New York and Southampton for the Caribbean, Bermuda, the Bahamas, West Africa and the Mediterranean. The *Mauretania's* last cruise started from New York on 15 September 1965 to the Mediterranean and then on to Southampton. Shortly after that the *Mauretania* left Southampton for Inverkeithing and the scrapyard under the command of her final master, Captain John Treasure-Jones.

The *Scythia* took war brides and their children to St John's, Newfoundland, and on her return brought German POWs to work in England. After other repatriation trips to other parts of the world she returned to the North American routes in 1950. However, in November 1955 she was again used for trooping duties, taking Canadian troops from Europe to Quebec. In 1958 it was *Scythia's* final voyage from Halifax to Southampton via Le Havre and Rotterdam, and she was then sold to the British Iron & Steel Corporation. Captain Geoffrey Marr, her final Commander, delivered the *Scythia* to the ship breakers at Inverkeithing, arriving on 23 January 1958.

By 1950 the *Samaria* had been refitted and returned to Cunard, The passenger accommodation was changed to 250 first-class and 650 tourist-class passengers, and the *Samaria* made her first voyage to Quebec from Southampton, calling in at Le Havre on 12 July 1951.

Nursing Sister Jean Edwards sailed on the *Samaria* in 1955: 'My first trip on the *Samaria* was pretty bad because a haemophiliac who was seasick became ill, and we had to take blood from 15 crew members who were O-negative. When we got to the St Lawrence River I went ashore with the pilot boat with the patient and went out by ambulance to Quebec, where he made a rapid recovery. His wife was with him and there was one of the other ladies who had pneumonia, and luckily for them they were in hospital as they were part of the Mormon Tabernacle choir. The plane taking the remainder of the choir and other passengers crashed and all were lost.'

This was the United Airlines Flight 409, a Douglas DC-4, from Denver, Colorado, to Salt Lake City, Utah. The plane was due to depart at 6.33am on 6 October 1955 but was over an hour later leaving than its scheduled departure time. The aircraft crashed into Medicine Bow Peak, Wyoming, killing all 66 people on board (63 passengers, three crew). The crash was at the time the worst crash in the history of US commercial aviation. The victims included members of the Mormon Tabernacle Choir, who were returning from a European tour.

There was no radar coverage in those days and radio contact was lost with the aircraft. The crash investigators could not establish the reasons for the crash, but the accident was instrumental in the improvement of airline safety with the introduction and use of radar for civil aviation.

The *Samaria's* last Quebec-Havre-Southampton crossing commenced on 23 November 1955, and she was finally scrapped at Inverkeithing in January 1956.

Cunard Builds a New Class of Ships

Cunard decided to build a new class of ship in 1951 for the Liverpool to Montreal route and these ships were to be the *Saxonia, Ivernia, Sylvania* and *Carinthia*. All were built by John Brown's Clydebank yard, and the first to be launched was the *Saxonia* and then the *Ivernia*, both in 1954.

When Gus Shanahan left the *Media* he went on the *Saxonia* as the ship's carpenter in June 1955, sailing on the Canadian service from Liverpool to Quebec and Montreal: 'The *Saxonia* was one of the four ships built in 1954–55. On the first trip

The *Saxonia* (21,637 GT) in ice on the St Lawrence River. She was built in 1954 by John Brown & Company, Clydebank. Between 1962–63 she was refitted and renamed *Carmania*. In 1973 she was renamed again as *Leonid Sobinov*. She was broken up in Alang, India, in 1990. (Dorothy Cadman (Lee) Collection)

The *Ivernia* (2) (21,717 GT) was built in 1955 by John Brown & Company, Clydebank. She was refitted in 1963 and renamed *Franconia*. (John Merry Collection)

the *Saxonia* came down the St Lawrence River a bit too fast and the propellers' wash caused the boats of the people living along the riverside to be washed ashore. They complained about it and so after that the ship would come down the St Lawrence River much slower.'

There were difficulties with industrial disputes in 1955, and by 1957 the *Saxonia* and *Ivernia* had transferred to Southampton. However, the third vessel was the *Carinthia*, which was launched in 1955 and remained based in Liverpool.

John Merry was an engineer on the *Ivernia* and remembers one crew member who was in fear of the pet he had brought on board: 'We had a crew member on the *Ivernia* who bought an alligator in New York and brought it on board. The alligator was about 3–4 inches long and he kept it in one of the baths, which put that bath out of action. About three trips later the alligator was getting bigger and snappier. The crew member started to get frightened himself and eventually had to get staff from a zoo to take the alligator away.

'On the *Ivernia* I was second in command in the engine room. There was a third engineer in the boiler room, a second engineer in charge of the watch and a fourth engineer with a junior under him.

'There were some major incidents on the *Ivernia*. One was when we were going to New York in the wintertime and we caught the edge of a hurricane. It was very rough and it was the only time I was really worried because the ship went over, even with the stabilizers out.

The other incident was an emergency. We were steaming along quite nicely, and it was in the middle of the night and we were watching the gauges. All of a sudden all of the gauges went down and the back-up cut in. I tried to get through to the boiler room but with no success. The Chief Engineer shouted, "Stop the engines!" as the boiler room hadn't heard the phone. We had calls from the bridge asking what was going on. Anyway it was all sorted out and we continued on the voyage.'

After being second in command in the engine room on the *Ivernia* John Merry joined the *Queen Mary*. He was surprised by how much he was paid for the task he was allotted to: 'When I joined the *Queen Mary* from the *Ivernia* I was put in the after engine room. And my duties were just to look after two water-feed pumps, and for that I got more money!' The *Ivernia* was rebuilt for cruising in 1963 and renamed *Franconia*.

In 1962 the *Saxonia* sailed to the Clyde, where it was to be refitted for the cruise market. This led to the ship's tonnage increasing to 22,592 GT. The decision was taken to rename her *Carmania* (3) in 1963. The refit had included air conditioning and adding a lido and sun terrace. The passenger accommodation was also upgraded to carry 600 peole.

Pat Royl was with the *Saxonia* when the ship was taken out of service and taken to Clydebank, painted green and renamed *Carmania*: 'I went up to Clydebank with her with just a skeleton crew and then I was redirected back to the *Queen Elizabeth*. That was when the *Queen Elizabeth* did the first and only cruise out of New York at Christmas to the Bahamas. The ship was packed solid with Americans. I was working at the first-class restaurant and was with her until the *Carmania* was ready to leave Clydebank. I remember the crew going up to Clydebank on a Hants and Dorset bus and what an uncomfortable journey that was, especially as there was no food provided!

'When we got to Scotland there was no catering. All we had when we got there was a bottle of Scotch. That was all we got for breakfast because the catering staff hadn't turned up.

'We sailed down to Southampton and then straight out to Fort Lauderdale and stayed there for six months. From Fort Lauderdale we did Caribbean cruises. That was in about 1964 and we couldn't get in to Bermuda on the way back because the weather was so bad and it was snowing when we eventually arrived back.

The *Britannic* (26,943 GT) leaving for the breakers' yard in December 1960. The *Britannic* was the sister ship to the *Georgic*. (Courtesy of Gus Shanahan)

'At that time it was expensive to dock because the port dues were so high in Southampton. After a four-hour drop-off in Southampton we went across to Rotterdam and stayed until Tuesday. We returned to Southampton to pick up passengers and then went back to Canada for the summer.

'I remember once there was a waterspout in the Caribbean, I think around Christmas. This was on the *Carmania* and the bridge notified the passengers that there was a waterspout over on the starboard side. It was about lunch time and we had a deck buffet going, and all of a sudden this waterspout came towards us, and the bridge told the passengers that they were making a manoeuvre, but it was too late. The waterspout hit the ship and the swimming pool was full of glass, plates, food and deckchairs all over the place. It was scary, but it happened very quickly and was over in a matter of seconds. The waterspout passed over the aft end of the ship, and afterwards there was steam coming off the aft end, but by the afternoon you wouldn't think anything had happened.'

It was originally planned for the *Carmania* to sail from Europe to Montreal and spend the winter cruising from Florida to the Caribbean, but as a result of continued industrial strikes the travelling public began to change to other means of travel. The *Carmania* struggled on, spending most of her time cruising.

By December 1971 the *Carmania* was laid up at Southampton, but in May 1972 both the *Carmania* and her sister ship, *Franconia*, were moved to be laid up at Falmouth. Eventually the *Carmania* was bought by a Russian shipping company and renamed the *Leonid Sobinov*. She spent some time cruising from Australia, but as a result of the Russian invasion of Afghanistan the vessel was banned from Australian ports and was moved to Vladivostock, but from then on very little was known about what happened to the ship.

Bert Moody: 'There is no mystery to what happened to these two ships. *Franconia* was also sold to the Russians and renamed *Fedor Shalyapin*. In 1973 both ships were operated by Nikreis Maritime Corporation of Panama, acting as agents for the Russian's State Shipping Company.'

During the 1980s both vessels were cruising mainly in the Mediterranean and the West Indies. In 1980 *Leonid Sobinov* was operating under the Maltese flag by Trans-Orient Overseas. By 1996 both ships were laid up at Ilyichevsk in the Black Sea in need of repairs for which the owners did not have the money. On 30 January 1999 *Leonid Sobinov* sailed for the breakers' yard at Alang in India and *Fedor Shalyapin* was broken up afterwards.

After the war the *Britannic* returned to the Liverpool-New York service in 1948, but by 1950 Cunard-White Star changed back to the Cunard Line. Both *Britannic* and her sister ship, *Georgic*, remained as the last White Star ships in service. The *Georgic* had been requisitioned for war service in 1939 but in 1941 was beached in shallow water after being hit by German bombs at Suez which caused her to catch fire. However, it was decided to raise the vessel and she was towed first to Bombay for repairs and then sailed under her own power to Belfast for a complete refit. The *Georgic* was sold to the Ministry of Transport in 1943, although she was still managed by Cunard-White Star, undertaking trooping duties until 1948 when she started taking emigrants from Liverpool to Australia and New Zealand. She again returned for a short time to the Liverpool-New York service but was used for trooping for the Korea War from 1950–53. She finally made her last voyage under the White Star flag in 1954 and was scrapped at Faslane in 1956.

When the *Britannic* left New York for her final transatlantic crossing in November 1960 she was the last ship to fly the famous White Star Line houseflag, and it was also the last transatlantic crossing of a White Star ship. The *Britannic* left Liverpool on 15 December 1960 under her own power to be scrapped in Inverkeithing. When she arrived on 19 December there was a decorated Christmas tree alongside the main doors of the first-class restaurant that would never see Christmas.

When the work started on breaking the *Britannic* in February 1961 the interior fittings were stripped out and many sold at auction. The *Britannic's* bell and her steam-operated triple-chime whistle are now stored at the Merseyside Maritime Museum.

In 1957 Cunard announced that it had reserved a berth at John Brown's Clydebank yard to build a replacement for the *Britannic*, but with an increasing number of passengers changing over to air travel this was cancelled. The Liverpool-Cobh-New York service was taken over by the *Sylvania* and *Carinthia*. Both were on this service from 1957 and remained on the transatlantic route until the final sailing in November 1966.

Ile de France returns to the French Line

At the end of the war the *Ile de France* was managed by Cunard but on 3 February 1946 she was returned to the French Line, and her first commercial service from Cherbourg to New York commenced on 22 October 1946. The *Ile de France*

The *Monarch of Bermuda* (22,424 GT) was completed in 1931 by Vickers-Armstong, Barrow-in-Furness. In 1947 she was badly damaged by fire. She was rebuilt by J.I. Thorneycroft, Southampton, and renamed *New Australia* in 1950. (Bert Moody Collection)

went into dry dock in 1947 and was rebuilt to 46,356 GT with two funnels, her dummy funnel being removed and passenger accommodation made for 541 first-class, 577 cabin-class and 227 tourist-class passengers.

The transatlantic service from Le Havre to Southampton and on to New York recommenced on 26 July 1949. On 25 July 1956 the *Andrea Doria* was approaching Nantucket bound for New York. She had reduced speed because of dense fog when she was in collision with the Swedish American Line *Stockholm* that was outward bound from New York. However, the *Ile de France*, which had passed the *Andrea Doria* hours before while sailing to New York, turned around and rescued 733 survivors from the sinking ship.

On 10 November 1958 the *Ile de France* sailed to Osaka under the name of *Farenzu Maru* in preparation for scrapping but was renamed the *SS Claridon* and sunk for the filming of *The Last Voyage*. Later she was refloated and scrapped in Osaka, Japan.

Shaw Savill on the *Monarch of Bermuda*
The *Monarch of Bermuda* was 22,424 GT and 579ft (176.5m) long, with a beam of 76ft (23.2m). She had three funnels, two masts and a cruiser stern. Her engines were turboelectric, which powered four screws at a service speed of 19 knots. The passenger accommodation was provided for 799 first-class and 31 second-class passengers. She carried a crew of 456. After being launched on 17 March 1931 the *Monarch of Bermuda* sailed on the Furness, Withy & Co.'s New York to Bermuda run from 1931 to 1939.

In 1946 the *Monarch of Bermuda* was used to carry Canadian war brides across the Atlantic. The vessel was gutted by fire on 24 March 1947 while undergoing a post-war refit. The Ministry of Transport decided to rebuild the ship. She was structurally sound and was rebuilt in Southampton.

In 1949 the old *Monarch of Bermuda* had been rebuilt and was renamed the *New Australia*. The *New Australia* was 20,256 GT and was 553.2ft (168.6m), with a beam of 76.7ft (23.4m), and could accommodate 1,600 as one class. Shaw Savill was asked by the Ministry of Transport to manage the vessel.

New Australia
It was on 15 August 1950 that the *New Australia* made her first voyage from Southampton to Sydney, taking migrants from Britain to Australia. For her return journey she sailed to Japan and brought British troops of the British Commonwealth Occupation Force (BCOF) back to Britain.

In 1952 the *New Australia* took troops of the 1st Battalion of the Royal Australian Regiment to Korea. She returned again to Korea in 1953, and this time she brought the 2nd Battalion of the Royal Australian Regiment to relieve the 1st Battalion. However, she was caught up in a severe typhoon off the Philippine coast while taking more troops.

The *New Australia* (20,256 GT), formerly the *Monarch of Bermuda*. In 1958 she was sold to the Greek Line and renamed *Arkadia*. She was broken up in Valencia in 1966. (Mick Lindsay Collection)

John Fahy joined the *New Australia* for his first voyage to sea in 1955: 'My first ship was the *New Australia* as assistant steward, but in those days we had no training and I was put to work with another steward. We had a table of 14 and my job was to take the orders, go and get them from the galley, and bring them back for the steward to serve. The steward's job was to look after the passengers while I was taking the orders and getting them from the galley, and then he would serve them. I was happy with that because it took a load off me. All I had to do was to go out and get the orders from the galley.'

John Fahy had two trips on the *New Australia*, returning again in 1957 for the second trip: 'The *New Australia* was a beautiful ship, even better than the liners I later worked on. It was one of the best ships I was on for accommodation, and the most berths were two to a cabin, while on the *Queen Mary* and *Queen Elizabeth* there were 8–10 to a cabin.'

In 1957 the *New Australia* was used again as a troop transport. However, one day, in the late afternoon, she was passing through the Torres Strait between North Queensland and New Guinea when she collided with an oil tanker. Fortunately the damage was not severe and there were no casualties.

Voyages while serving on the *New Australia* were mainly happy times and John Fahy has memories of some of the places he visited while on board: 'They were good times and in 1955 we went to Australia – Perth (Freemantle), Melbourne, Sydney, Townsville – where we would pick up troops. We went to Korea in her as well, and picked up a load of Australian troops to take them home, but we then went to Japan, just five miles from where the atomic bomb was dropped on Hiroshima. I had the opportunity to go there. That was in 1955 and it was still devastated then. Then we called in Penang, Malaysia, and picked up another load of British soldiers to take home. We went back to Townsville, dropped all the Australian troops, and then carried on back down to Sydney, picked up stores. We had the British troops still on board and we came down to Freemantle, took on fresh water, and a dash across the Indian Ocean to Columbo, Ceylon, then carried on to the next port of call, which was Aden. We used to go in there and buy anything: cameras, watches, diamonds and sapphires. You could buy anything and there were some wide boys on board ship who knew exactly what they were after. It was a duty free port and they would buy goods to take back to England to sell because there was no tax on them. We then went back through the Suez Canal to Port Said and then back to Southampton.'

Andes and the *Magdalena*

Harold Lloyd worked as a seaman for the Royal Mail Lines and was due to join the new *Magdalena* but finished up signing on the *Andes*. Harold Lloyd: 'I was due to join the *Magdalena*, which was a brand-new Royal Mail ship, but I had trouble because I didn't have my seaman's book when I said that I was to sign on for the *Magdalena*. They told me in the office that they were filling up one ship at a time and the next ship available was for the Union-Castle Line. I said

The *Andes* (2) (26,689 GT) was completed in 1939 by Harland & Wolff, Belfast. She was refitted by De Schelde in 1959 for cruising and given a white hull (as shown). She was broken up in Ghent in 1971. (Mick Lindsay Collection)

I was working for the Royal Mail Line so I went over to the Royal Mail Office and saw a man in there. He phoned up and told the person I had seen that he was sending me over for the *Magdalena* and to get on with it. If I didn't do that he would also be looking for a job. However, I was too late and didn't make the *Magdalena* and so they put me on the *Andes*. The *Andes* was going down to Buenos Aires, Argentina, to load up with a cargo of beef, although she did carry quite a few passengers as well.

'I was lucky that I missed the *Magdalena* because she went down off Rio de Janeiro on her maiden voyage. She hit the rocks coming out of Rio de Janeiro while homeward bound. We actually saw the ship as the *Andes* went past while sailing into Rio de Janeiro.'

The Royal Mail's first new, post-war, intermediate passenger liner, *Magdalena*, built by Harland & Wolff, had left London on 9 March 1949 bound for Buenos Aires for her maiden voyage. On 25 April she ran onto rocks on the Tijucas Reef while homeward bound. The bow section broke away and sank, but the stern section remained afloat and was later sold for scrap. Although she was refloated the next day she broke her back with the stern section remaining afloat, but the bow section sank straight away. The stern section was later sold for scrap.

In June 1953 the *Andes* sailed from Southampton to the Coronation Review at Spithead to represent Royal Mail. Just two years later Jim Taylor, who had left his first ship, the *Scythia*, joined the *Andes* as a bellboy, otherwise known as a page boy, on 2 March 1955 for his first two trips: 'As a bellboy I had a small hat and many buttons on the front of my uniform. The *Andes* was a lovely passenger ship and her regular Royal Mail run was from Southampton to Buenos Aires carrying passengers, mail and freight. We had refrigerated cargo holds which we used to bring back frozen lamb and beef. I always remember when we sailed into Montevideo we could still see the wreckage of the Deutschland class cruiser *Graf Spee* where she had been scuttled in the bay by her captain.

After a very happy two and a half years on the *Andes* Jim Taylor had worked up from assistant steward, where he was serving the engineers, to a first-class waiter: 'All the time while you are assistant steward the Chief Steward and 2nd Steward were keeping their eyes on you. I was then promoted as a first-class waiter in the restaurant, based on the recommendation of the Chief Steward, who said I did a very good job.' On the last three voyages Jim Taylor had the job of 'Boots and Baths,' but finally left the *Andes* on 1 August 1958.

The *Andes*'s South America service was ended in November 1959, and after a major refit at the De Schelde shipyards at Flushing in Holland she began a year-round cruise service as an all first-class ship on 10 June 1960. The *Andes* was now catering for the very rich, who returned year on year because of the high-quality service and almost one-to-one service, with passengers being looked after by an equal number of crew members.

The *Nieuw Amsterdam* (36,287 GT) was built by the Rotterdam Dry Dock Company and launched in 1937. In 1957 she was repainted with a grey hull. She was broken up 1974. (Bert Moody Collection)

This service was only to last for a decade and by the end of the 1960s, with the high running costs and fewer passengers taking the cruises, it was decided to scrap the *Andes* in Ghent, Belgium, in 1971.

Holland America Line *Nieuw Amsterdam*

The *Nieuw Amsterdam* was 36,287 GT and 758ft (231m) long, with a beam of 88ft (26.8m). Her engines were steam turbine powering twin screws at 20½ knots. She was built for the Holland-America Line by the Rotterdam Dry Dock Company and launched on 10 April 1937. Her passenger capacity was 556 first-class, 455 tourist and 209 third-class passengers.

The *Nieuw Amsterdam's* maiden voyage was from Rotterdam to New York, calling at Boulogne and Southampton on 10 May 1938. During the war she carried out troopship duties under the management of Cunard. In 1946 she was released from war duties and returned to Rotterdam to a hero's welcome. By 1947 she had been refitted for commercial service on the transatlantic crossings. After a number of other refits and the installation of air conditioning in 1957 the *Nieuw Amsterdam* returned to a regular service with the *Rotterdam* and *Statendam*, sailing from New York every Friday for Southampton, Le Havre and Rotterdam. However, the era of the jet aircraft had come to the fore, both the *Statendam* and *Rotterdam* changed to cruising, and it was only the *Nieuw Amsterdam* that sailed out of Rotterdam. She was broken up in Taiwan in 1974.

The second *Nieuw Amsterdam* was built in 1983. She was acquired by the United States Line in 2000 and renamed *Patriot*, but this was not to last and the name was changed back again to the *Nieuw Amsterdam* and she went on charter to the Carnival Group. She was then renamed *Thomson Spirit*, and joined her sister ship, the *Noordam*, which became the *Thomson Celebration*.

The *Nieuw Amsterdam* (33,930 GT), built in 1983, was renamed *Thomson Spirit* in 2002. The picture shows the *Thomson Spirit* leaving Southampton. (Richard de Jong Collection)

CHAPTER 6
SAILING ON THE QUEENS AND OTHER CUNARDERS IN THE 1950S AND 1960S

Introduction to the Queens

Douglas Ward is the author of the Berlitz *Complete Guide to Cruising and Cruise Ships* and remembers his time working on the 'Queens':
'The *Queen Mary* and the *Queen Elizabeth* were built for transatlantic travel; they had thicker hulls and deeper draught than the *United States*. The *Queen Elizabeth* was a somewhat larger ship of the time and to me she had much nicer interiors than the *Queen Mary*. I think the *Queen Elizabeth* had 52 varieties of African woods for the interiors. She also had a Press Relations Room, which was really richly panelled and a very long table for interviews.

'In the 1950s there was some competition from aircraft and this was the death knell for the ocean liners, but the one advantage that ocean liners had over jet aircraft was that you could carry as much luggage as you wanted. The *Queen Mary* allowed 2.5 tons of luggage and this was ideal for people relocating between continents.

'As the vessels changed from the transatlantic line service, with the occasional cruise, to more cruising so the interiors needed to be changed to suit the warmer weather cruises. In 1966 they decided to send the *Queen Elizabeth* cruising in the wintertime and she went into dry dock to be totally refurbished and have a complete refit which involved installing air conditioning and an open-air swimming pool on the stern deck.

'The first cruise was for 30 days to the Canary Islands and North and West Africa. It was a very successful cruise so they decided to send the *Queen Elizabeth* on more, and that is how Cunard evolved from transatlantic service to cruising.

'There is one thing I remember about those ships and that was that they had DC (direct current) for power and you needed a converter for AC (alternating current). When we were in New York we would sometimes have a Mayor's Ball on board. We had five bands on the *Queen Mary* and I was the band leader of one of the two first-class bands. I've never worked in cabin class or in the tourist class, but I do remember that the American agencies sometimes sent cabaret trios for these functions. They would plug their amplifiers into the mains on board and they would just blow up because they didn't realise it was DC and not AC.

'It was while we were crossing the Atlantic in 1967 and passing the *Queen Mary* at a distance of about five miles when we had an announcement on the Tannoy system from the Cunard chairman saying that due to the economic situation, changing markets and competition from jet aircraft, Cunard had decided to retire the *Queen Mary*.

'The *Queen Mary* was to be withdrawn first and the *Queen Elizabeth* a year later. Everybody was a bit dismayed after the announcement.'

Life On Board the *Queen Mary* for the Officers and Crew

It was during the *Queen Mary's* conversion to peacetime service that the passenger accommodation was changed to 711 first-class, 707 cabin-class and 577 tourist-class.

The first post-war voyage was from Southampton to New York on 31 July 1947. However, this was the period when industrial disruptions to the service occurred, and although land-based wartime airfields were being developed for commercial passenger services, causing the demise of the flying boat service, air travel had not yet become a serious threat to the transatlantic ocean liner services.

There was a gradual change in passenger attitude to transatlantic travel, from the almost pampered luxury of the liner crossing to the much quicker jet air travel. On 1 January 1949 the *Queen Mary* ran aground at Cherbourg and had to return to Southampton for repairs. When she arrived in Southampton a number of passengers decided to leave the ship and fly from London to America. This was an indication of the choices that passengers were beginning to make between sea travel and air travel.

The problem in Cherbourg was that the *Queen Mary* was anchored in the harbour when one of the anchors became entangled in the World War Two fuel line PLUTO (pipeline under the ocean), laid to supply fuel to the D-Day invasion forces in 1944. However, the weather got worse and Captain Harry Grattidge decided to lower the port anchor to prevent the liner drifting on to the rocks, but she went aground and stuck in the mud. After working all night the crew freed the liner and she returned to Southampton and sailed into the dry dock. There was some leaking, but workers employed a similar temporary repair to the one undertaken after the collision with HMS *Curacoa* in the war. Tons of cement were used to seal the damaged area and the *Queen Mary* proceeded to New York.

Getting work with Cunard

To get a job working for Cunard you either had to know someone already working for them or someone who could introduce you. It was in the early 1950s that Barbara Pedan heard about the possibility of a post with Cunard and was lucky because her father had links with Cunard: 'You could only get a job with Cunard by introduction, and as my father's firm had done business with Cunard I was able to get an interview for the post of Assistant Lady Purser.'

After brushing up on her shorthand and typing skills Barbara Pedan joined the *Queen Mary* in 1953: 'It was like entering another world, but all the crew were very welcoming and I very quickly settled in and found my way round the vast ship.'

The origins of the Lady Pursers

Barbara Pedan talks about how the Lady Pursers' role developed and the work while on board: 'During World War Two there had been WRENS on the 'Queens' and several of these stayed on when they returned to their passenger roles, becoming the first Lady Pursers. For each of the three classes on the old 'Queens' there was a Purser in the office with two to seven assistant pursers and one lady purser.

When Barbara Pedan joined the *Queen Mary* as an assistant lady purser she spent several years in the first-class office: 'This was a large office with shutters all round on B Deck, which was approximately in the middle of the ship. It was interesting to be stationed there where you could see everything that was happening, such as the captain greeting the famous people as they came on board on embarkation day, the beautifully dressed women, the smell of perfume and cigars, or the Queen Mother coming down the grand staircase opposite on her way to the first-class dining room. However, to all the purser's staff it was something of an ordeal and we all preferred the tourist-class office or the cabin-class office, which was halfway between the two worlds. Mostly English people, regular passengers, would travel cabin class.'

While at sea the work of the pursers would be to prepare all the details needed for the manifests, a massive task that was important for American immigration. Barbara Pedan: 'The American Immigration were very tough compared to ours and the officers presented a very forbidding appearance as they swarmed on board, but over the years we got to know them all and never had any difficulty with them. Along with immigration the shore staff from Cunard in New York came aboard to help smooth out any arrival difficulties and to help the VIP's through the 'formalities' quickly.

Disembarkation would take the best part of the day. If we arrived at 6am you could reckon on the ship being finally cleared about 3pm, and then you would breathe a sigh of relief and look forward, on the Queens at any rate, to a night or two in New York.'

One of the other duties of the lady pursers was to be available to do any stenography that was required by passengers. Barbara Pedan remembers her first assignment very well: 'Just imagine my horror when I found that my very first assignment was to take down a play which was in cockney dialect. Straight language would be bad enough but a dialect! Fortunately, he was an extremely nice man and I told him this was my first dictation.

'He went very slowly and I managed to get most of it down and quickly pencilled the dialect above, but we had terribly rough weather. It was my first trip and I was seasick most of the time, and I still have horrible memories of that play. Years later I heard the very play on the radio. I had worked so hard getting the play down I more or less knew it by heart and had no doubt that that was it.'

The play was Angus Wilson's *The Mulberry Bush*, which was first performed by the Bristol Old Vic Company on 27 September 1955 and at the Royal Court Theatre on 2 April 1956, directed by George Devine. The play was also televised in 1957.

Barbara Pedan: 'Other passengers I worked for were the scientist Julian Huxley, but much of this was copy typing and reading his writing was quite a feat. I did work for Billy Graham, the American evangelist, and for the founder of Toc H, the Reverend Philip Clayton, better known as the Revd 'Tubby' Clayton.'

The Male Stewards

The male stewards did not have an easy time when in port, as John Stamp explains: 'If we were to call at Cobh, Cherbourg or one of the other ports we weren't just stewards, we had to load and unload stores. In Southampton we would be carrying linen, fresh laundry and provisions which we would carry on board the ship. In those days on board there was only so much accommodation, and no room for cleaners, so the waiters did the cleaning as well. While the deckhands cleaned all the decks, polished rails, brasswork and paintwork, generally keeping it all tidy upstairs, we had to do the same inside ship.

'If you were a steward you would be in a cabin on D deck with 12 others, but the cabin we had was over the engines and, believe me, in winter time it was not the place to be with the pounding of the engines. In rough weather the stern lifted out of the water in the middle of a hurricane and the screws would start revolving around before they hit the water again. It was a bit hairy I suppose, but we accepted it.

'You would be working 12 to 14 hours a day, sometimes split shifts. I don't know if it was a blessing in having the top or the bottom bunk, but you had a little locker about a foot wide where you had keep everything in, including cleaning gear and you had to look smart and tidy. Not easy when in the first class – during the daytime we would wear white jacket and blue trousers and at dinner in the evening white tuxedos. There was quite a bit of cheating going on where some waiters would be wearing collars, studs and white fronts with nothing underneath. However, a majority of us did wear a shirt.

'On board ship we had some wonderful times. We had some laughs and also met some very famous people, but having said that life was hard at times, winter time especially. In the winter the ships used to sail light of crew and quite a few of us were contracted to Cunard. They would contract some crew because they like to have a steady crew that could stay on in the winter. Cunard's regular crew could be spread around the other ships, such as the *Mauretania* and *Caronia*, who were two cruising ships during the winter time.'

To pass the time the crew would have little bets on the time the *Queen Mary* sailed from Southampton to New York and also on the return trip. The measurement was time between Nantucket Island and the Nab Tower. Gordon Brown: 'You used to write down the estimated time of arrival at Nantucket Island off of New York and the Nab Tower, off the Isle of Wight. It was a £1 a time and the correct estimate got the lot.'

The Glory Hole Steward

The crew cabins were called the glory hole and there was a steward whose job was to look after the crew in the cabin. Gordon Brown: 'You didn't look after your own bed, you paid the glory hole steward £1 a trip to make your bed, change your linen and keep the place tidy.'

The stewards would be called at 6am by the glory hole steward and would dress and begin scrubbing floors using buckets of soapy water while using rolled-up carpets as kneeling pads. The big lino floors with crazy patterns and the big areas outside the shops and staircases would be scrubbed and polished clean.

John Stamp: 'You had to lay your table up, as there was no laying up overnight and it all had to be done in the morning. When there was the bad weather you would lay your tables and place only the cutlery. Otherwise you'd have to put your 17 pieces of silver per person, including fruit knives and forks, four crystal glasses and other items. Then you would have to go down, get dressed up and put on the uniform and come back to serve breakfast. After breakfast had finished you would go down and change to scrub the restaurant again.

'Then there were the afternoon teas. The waiters had to do afternoon teas as well. They would go up topside and help topside stewards with the afternoon teas. Everyone hated afternoon teas because you didn't get finished till 5.30pm. You might get down, snatching one hour's rest, showering, shaving and changing into uniform, before going up to the restaurant to prepare for dinner. That was something else. I had to collect the napkins from the linen cupboard, fold them and lay the table. When we had finished at night the restaurant would have to be cleaned, all the silver washed, polished, and some of the waiters would be working the glass locker, cleaning and polishing all the glasses. You would have what you call 'pearl divers' outside to wash all the plates. All the silverware and silver service had to be cleaned and polished.

'There is a real preparation, and, in fact, when you think about it, there were really three meals a day in complete luxury. Even the cabin and tourist class had good standards. I don't think you can do that today.'

The Bellboys

Most of the bellboys on board the ships sailing from Southampton Docks originally came from Southampton, Portsmouth and the Isle of Wight. Their jobs on board the *Queen Mary* included carrying messages and telegrams from the pursers' office, walking dogs from the kennels on the sports deck, helping to carry passengers' luggage and opening doors for them. Although their monthly wage was not very much they would get many more times that in tips, especially from celebrities, who would always tip well.

The bellboys would have to get up early, like the other crew members, and scrub out before getting dressed into their uniforms. They would parade between 7 and 8am for inspection and have their nails checked as well as other matters of cleanliness and smartness, in keeping with Cunard's very high standards of staff presentation.

John Stamp was a bellboy and from his experience has his own view of them: 'Now there were the bellboys on board ship. At the tender age of 15 there were these little kids. They were all picked for their size, but all the American women used to think they were orphans. They made a fuss of them and wanted to adopt them, but trust me, these bellboys were the biggest gangsters in the world! They were certainly seawise, or streetwise as it is called today. Trust me, I know, I was one!'

The Verandah Grill

John Fahy joined the *Queen Mary* for the first time in 1958 and was first working on the night gang. He was then moved to the deck pantry, making sandwiches for the passengers, and then he got a job as a steward in the cabin dining saloon: 'I also worked in Verandah Grill on the *Queen Mary*, which was on the upper deck at the after end. This was a top place on the *Queen Mary* and passengers had to pay extra for their meal. The restaurant in the Verandah Grill was exclusive and there was a 12s 6d cover charge for first-class passengers who dined in the grill restaurant. In the evening this area became a night club, but it had its compensations in the numbers of famous personalities sailing on the *Queen Mary*. It was quite an experience, and the dancing used to go on sometimes until 04.00 or 05.00. I used to love the atmosphere in the grill. You would see all the famous people there and the best musicians used to play there. Geraldo used to run the music agency and he had all the best musicians playing on board. There would be a change of one or two musicians every trip because they used to take their holidays from the Savoy Hotel, join the *Queen Mary*, do one trip, which was two weeks, go back to their own job in the Savoy Hotel, and then somebody else would come on a trip. While working in the Verandah Grill I used to start at 5pm and finish some nights at about 4 or 5am, and then you had to 'turn to' again at 7am.'

Working in the First-Class Restaurant

John Stamp's promotion to first-class waiter was quite swift and not fully approved of by the restaurant manager: 'I was the captain's tiger commis waiter and was picked out because I got on very well. They made me into a first-class waiter, but that was something else. The restaurant manager at the time said I was too young at 18, "You can't take the boy and make

Carving the salmon in the first-class restaurant on the *Queen Mary* (80,773 GT). (Geoffrey Le Marquand Collection)

him into a first-class waiter. It is unheard of." However, the captain insisted and I was made first-class waiter and became the youngest first-class waiter in the fleet.'

John Stamp found working in the first-class restaurant during the summer very busy: 'During the summertime you would have as many as 150 stations in the first class, and first class meant first class. When you served the grapefruit in the morning you were struggling with six grapefruit on your tray, with silver bowls packed with ice and vine leaves around the outside.'

Geoffrey Le Marquand remembers his time as a first-class commis waiter: 'The first-class waiters in the restaurant used

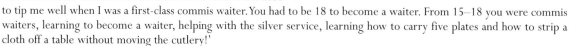

to tip me well when I was a first-class commis waiter. You had to be 18 to become a waiter. From 15–18 you were commis waiters, learning to become a waiter, helping with the silver service, learning how to carry five plates and how to strip a cloth off a table without moving the cutlery!'

When reporting to the head waiter in the first-class restaurant Geoffrey Le Marquand was informed of what he was required to do: 'I was told that my job was first to welcome passengers. I had to open the restaurant doors on the starboard side for the passengers when they entered. However, I soon learned the naughty trick of your age and how to gain a few extra dollars in tips from the passengers.

'The night before you docked in New York or Southampton would be gala night with a special menu. As the first-class passengers entered I would say "Good evening, sir, good evening, madam." I was very polite and they thought I was a nice boy. In the course of the conversation I would often be asked how old I was. I would say, "Well it is a coincidence, but it is my birthday tomorrow night, I will be 17." The gala night was always going to be my birthday! That was the night when money changed hands, and on that night when you opened the doors for them, not only did you get your tip but more often than not an extra $5 as a birthday present. You would do the same on the homeward bound voyage, but you had to be careful in case you got the same passengers on the return trip because you could only have one birthday!'

Once the passengers had been welcomed into the first-class restaurant Geoffrey Le Marquand would be on the smoked salmon trolley in the evening: 'There were two of us within the restaurant with a smoked salmon trolley, with one trolley at each side (port and starboard) of the restaurant. At first I had to go into the galley and get the smoked salmon trolley ready and then wait with the trolley in the restaurant until I would be called by one of the waiters to carve the salmon for the passengers who had ordered it at the table. You had to keep these trolleys under control when the *Queen Mary* was dipping and rolling in the rough weather.

'Your job was to be at the side of the passengers and on the trolley would be marble slate, and you would sharpen the knife before cutting the salmon. Sharpening the knife was all a bit of a show to "impress the passengers". Then I would carve the salmon razor thin, and when that was over you had the roast beef on the trolley with flames underneath to keep the beef warm.

'When this was over I was then expected to help the waiters around several tables with serving the rest of the meal. Once dinner was over and the passengers had left the restaurant we usually sat down to eat our meal. Did we eat well! We then returned to our cabins, got changed and back into the restaurant to help wash the floor. We would end up later in the Pig & Whistle (the crew's bar) for a chat with other crew members.'

The *Queen Mary* 'Roll' on Atlantic Crossings

Geoffrey Le Marquand remembers the rough Atlantic weather: 'By now the weather on the Atlantic crossings was beginning to get rough – the ship rolled and pitched for the entire voyage. Some passengers stayed in their cabins and the restaurant was often half empty.'

John Minto also remembers the rolling of the *Queen Mary*: 'Depending how rough the weather was the *Queen Mary* used to roll over, hold the position, sometimes quite a long time, and then slowly come back. Then she would roll the other way.'

To cope with the rolling when working the crew would have to stand a certain way, as John Minto explains: 'Most people who worked on Cunard had what was called 'Cunard feet', which were splayed out at 10 to 2.'

Ships' engineer David Main remembers one serious incident due to a rogue wave: 'I was in the mess room having a meal in 1961 and it was relatively calm with the ship rolling gently when a rogue wave came along and hit us. She started to slowly roll and over she went to 22° and stayed there for a long period of time before she righted herself. Then she went 15° in the opposite direction. When it all settled down everybody had to start cleaning up all the broken crockery and everything else that had been damaged, and that was quite alarming.' This is mentioned in the records of the *Queen Mary* in Long Beach.

The roll on the *Queen Mary*. (Geoffrey Le Marquand Collection)

Experienced passengers would soon be aware when rough seas were expected because the waiters would be seen dampening down the table cloths and locking the chairs.

New stabilisers were fitted in March 1958, but the ship still rolled in rough weather. Geoffrey Le Marquand: 'I was also on board as part of the standby crew when she was fitted with stabilisers, which took about 10 weeks to complete. Once the stabilisers were completed we set sail for the Bay of Biscay in search of rough weather. However, on this occasion the Bay of Biscay was calm and I believe we ended up off Ireland before we found rough weather to put the stabilisers to their test.

'In the winter arrival at New York we would find the Hudson frozen, making the Moran tugs work harder. They had to first break up the ice, then get the *Queen Mary* into Pier 90. While we were berthed in New York for the three days the *Queen Mary* was well and truly frozen in. The tugs had to break up this ice before attempting to pull the *Queen Mary* out into the Hudson, but once we were out and the ship was under way the *Queen Mary* soon pushed her way through the ice.'

Tips

Geoffrey Le Marquand remembers how low the wages were at the time and that other methods of helping passengers could get them more tips: 'Carrying passengers' cases on board and to their cabins both in New York and Southampton was another way of earning tips.'

Barbara Pedan remembers the 1950s when the first-class stewardesses were noted as the best-off of the ship's crew. Their basic pay meant little to them but it was the handsome tips that were handed out at the end of the trip by their passengers which made their incomes soar. A $200 dollar tip was quite common and in those days it was a lot of money, but they worked long hours during the daytime and evenings: 'I used to see them sitting in the alleyways immaculately dressed in their white uniforms, waiting for a bell to ring to summon them to one of their cabins.'

John Minto, who was a waiter on the *Queen Mary*, was very pleased with the tip he got from Paul Robeson: 'The best trip I had on the *Queen Mary* was when I was told I only had two 'bloods' (that's what we called passengers who tipped). Who should turn up but Paul Robeson and his manager! That was just after his passport was reinstated to travel and he was going off to Moscow. He was no trouble at all. Never came down for all the meals. The first thing I said to him was "Are there any special orders?" He said he would choose from the menu. He used to come down at 7pm every night on the button. No trouble at all. We arrived in Southampton and he didn't come down for breakfast that morning. His manager said to me, "He won't be coming down for breakfast" and handed me an envelope. I said. "Thank you very much." I didn't open it then but went down to the working alleyway, the Burma Road as we used to call it. They were all saying, "Come on, let's see what you've got." I hung about and eventually picked up the envelope and opened it. I counted $100...$200...$300...$400. That was my best tip all my time at sea, and he was no trouble at all.'

John Stamp: 'We had some good times, whatever fun we had on board it was basically made up ourselves. It was very much a different situation altogether in those days, when there was a great big barrier between officers and crew. As crew we worked long hours and had more contact with the passengers than the officers, who did a four-hour on, eight-hour off watch, and we tended to pick up a lot of tips, especially during the summertime. Therefore, it was a well-known fact that we were the ones with the cars and the officers had the bicycles. There was an old story that when the dockers needed to move the cranes when loading and unloading at different holds the message went out: "Would the stewards move their cars from the quayside and would the officers move their bicycles!"'

Famous Personalities On Board

The luxury five-star service on board the *Queen Mary* attracted many famous personalities. When Geoffrey Le Marquand first joined the *Queen Mary* he was very impressed with the interior design of the *Queen Mary*: 'The interior decor had to be seen to be believed. This was a liner built with so much to offer the passengers in levels of comfort. We had many famous passengers who would travel on the *Queen Mary*, and I was lucky enough to meet many of them during the course of my work.'

Many of the celebrities, including film stars and entertainers, who travelled on the *Queen Mary* would agree to entertain the crew in the Pig and Whistle. John Stamp: 'We used to carry many famous personalities on board ship, and they were very good to the crew and would come to the Pig and Whistle to entertain the boys. I saw the film star Victor Mature, who used to come in and have a drink with us. There was Duke Ellington and his band, and Ivor Novello used to travel regularly across the Atlantic, as did Noel Coward.'

Gordon Brown also remembers Victor Mature and Duke Ellington and his band: 'Duke Ellington brought 10 of his band because he couldn't get them all in as the Pig and Whistle was not a very big bar, but he gave us a very good jazz session.' He also remembers Liberace: 'Liberace was brilliant. We had an old honky-tonk piano and we all had a turn sitting alongside him twiddling the keys. The only one who wouldn't play in the Pig and Whistle was Bill Haley and his Comets. When asked if he would entertain the crew in the Pig and Whistle he replied, "How much are you going to pay me, man? You pay me, I'll play."'

John Fahy recalls other personalities who sailed on the *Queen Mary*: 'We used to get all the stars there. I saw Robert Mitchum, Elizabeth Taylor, Johnny Ray, Sgt Bilko and even Mister Ed, the talking horse. They built a stable alongside the Verandah Grill and one of the crew was designated to help look after the horse. I also saw Matt Busby when he was manager of Manchester United. Matt Busby was in the first class, but all the team were in the second class. We used to also get famous jazz musicians, and I remember Ella Fitzgerald singing to the guys in the Pig and Whistle.'

Bob Hope was always a favourite and was often quick with his replies. Bill O'Brien remembers him boarding a ship when one of the dockers, holding up his hook for moving cargo, asked Bob Hope where his hook was. Hope pointed to his nose and said, 'There's my hook!'

This was not the first time Bob Hope had referred to his nose. After VE Day on 8 May 1945 the US government was concerned about their war-weary American soldiers in Europe, especially after being part of a very tough war to defeat Germany. A decision was made to send Bob Hope and a group of entertainers to England to entertain the troops. In his words, 'they were a bunch of tough, war weary, confused guys who did not know if they would be returning to America or whether they would be sent to the Pacific to prepare for an invasion of Japan.'

Bob Hope: 'We left New York on the *Queen Mary*, a ship fast enough to outrun anything in the Atlantic except a frightened comedian. The captain tried to calm me by explaining that there was no danger, the German submarines had surrendered and the Japanese submarines were in the Pacific, but I was no good at geography. I kept seeing periscopes in front of us until I realised it was my nose!'

The first show was at the Albert Hall, London, on 4 July 1945 before 10,000 GIs. Bob Hope: 'After the first laugh I stopped being nervous. More than ever now, our group represented home to them, the one place in the world they wanted me. I guess a lot of the laughter was homesickness, but, like I said, I'll take 'em anyway I can get 'em'. (From Bob Hope's autobiography, *Don't Shoot, It's Only Me*.)

The Burma Road

To get from one end of the *Queen Mary* to the other the crew would use the working alleyway, otherwise known as the Burma Road. John Minto: 'A lot of ex-servicemen who joined the *Queen Mary* as crew members had been in Burma during World War Two and had named the working alleyway the Burma Road. You used to come down from the first class, cabin class or tourist class as it was known then, and use the Burma Road to get from one part of the ship to another. The alleyways were very narrow and we used to go along the Burma Road to get down to the Pig and Whistle.'

When Gordon Brown joined the *Queen Mary* as an assistant butcher, his job was to prepare and send trays of steaks to be used for the whole day. 'The butcher's shop was off the working alleyway, where there was the laundry, vegetables and everything needed for the ship. You would go through with a trolley and into the huge lifts. If you had a trolley load and the ship started to roll then you had problems.'

It was also the butcher's job to look after the dogs and exercise them on deck. Gordon Brown: 'I looked after Joan Crawford's dogs. Dogs weren't allowed in the cabins but she had hers in her cabin because she was so famous.'

Opportunities Not Available Now

At that time it was possible to join the onboard catering departments without qualifications, and that was what interested Gordon Brown. 'Today if you wanted to be a cook you would need all sorts of qualifications.' It was after his first trip as assistant butcher that Gordon signed on as a kitchen porter, a job that involved mainly washing pots and pans: 'I was not happy with the job and Teddy Wren, who was a lovely head chef, asked me what I wanted to do. I said that I wanted to be a chef, not wash pots and pans. Teddy said that when we got to New York if I really wanted to be a chef I was to draw my money out and buy my checks, whites and hat and that would prove how much I wanted to be a cook. This I did and he put me on the vegetable corner to start with. On the *Queen Mary* there was a large kitchen with different areas that specialised in a particular area of cooking. There was a vegetable corner, the soup, sauce cook, roast cook, grill cook, fish cook, next to the sauce, confectionery shop and bakery. The waiters would come in from the restaurant, place their orders at each area and then go back to collect the food to deliver to the tables.'

Working in the Engine Rooms on the *Queen Mary*

David Main was an engineer on board the *Queen Mary* and gives his own account of what life was like working in the engine rooms. It was often four hours of gruelling work on the watch, especially in times when there were rough seas, and a much-needed rest for eight hours afterwards.

Following the disappointment of having missed the world cruise on the *Caronia*, David Main was finally assigned to work as a junior engineer on the *Queen Mary*: 'My first job was in the propeller shaft tunnel on a four-hour on, eight-hour off shift, looking after all the propeller shaft bearings, keeping the water level down in the bilges and looking after the sewage plant. It was not very pleasant, but it gave me a great incentive to get promotion!' He advanced quickly from the propeller shaft tunnel to the after engine room: 'There were two engine rooms in the ship. The forward engine room had two engines in, and they drove the two outboard propeller shafts, and the after engine room had another two engines in, and they drove the two inboard propellers. So we had four engines and four propeller shafts.

'There were only three of us to operate the main engine room and it was quite daunting really to start turning the largest steam control valves which admitted steam to the turbines to start moving the ship, either ahead or in a stern direction when leaving port, either Southampton or New York. When first you operate the steam control valves you do it very carefully but are soon under fire from the chief engineer because you're not doing it quick enough, and that could cause the ship to hit something. You learn very quickly on how to operate those main engines!

'I spent quite a number of voyages in the after engine room and one memorable one was when we were on our way across to New York, and it was during a hurricane season. We came face-to-face with Hurricane Donna in 1960. We heard it was coming up the east coast of America and then it would swing out into the Atlantic. I was on watch in the engine room during the best part of the hurricane and one of the engineers got hurt. He had to go up to the hospital and that left two of us down below. We had no replacement and the other engineer and I were left to manage the engines. This meant speeding up, slowing down for the whole watch just to keep the steerage on the ship, so she could maintain the bow going into the storm. The rolling and pitching were quite considerable. It was a long watch but quite an experience, I must say!' (Hurricane Donna was the most destructive hurricane of the 1960 hurricane season after reaching Category Five strength in the open ocean in early September. Category Five, measured on the Saffir-Simpson Hurricane Scale, is the highest classification in the scale, used to describe the most catastrophic hurricanes that can form in the Atlantic Ocean. Hurricane Donna had winds of 160mph (260kph) and 140 knots.)

David Main: 'From the after engine room I was promoted to the forward engine room where I did the same thing as I did in the after engine room.' Further promotion from the forward engine room to the No.1 boiler room followed: 'We had five boiler rooms. No.1 boiler room was almost under the bridge and had three Scotch boilers in it that were used for providing all the domestic steam for the ship and a lot of the machinery in the after end room for the auxiliary equipment, the laundry and kitchen. The foghorn and heating were provided from the boiler room. It also provided the steam from the forward turbo generator room which had three 1.3mw turbo generators in it that provided all the domestic electrical power for the ship. Then there was No. 2, 3, 4 and 5 boiler rooms, which had six water tube boilers in each boiler room with seven oil burners per boiler.'

Those were the worst trips for David Main as he was working in the forward part of the ship and he would be sick from the time he went on watch until the time he finished, but he didn't stay long in that boiler room. He was promoted again to No.5 main boiler room, which fed steam to the after engine room: 'I had no experience in there and Cunard training was nonexistent. You are expected to go in and just do it. It was within two hours of sailing and I had six boilers nearly up to full pressure. During those two hours I was rushing around like an idiot, trying things to see what would happen and making sure what I was doing was right. Now, when you think, you've got all this happening down below and there are people up there on the top deck sipping their champagne, oblivious that the guy hasn't got that much clue at as to what he is doing. Anyway, I didn't burn any boilers out during that initial period. However, you do have thoughts about what career you could take up if you sunk the ship!

'I did survive and the Cunard trips continued on as normal. I think I did about 50 trips across the North Atlantic.'

The Captain

John Stamp: 'The captain commanded respect and I remember a time when the captain walked into the restaurant and sat down to eat. There was a small section where the officers would eat and when the captain walked out the restaurant the officers would have to get up and leave as well. This was regardless of whether they had finished their dinner or not. The protocol was the captain was on time, the captain leaves on time, and everyone was supposed to do the same.'

One of the *Queen Mary's* captains in 1952 had the problem of docking her without the aid of tugs, due to a tugman's strike in New York. He was Captain Donald Sorrell, and it was an amazing feat because it would normally have needed five tugs to dock the vessel, but Captain Sorrell managed to dock the *Queen Mary* successfully. Captain Sorrell was a very popular captain with his officers and crew. He was just 5ft 4in tall and was described by one of the *Queen Mary's* stewards as 'half-pint size with a pint-size heart'. When Captain Sorrell retired it was nursing sister Jean Edwards who presented him with his farewell present.

Church Service

Geoffrey Le Marquand remembers assisting with the Sunday church service, which the captain would lead: 'Sundays, after breakfast was over, I was required with three other lads to attend the church service that was conducted by the Captain. We had to give the passengers the service sheet and show them to their seats, then when required we had to pass the collection plate around, and after the service with one of the pursers (who kept his eyes on us, just in case we thought about taking the odd dollar from the collection plate) returned to the pursers' office with all the collection plates.'

Apart from the experiences of visiting New York, going to Radio City, shopping and other entertainment venues, the crew of the *Queen Mary* had many opportunities to bring various items back to England where they could make a profit.

Captain Donald Sorrell with officers and nursing sisters on the *Queen Mary*. (Jean Edwards Collection)

Quite a few have remarked how they had sports cars and often were the first to have a car in their street when at home or often changing their motorbikes for more upmarket ones.

In the early 1950s, when transatlantic crossings were at their height, the crew were particularly pressurised when in Southampton because turnarounds would be very quick. Often the ship would arrive one day and sail again the next day.

On the big liners there were three shops, one for each class. There was also a very busy beauty salon where facials could be given, hands manicured and hair styled. The liners would also have a children's nursery where parents could leave their children under the care of a trained children's nurse. For the even younger children there was often a nursery where the babies were watched in their cots and given their bottles and orange juice when required. The nursery would be equipped with slides, Wendy-houses, swings, bricks and other toys. The climax of every trip would be the children's party, where the excited and often yelling youngsters would be given party hats and presents under the supervision of an exhausted nursery nurse by the end of the party.

Officer Status for Nursing Sisters and Assistant Lady Pursers

The nursing sisters, along with the assistant lady pursers, had officer status and as such had certain privileges, such as having their meals in their cabins or in the first-class dining rooms. Their cabins were mainly situated in the passenger accommodation rather than in crew quarters.

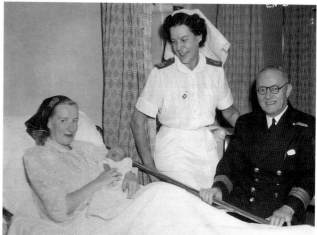

A baby was born on the *Queen Mary* while at sea in 1955. (Dorothy Cadman (Lee) Collection)

The passenger ships always had one doctor and at least one nurse, but on the Queens there were three doctors, seven nurses and one physiotherapist. Nurses had to be fully qualified and preferably certified midwives. Barbara Pedan: 'They were very much a race apart in their sparkling white uniforms. Some trips they would be very busy, maybe a tummy bug would sweep the ship and they would be on the go for 15 hours a day. A birth happened occasionally, but nearly every trip there would be a death and this involved many cables and formalities, for which we in the pursers' office were responsible.'

Nursing sister Jean Edwards remembers her transatlantic trips on the *Queen Mary* well: 'It was fantastic. I wouldn't have missed it for the world. Terrifying when you're looking up at the wave and it looked about 100 foot above you, and the next minute you're looking down on it. There was this great big wave of electric blue-green, fantastic. I was never seasick and I think that was because the work took my mind off it'.

USS *Somersworth*

In July 1957 the doctors and nurses on board were engaged in treating badly injured US Navy sailors after an explosion on board their ship. A TNT device had exploded on the USS *Somersworth*, a PCR-849 Class (Patrol Craft Escort Rescue) ship while she was on a routine mission off Long Island. Three crewmen were killed and four seriously injured. In response to radio calls for medical assistance, doctors from the *Queen Mary* boarded USS *Somersworth* and supervised the transfer of the four injured to the liner.

The *Queen Mary* had just left New York when she had a message that a US Navy ship had had an explosion on board and needed medical help urgently. Jean Edwards remembers it well, as she had decided that month that she would be leaving the *Queen Mary* after the voyage from New York to Southampton: 'We found out that we were turning back because there had been an explosion on an American Navy ship and there were injured that needed urgent treatment. Three lads had been killed and four had been severely injured. We brought them over to the crew ward and had to amputate one leg, stitch back on a foot, and take shrapnel out of an elbow and a knee. The poor lad who had lost his leg was only 18. The working alleyway was full of crew offering their help and their blood. We didn't have time to take any blood from them. Later we all got a little citation from the American ship. That was my last trip.'

Arrival at Southampton

Geoffrey Le Marquand: 'We would leave early from Cherbourg in the morning and then come up the Channel, but when the *Queen Mary* came into the Solent the Customs would get on board at the Nab Tower looking for cigarettes and nylons.'

John Stamp: 'All the catering staff would be involved in cleaning the ship when we arrived at Southampton. As we were coming up Southampton Water we would have to clean all the brass portholes, and to do that we would have a box of oil, sand and rags to polish all the brass so that the ship would be spotlessly clean when she arrived at the dockside.' Geoffrey Le Marquand used to earn some extra money by cleaning the portholes for the bedroom stewards, but was well ahead with his preparation for arrival at Southampton: 'I also used to clean portholes when we docked either in Southampton or New York for the bedroom stewards and got paid $1 per cabin. My trick was to clean them in New York with Brasso, and then give them a coat of Vaseline so that when we got to Southampton I only had to remove the Vaseline!'

Cunard decides to use the Queen Mary for cruises

During the 1960s the numbers of passengers began to drop on the *Queen Mary* due to the competition from the airlines, and in December 1963 she went on her first cruise, a week's run from Southampton to Las Palmas, the Canary Islands, and back. Other cruises included voyages from New York to the Bahamas and also to the Mediterranean in 1966. This was a month's cruise leaving Southampton and calling at Madeira, Lisbon, Gibraltar, Palma, Cannes, Naples, Piraeus, Tangiers, Las Palmas, and back to Southampton. However, the disadvantage for the *Queen Mary* was that she was built for the North Atlantic passenger trade and not for a cruising role. She did not have air conditioning or swimming pools on deck that cruise passengers expected when sailing in the tropics.

John Stamp also found it uncomfortable: 'In the summertime you had your full complement of crew, but there was no air conditioning on board and it was so hot, especially down on the deck. You couldn't sleep at night because you were so hot. We had to get up, take a quick shower. The showers, unfortunately, were a long way away from the cabin.

'When the *Queen Mary* eventually went cruising she couldn't go through the Panama Canal so they had to go round Cape Horn, as they did during World War Two. However, this was an important decision when building the *QE2*, who was built to go through the Panama Canal, albeit with only a few inches on either side.'

Final Years of the *Queen Mary*

In 1966 the six-week seaman's strike caused irreparable damage to the *Queen Mary's* future. All the major ports were affected and, apart from cargo imports, many of the passenger fleets were out of action. It was just one year later, on 16 September 1967, that the *Queen Mary* made her last transatlantic crossing.

The *Queen Mary* bade her final farewell to Southampton on 31 October 1967 with 1,040 passengers for her final cruise to Long Beach, California. John Bratcher remembers well the day the *Queen Mary* sailed out of Southampton for the last time and he wanted to give her his own farewell: 'I used to keep my boat on a mooring in Husbands shipyard. My friend Jack and I went out on this particular morning as the *Queen Mary* was due to sail for the last time and we couldn't let her go without a send off.

We got up at some ridiculous hour and rowed out to the mooring. As we didn't have any signal flags in those days we bought lots of balloons of various colours. We sat down on the boat blowing them all up, tied them together with string and formed an A shape. We hauled them up the halyards and went out to the stern of the *Queen Mary* to see her off. We sailed as far as Hythe Pier following her, but the Royal Marines were there keeping us away. She had a long paying-off pennant and two London buses on deck. The next day the *Daily Express* reported that a keen local yachtsman had dressed his yacht all over for the farewell of the *Queen Mary* from Southampton.'

The final cruise was a cruise to be remembered and took 39 days. After leaving Southampton the *Queen Mary* made ports of call at Lisbon, Las Palmas, Rio de Janeiro, Valparaiso, Callao, Balboa, Acapulco and then on to her final home at Long Beach, arriving on 9 December 1967. Two London red double-decker buses were lashed down aft on the *Queen Mary*. The plan was to use them in Long Beach to take visitors to and from the *Queen Mary*. However, one of the highlights for passengers was sitting on the two buses as the *Queen Mary* rounded Cape Horn and to be able to say that they had gone around Cape Horn on a bus!

Visits to the *Queen Mary* in Long Beach in the 1990s

Geoffrey Le Marquand: 'In April 1995 I voyaged back in time when I revisited the *Queen Mary* in her retirement home of California and walked up the old Cunarder's gangway once more to relive the time when I was on this great ship. The *Queen Mary* is still an impressive sight at Long Beach with her huge size and majestic funnels. Her general appearance looked good, as though she could be ready to sail tomorrow.'

David Main also visited the *Queen Mary* in Long Beach, but his association with the liner was to be extended into a yearly visit to talk to visitors and demonstrate his work as an engineer while serving on board: 'In 1996 my son alerted me that there was a trip going to the *Queen Mary* in Long Beach. I was born three days before the *Queen Mary* sailed on 27 May 1936 for her maiden voyage. My son said I should celebrate my 60th birthday on the *Queen Mary* since leaving her in 1961.

'It was quite an emotional experience being on board, especially in the engine room holding on to the machinery that I had operated many years previously to start and stop the engines. I spent a lot of time down there on my hands and knees looking around the floor to see if my footprints were still there. I got a gathering of Americans watching me and we started talking about my experiences and I found this went down very well. My offer of help was accepted and I have since spent two months a year explaining to visitors to the *Queen Mary* in Long Beach the workings of the engine room. However, after nine years, and with age catching up, I have started to reduce my time to one month.'

John Stamp is reminded of what the life was like on the *Queen Mary* at the time: 'Talking about it now brings back to me what a fantastic operation it was. I can tell you how professional men were in those days. I think every seaman has been made richer by serving on the *Queen Mary*.'

Life as a Passenger on the *Queen Mary* in the 1960s

Margaret Dines travelled on the *Queen Mary* in 1960 and thoroughly enjoyed the experience: 'It was on 3 November 1960 that I made my first transatlantic crossing on the *Queen Mary*. I do remember clearly that there was a full complement of passengers that time. I always travelled cabin class and it was very, very nice.

'When I got to the Ocean Terminal in Southampton I thought it was all very well organised. I had relations living in Southampton so I didn't have much of a journey to get there. My parents were at the Ocean Terminal to see me off and there were streamers flying. However, I do remember we were delayed in the Channel for a very long time because it was very bad weather. There were stabilisers on the *Queen Mary*, but in bad weather they used to put the sides up so that the crockery didn't fall down and break. Although it was rough I didn't get seasick. That was because I come from the Isle of Wight and was quite used to sea.

'Once on board you quickly learn to find your way around the ship, and in cabin class you had your own area. We were very well looked after and during the day you could be sitting on deck and the deck stewards would offer you beef tea if you didn't feel too well.

'You could play deck quoits, but as it was November we didn't have very nice weather. I can't remember if I went to the cinema, but there was an indoor swimming pool. For lunch there was always a buffet, but there was always food available for the passengers.

'I used to spend quite a lot of time in the writing room and liked the very nice writing paper we could use. It was a very nice place to congregate and also had newspapers and the daily bulletins, which informed you what was happening on board that day, which was always fun and interesting. I think the pursers' office was nearby if I remember correctly.

It was all quite a new experience for me and on my first crossing in November 1960 I thought the food was wonderful and here were lots of people on board. I was well looked after and at dinner you would have the captain or one of the officers at your table every night, and it was most enjoyable. The ship's doctor used to join us quite a bit. I do remember that the dining room was quite large.

'I had a cabin steward and the service was excellent. Somehow it seemed quite easy in cabin class as it was a very nice lifestyle.

'I do remember going down to the engine room. It was a magnificent experience to see the huge pistons going backwards and forwards. There was an incredible noise in the engine room which we didn't hear on deck.

'We arrived in New York five days later and I remember the beautiful shoreline and the Statue of Liberty. Once the *Queen Mary* had docked at Pier 90 all our luggage was sent ashore and John (Margaret's future husband) was there to meet me. There were always a lot of people around who wanted to look at the ship because she was a spectacular sight, and when you left the ship there were many people at the dockside.

'We travelled home quite a bit on the *Queen Mary*, mainly to see parents and also because we liked the ship. However, from March to May 1963 I had to do a number of transatlantic trips because my mother had suddenly passed away. I noticed that the passenger lists were getting smaller with fewer people travelling. That was because more people were changing to air travel and it changed the atmosphere on board ship quite a lot. At that time that was what you did. It was just five days of cruising really, and it was before I started flying.

**Margaret Dines taking afternoon tea.
(Courtesy of Margaret Dines)**

The New York skyline. (Courtesy of Margaret Dines)

We had lived in America for six years and my homeward voyage on 19 October 1966 was on the *Queen Elizabeth*, where I again travelled cabin class. On board it was a similar routine to the *Queen Mary* but much quieter as fewer people were travelling, but the service was just as good.

'I cannot stress enough how much I enjoyed all my transatlantic crossings and how pleasant and comfortable the officers and crew made everything. It was luxury!'

Southampton to New York on the *Queen Mary* in 1964

John and Fay Bratcher travelled on the *Queen Mary* in 1964. Fortunately, they were experienced sailors as the passage to New York was rough and they also ran into blizzards. Fay Bratcher: 'We sailed on the *Queen Mary* from Southampton on 9 January 1964, arriving in New York on 14 January. This was the same year as the Beatles toured America, and they were out there the same time as us. When we arrived at Ocean Terminal, Berth 44, Southampton Docks, our travel agent was there to meet us. Once we had checked in we were allowed to go on board.

'We were given our table when dining, and at that time it was an all-English crew and they all wore dark suits. It was all silver service in the restaurant, and when it was rough the sides came up on the tables. However, they were up most of the time because the crossing was really, really rough.

'The *Queen Mary's* interior was full of beautiful wooden panelling and artwork. There was the evening entertainment and I think I used to have a fancy dress and fancy headdress competition, which you made yourself. There was the cabaret and the bingo, where I won £19. Quite a bit in those days because I think at that time it did not seem very expensive to sail to America on the *Queen Mary*.

'Even though it was very rough no one had an accident or anything like that, but you couldn't sit on deck. However, I was a bit worried when they put up the steel windows, and everybody was told they weren't allowed on deck because it was too dangerous. They reckoned that because the wind was so bitterly cold if you went outside it would take your ears off!

'That is interesting because we have friends who have sailed transatlantic on the *Queen Mary 2* and they have said that they couldn't sit on their balcony because when the ship was moving there is a strong wind created. However, if you are in the Caribbean or somewhere warm like that it is a different story.

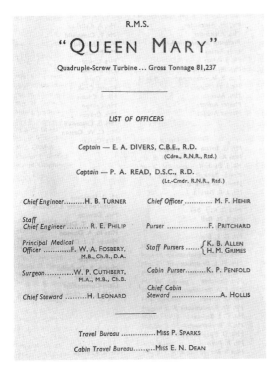

The *Queen Mary's* officer list, 1964. (John and Fay Bratcher Collection)

Embarkation arrangements and boat train times for January 1964. The *Caronia* travelled from Southampton to Port Everglades via Havre, Barbados, Kingston and Nassau; the *Queen Mary* and *Queen Elizabeth* went from Southampton to New York via Cherbourg. (John and Fay Bratcher Collection)

The programme of events for Tuesday 14 January 1964. (John and Fay Bratcher Collection)

'There were a lot of American forces and their families on board and they were returning to America, and, of course, many more children on board than normally.

'One of the crew members was a girl I used to go to church with, and she said that that the *Queen Mary* was very packed this time because of all the children on board. The American servicemen and their families were also in cabin class.

'You did get your sections when on board and we were in cabin class and you weren't allowed in the first class. There were doors that blocked the entrance.'

John Bratcher: 'We ran into a blizzard as we approached the New York coastline. The Verrazano–Narrows Bridge was being built and with its state of construction it was about three-quarters finished. The interest on board was that the *Queen Mary* had high masts and would she go under the bridge? Everyone had their fingers crossed and watched the mast go under the span of the bridge and I estimated we had just a foot (0.3m) to spare.'

The crew was not going to miss the snow and there were some snowball fights. Fay Bratcher: 'We were in the dining room and we saw that the floor was very wet. From previous experience, if there was any liquid on the floor it was mopped up immediately because someone could slip and have an accident. The floor was cleaned up and we found out that our waiter had been in a snowball fight and this was what caused the water on the floor.'

John Bratcher: 'Ice had built up on the rigging and I didn't know that salt water froze, but it does. I got out on deck and got some cine film which I was very pleased with.

The abstract of the *Queen Mary's* log on a Southampton to New York voyage in January 1964. (John and Fay Bratcher Collection)

'Ice floes were still coming down the Hudson River and when the *Queen Mary* turned to go into the pier the ice built up behind the ship and the tugs did a good job pushing her into the berth.'

Queen Elizabeth

The post-war overhaul and refurbishment of *Queen Elizabeth* to her commercial role as a luxury passenger liner was carried out in Southampton and also on the Clyde. However, on 9 March 1946, prior to her leaving for the Clyde, a fire was discovered on the promenade deck. It was fortunate that the fire was discovered early as the fire brigade was able to extinguish it before more damage could have been caused to the ship. It is thought that the fire was possibly started by an arsonist. At the end of March the *Queen Elizabeth* left for the Clyde to be repainted in the Cunard livery and then it was back to Southampton from 17 June for the interior refurbishment.

At last the *Queen Elizabeth* was able to make her first commercial passenger voyage to New York on 16 October 1946. However, there was the speed trial to complete and once that had been successfully achieved she was visited by the Queen, accompanied by Princess Elizabeth and Princess Margaret.

Once back in Southampton the *Queen Elizabeth* set out on her maiden voyage to New York, but despite being faster than her sister ship there was no attempt to take away the Blue Riband from the *Queen Mary*.

There were some mishaps, one being the *Queen Elizabeth* running aground on the Brambles Bank in the Solent while making for Southampton Water in thick fog on 17 April 1947. There was no damage to the ship, but the passengers had to disembark while the fuel was pumped out. Another time was when the *Queen Elizabeth* was in collision with a cargo ship in the Ambrose Channel. This was on 29 July 1959 while outward bound in thick fog from New York and she was struck on the starboard bows by the *American Hunter*, a United States Lines cargo ship that was also outward bound. The damage was slight and temporary repairs were carried out in New York, allowing the *Queen Elizabeth* to continue with her transatlantic service.

There were other times when the service was interrupted, one being in 1948 when industrial disputes found the *Queen Elizabeth* stranded at New York for two weeks. However, she continued on her transatlantic crossings, completing her 100th crossing by September 1951.

The *Queen Elizabeth* (86,673 GT) alongside the old Ocean Terminal, Southampton. (Jim Brown Collection)

The *Queen Elizabeth's* promenade deck. (Dorothy Cadman (Lee) Collection)

**The cabin-class restaurant on the *Queen Elizabeth*.
(Dorothy Cadman (Lee) Collection)**

Further improvements were made to the *Queen Elizabeth* in January 1952, when she had her fuel capacity increased and was also fitted with air conditioning. Three years later, in January 1955, she was fitted with Denny Brown stabilisers to make the often rough crossings of the North Atlantic smoother.

This was a period when air travel was becoming more popular than sea. The shipping lines began to find that their potential passengers were now choosing between the longer, although luxurious, crossings of the North Atlantic and the speedier crossing by the jet airliner. By the late 1950s and early 1960s more passengers were travelling by air than by sea.

Leaving Union-Castle for Cunard

Roy White: 'I decided I wanted to work on a steam turbine ship for Cunard so I left Union-Castle and joined the *Queen Elizabeth*. Although the *Queen Mary* was always held in affection the *Queen Elizabeth* was really the flagship of Cunard.

'It puzzles me why she wasn't thought more of. She had beautiful bridge superstructure and was a better-looking ship by far. Down below she had fewer boilers but was more modern and more powerful.

'If you go up to the funnel deck on the *Queen Mary* there were stay wires supporting the funnels and the *Lizzie* had none. However, down below, I know she was a newer ship, but her generator room was not so well kept, whereas the *Queen Mary* had all these firemen and greasers who had served on her for a long time and treated her like their home. Everything was polished up to perfection, but the *Lizzie* was not up to those standards. That was my observation.

'I did a few trips on the *Queen Elizabeth* as a junior engineer and also worked on the *Queen Mary*. When you came back from New York you always had a following sea and the *Queen Mary* would slowly roll over and then back the other way. This would go on day and night.

'On the *Lizzie* the engineers' mess was about the highest accommodation on the ship, just behind the after funnel. It was a big dining room and I remember one morning I was sat at a table and the *Lizzie* was dipping and rolling. She must have gone right down and all of a sudden all the crockery smashed and really frightened me.

'On the Queens we had about 60–70 engine room staff, whereas today there are fewer engineers needed because of computer technology.

'After a number of transatlantic crossing to New York I started to get bored, but I had been courting a girl for about four years, and when we got married I decided to come ashore'.

Pat Royl Talks About his Time On Board the *Queen Elizabeth* in the 1950s and 60s

In the mid-1950s, after working on the Union-Castle Line, Pat Royl transferred to Cunard: 'I was fortunate to get a job on the *Queen Elizabeth* as a commis waiter. There were 14 of us boys in the cabin over the propellers. In rough weather in the Atlantic it was really noisy when the propellers came out of the water. Later we graduated up into cabins of about eight. I found that time was the happiest time of my life.'

Pat Royl comments how tight the discipline was, and that was to maintain the high standards required by Cunard: 'It was really good training and after working with Cunard you could get a job anywhere. A guy called Nobby Clark was in charge of all the boys in the restaurants and made sure we were up to scratch. Every morning and every mealtime the boys used to line up and the head waiter would check your fingernails, check

Two of the *Queen Elizabeth's* first-class waiters, Pat Royl and Brian Scorey, dressed for evening dinner with dark suits, stiff collars and white waistcoats. Day wear was a tuxedo, soft shirt, black bow tie and a waistcoat. (Pat Royl Collection)

your socks, check your vest, your arms and if you were a bit 'sniffy' you would be told to get a shower and change to a clean coat. That was all part of the training.

'All the boys did their training in the first-class restaurant. That was full silver service. Six head waiters in the first-class restaurant, three saloon stewards and the restaurant manager, Mr Mullins. My training was done in 1958. I was on £12 a month then and still had to send money home to my mother.

'There were about 800 passengers at one sitting in the first-class restaurant, and we used trolleys for serving purposes to serve smoked salmon and hors d'oeuvres. At breakfast there were all the jams and marmalade you can imagine on trays and served by hand to the passengers, there were no plastic pots then.

'Across the front of the restaurant was where all the coffee was brewed. The boys would do that and serve the coffees. That was how the boys made their money because the waiters used to make the money through the tips they received and then pay the boys. The bar boys used to make their own money, but the commis waiters made theirs from helping the restaurant waiters. The waiters used to pay them for their help.

'At 18 you got a rating and became a staff steward. I used to look after the engineers, the nurses and the band. You were not with passengers at the start, but then you graduated to tourist restaurant, cabin restaurant and possibly back up to the first-class restaurant.'

'Our day would start at six o'clock in the morning, getting up and getting the tables ready for breakfast. There would be two sittings in the restaurant, which took until about 10 o'clock. At 11 o'clock I used to be on deck helping with the teas. Then at 12.15pm there were two sittings for lunch, then afternoon teas and finally two sittings for dinner in the evening. All these jobs, including laundry and scrub outs, they all had to be done. We used to finish about 11pm at night. Sometimes we used to have an hour off in the afternoon when we used to crash out.

'With the scrub outs we used to have bits of carpets tied round our knees. They used to be done at night and then the night gang would come on with buffers and buff it all. This was mainly the restaurant because we didn't have carpets as it was mainly polished lino. It would have been difficult if there were carpets in the restaurant because you would have a job pushing trolleys around on carpets.

Off the main dining room there were three PDRs (private dining rooms) where people could have private parties. They would allocate a couple of waiters to them.

It was a good life; we had the Pig and Whistle where we could go and get a drink. It was wealthy people who used to travel in those days, royalty, sportsman and celebrities. All the stars and the bands that travelled in those days used to come down to the Pig and Whistle to entertain the crew, that is except for Bill Haley and his band, who wouldn't come down because they wanted to be paid.' (This is not the first time this has been mentioned by an ex-crew member – apparently Bill Haley did the same on the *Queen Mary.*) We had the Ted Heath Band, Duke Ellington Band, Lena Horne, Jack Hawkins, Michael Wilding and Liberace. Many other famous people travelled on the Queens including Viscount Montgomery, Queen Soraya of Iran, and also Elizabeth Taylor and Eddie Fisher came on board, but I don't think they came into the Pig and Whistle.

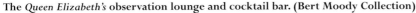

The *Queen Elizabeth's* observation lounge and cocktail bar. (Bert Moody Collection)

The smoking room on the *Queen Elizabeth*. (Dorothy Cadman (Lee) Collection)

At the time I was working at the first-class restaurant with a Liverpool lad, Billy Tyler, and the Liberace family of six was designated to our station, but he never ate in the restaurant. He ate in the Verandah Grill. His mother and brother ate in the restaurant. We only had him for about two meals and had a £60 tip at the end of the voyage. That was an awful lot of money in those days. Liberace and his brother used to come down to the Pig and Whistle to play darts, with his jewellery on and all that. Most of the celebrities didn't mind coming along and slumming it with the boys. They used to like having a big pint put in their hand!'

Jim Taylor joined the *Queen Elizabeth*, sailing from Southampton on 30 August 1960 for New York, but on the return voyage to Southampton there was a fire on board: 'On the *Queen Elizabeth* we all would have an afternoon kip. This was called the 'choir hour'. We were all in bed asleep coming back from New York to Southampton, but when you are on the ship there is this continuous sound of the engines, combined with a continual vibration. It never stops, but we were used to the sound and rhythm of the engines. However, the glory hole steward came around to give us a shake at about 3pm, which was well before the time he would normally wake us. The engines had stopped and it was quiet. There was no vibration and she was lying still in the water. This never happens and immediately we knew there was something wrong and all had our stations to go to. I was allocated the staircase outside the first-class restaurant, which went right up to the top of the ship. When I got there smoke was coming down the stairwell, but after a time I was told I was wanted on the pursers' deck. I was worried about going up through the smoke so I went and got some table cloths and threw some jugs of water over them, put them over my head and went up through the smoke safely that way.

'The captain, his deck officers, and some able seamen were there, but it was quite frightening with the roaring noise given off by the fire.

'It was the main junction room from the generators that had caught fire. The first-class suites were on either side and they had beautiful oak panelling with hanging tapestry. I was given a very large axe and told to go down to the port side cabins and break into the oak panelling, looking to see if there was any flames behind. After a destroying the beautiful oak panelling in the first few cabins I was exhausted, but no fire was discovered. Many of the passengers were on deck with their lifejackets on alongside the lifeboats. The deck was very hot, but that was thought to be the wiring, and for months afterwards we had Harland & Wolff workmen on board to replace a lot of the wiring.'

The Queen Mother, accompanied by Dr M. Rust and Sister D. Lee, visits the *Queen Elizabeth* surgery while on a transatlantic crossing to New York. (Dorothy Cadman (Lee) Collection)

The fire had broken out in an electrical switchboard, and the heat was so intense that some cabins were damaged. Commodore Donald MacLean had turned the *Queen Elizabeth* into a position that was a protection from the wind that could cause the fire to get worse. The fire was eventually brought under control within three hours, and the *Queen Elizabeth* resumed her voyage to Southampton.

Jim Taylor continued for a short time as a first-class waiter before his career at sea ended. After he came ashore he finally chose a career that was possibly influenced by experiences while at sea, especially on the *Queen Elizabeth*: 'I came ashore and after a few jobs I eventually served 27 years as a firefighter.'

John Merry: 'My father was in the war and was torpedoed twice and was on board the *Empress of Britain* when she was bombed. After the war he transferred to the Queens. I remember all through the war years I never saw my father, and even in peacetime when he was on the Queens we saw very little of him, and I made a conscious decision that when I got married I would come ashore to be with my children.

'We have much to thank Cunard for, because when my dad died his ashes were carried on the *Queen Mary* and a service was held when the ship slowed down and his ashes scattered at sea. Cunard later sent a map with a cross where my father's ashes were scattered and photographs of the ceremony.'

Life as Passengers on the *Queen Elizabeth* in 1965

Christine Young sailed transatlantic on the *Queen Elizabeth* in 1965 with her friend to emigrate to Canada, and what an experience they had on that voyage.

Christine Young: 'It was January 1965 and a friend and I were emigrating to Canada. We were originally thinking of going to America, but I was refused a visa because there was a temporary ban on office workers. My friend was a hairdresser and she said, "What about Canada?" My aunt had been there for years and loved it.

'The night before we sailed my mother read in the *Daily Echo* that Tommy Steele was sailing in the *Queen Elizabeth*, the ship we were sailing on. The *Daily Echo* in those days was giving details of all the famous people that were travelling on the ocean liners.

'The next day we boarded the ship, we were very excited, we were young, and it was a big adventure. We both intended to go just for a year, but we had to emigrate to have the visa to go, plus £100 in the bank. I was so proud because I had £105 in the bank.

'So we set off and because it was January not many people were sailing the Atlantic, so they had the doors open between first class and tourist. We could wander between first class and tourist class, and in fact our cabin was an interchangeable, and was very nice for tourists.

'The second or third day out we had seen the film in the tourist cinema and thought we would wander over to the first class. As we were coming out my friend tripped and somebody behind us said, "Did you have a nice trip?" We turned round and found it was Tommy Steele and two men, who we found out later were David Heneker, the British lyricist who wrote

the score for the musical *Half a Sixpence*, and Tommy Steele's manager, Larry Parnes. They were taking the musical over to New York.

'Anyway he stopped and said, "Are you girls doing anything special this evening?" We said we were not without appearing too overly keen. He said, "Would you like to come up to the Verandah Grill tonight for a meal with us?" We said we would be happy to and went back to the cabin and our stewardess was excited as we were. We were deciding what we were going to wear and my friend, being a hairdresser, was able to do my hair.

Christine Young with her friend, Janet, on the *Queen Elizabeth* in January 1965. (Christine Young Collection)

The menu for dinner on 18 January 1965 on the *Queen Elizabeth*. (Christine Young Collection)

'Off we went up to the Verandah Grill. I can't remember exactly what we ate, but he did ask us if we had tried caviar and we said no. So he ordered caviar. The Verandah Grill was somewhere special for first-class passengers, because I believe they had to pay extra to eat there. So there were the five of us sitting down for dinner and six waiters hovering around.

'Afterwards we went into the ballroom first and they had a bit of bingo. Who should win but Tommy Steele! I think it was about £15, which was quite a bit of money in those days.

'Tommy Steele was very easy to talk to and it hadn't been very many years since he had been a seaman himself on the *Mauretania*. He did say to us that he still felt he should be going up the crew gangway instead of the passenger gangway.

'Later on that evening he introduced us to Tab Hunter, who was a movie star and a singer, who had a hit record in 1957 with *Young Love* and *Red Sails in the Sunset*. He had been to Germany to buy a Mercedes car, which was on the ship at the time. I remember we bumped into Tab Hunter and he said that he hadn't been feeling too well because of the rough seas. At one stage we had 35ft high waves, and I was going out with an electrical engineer before the ship sailed and I used to meet him. The passengers were not allowed to meet the crew, but he used to come off watch at 12 o'clock and I used to meet him. I was told after about the third night that I was like Cinderella, because I used to disappear at 12 o'clock each night.

The abstract of the log for the transatlantic voyage of the *Queen Elizabeth* on her voyage from Southampton to New York from Wednesday 13 January to Tuesday 19 January 1965. (Christine Young Collection)

'However, when we met Tab Hunter later in the voyage he was a little bit worried because there was a longshoreman's strike in New York, and he was concerned that his new car would not be able to be taken off the ship.

'When we did get to New York the American TV and radio people were running around with microphones because they had heard that there had been 35ft high waves and they wanted to know if people were lost overboard and things like that. We told them that it was impossible as all the doors were locked, so we couldn't go out on deck.

'I remember the night we were with Tommy Steele he said that the weather was going to get rough because they were putting the ledges up on the tables and putting ropes around. We didn't see him again during the trip, but it was a very nice experience. We had something to tell friends when we dined out later. Our moment of fame when we had dinner with Tommy Steele, but I think he was just glad of some other company. It was very nice.

'When the musical *Half a Sixpence*, starring Tommy Steele, came to Toronto my friend and I got tickets to see it.'

Tommy Steele

In 1952, at the age of 15, Tom Hicks (better known as Tommy Steele) joined the Merchant Navy and worked for the Cunard Line for four years. He trained for a short time at the Gravesend Sea Training School and was soon aboard the *Scythia* as a cabin boy on the Southampton to Quebec route. On 5 June 1952, shortly after joining the ship, the *Scythia*, with 875 passengers and outward bound for London, was in collision with the Canadian steamer *Wabana* in thick fog in the Gulf of St Lawrence. The *Scythia* was towed by tugs back to Quebec where temporary repairs were carried out to the bow.

While on shore leave Tom Hicks was taken ill and spent some time in hospital. It was while in hospital that he was given a guitar, which he started to learn to play. When he was back on board ship he was taught the 12-bar blues chord sequence, and he started to entertain other members of the crew and later the passengers on the *Mauretania*. Tom Hicks left the *Mauretania* in August 1956 and started a career as Tommy Steele, musical entertainer. By 1963 he was performing in the role of Arthur Kipps in the musical *Half a Sixpence*. It was in 1965 that Tommy Steele travelled on the *Queen Elizabeth* from Southampton to New York to take *Half a Sixpence* on to the Broadway stage.

The Queens and *Ascania* (2)

Southampton developed and thrived as a maritime city and great emphasis was given to it being the 'Gateway to the World'. Both cargo and passenger ships left Southampton Docks to travel to port destinations around the world. However, it was the Golden Years that brought Southampton to the forefront, when transatlantic travel was at its height and the rich and famous arrived at the docks on the transatlantic liners. In the post-war years transatlantic travel was again taken up by the travelling public and the Queens were a major part of that era.

John Stamp: 'There was a weekly service between New York and Southampton. We used to meet the *Queen Elizabeth* halfway across the Atlantic. In those days you had two days in New York and Southampton, which made the seven days weekly service.' (It was two days in Southampton then five days crossing the Atlantic, followed by two days in New York and five days back. The round trip took two weeks.) 'The two main shipping lines at the time were the Union-Castle Line and Cunard Line. Of course, going back many years Cunard had 16 ships in the fleet, from small cargo ships to passenger ships. One of the smallest ships in the fleet was a passenger liner called the *Ascania*. She was only 14,000 tonnes. In fact, I was on the *Ascania* and during the winter crossing it was just like if you threw a flat stone on the water, she would skim across the top of the water.' After her wartime service *Ascania* returned to Cunard in September 1947 and made her first post-war voyage, from Liverpool to Halifax, on 20 December.

Restructuring of the passenger accommodation was carried out in 1949, making it 200 first-class and 500 cabin-class passengers. The *Ascania* continued on the Liverpool to Montreal route to serve the large number of passengers emigrating to Canada at the time. In 1955, after the *Saxonia* and *Ivernia* had taken over the Liverpool route, the *Ascania* was transferred to Southampton.

Mavis Carter was on one of the last voyages from Liverpool just before the *Ascania* was transferred to Southampton: 'I emigrated from Liverpool to Canada on the *Ascania* in May 1955. It was quite a small ship compared to the ships these days. It was all very exciting and I paid £70 to travel first class. First class, that's a laugh because I think there were about four bunks in that small cabin. When we were on the Atlantic we had a hurricane and in those days there were no stabilisers. We were going up and down and side to side with many people sick, but I was a sailor. My whole family were good sailors and so I wasn't sick, just had a heavy head. I sat at the doctor's table for my meal during the storm. The doctor asked me if I was alright, looking rather surprised!

'It was all good fun and then being first class we were with the officers as well. It was all very exciting as many people were emigrating. One of the ladies was going out to see her husband on the west coast north of Vancouver and another was going to Montréal to meet her husband.

'We all got on very well together and would go and play dice with the officers. It was all good fun and we were able to go down to the ship's engine room, which was absolutely immaculate.

'Captain Marr was very nice. I went to his cocktail party. Sounds grand but it was just a little gathering to meet the other first-class passengers. That was a very pleasant journey and we played games. Being a smaller ship you couldn't play so many deck games as you could on the larger liners.

'Then we arrived at the St Lawrence River, and although it was May there were still ice floes on the river.

'Service and the meals, as far as I remember, were always very good. And it was a very happy time on board. I enjoyed it and everyone was well looked after. Of course, being on the rough seas, when you arrived in Montréal for days you would be walking from side to side, quite a funny experience. My brother met me at the docks in Montréal and I then stayed at the YWCA for about two weeks. I went to the labour exchange to sign on and the Canadians were very good, and I soon found a job without any problem.

'I returned in May 1966 on a Canadian Pacific ship to Southampton, I can't remember its name, but it was quite a different experience on the way back. This time I had a cabin with a bunk bed and washbasin to myself.'

The Queens versus the *United States*

Although the *Queen Mary* was capable of a fast crossing of the North Atlantic she was unable to compete with the faster *United States*, which did her maiden crossing from New York to Southampton and took the Blue Riband in July 1952 with an average speed of 35.59 knots.

John Stamp: 'When the *United States* came along there were many comments made many years after the war, saying that the *United States* was the fastest in the world. Well she was, in fact, fast, but I was on the *Queen Mary*, and both would leave Southampton within one hour of each other. The *Queen Mary* would pick up passengers at Cherbourg, and an hour or so after the *United States*. When they said the *United States* was faster that meant nominally faster. In the summer we would be in sight of each other for about three days in the Atlantic, then she would slowly pull ahead and arrive in New York five or six hours ahead of us. That was fantastic, that was great and everybody said she is the fastest ship and she made the running for the Blue Riband and everything else, but that was summertime, when the going was easy.'

Douglas Ward also remembers one rough transatlantic crossing from New York to Southampton: 'I remember sailing across the Atlantic in a severe storm, which was almost a hurricane. The *United States* had left New York ahead of us and was due to arrive at Southampton a couple of hours ahead of us. The storm lasted three days and was so bad that we had to slow down to 6½ knots when the normal service speed was 29½ knots. However, the *United States* had to slow right down and ended up in Southampton 24 hours behind us.

The *United States* (53,329 GT) was completed in 1952. She gained the Blue Riband in the same year and still holds it. She was withdrawn from service in 1969 and since then has been laid up in various ports. (Mick Lindsay Collection)

John Stamp: 'Now, when it came to the winter time it was a different situation altogether. We actually left Southampton within the hour of each other to Cherbourg again. Then we would start the Atlantic crossing in the middle of winter, and that can be very hairy, very hairy indeed. The Americans will always play down the fact that the Queens would go through the Atlantic waves, the Atlantic storms, keeping their speed and arriving in New York on schedule. I've actually known the *United States* to arrive in New York 36 hours after us because she couldn't take the heavy weather. The Queens could, notwithstanding that there was a time when we lost our rails and the forward deck had sustained quite a bit of damage in the hurricane coming back to Southampton. In fact, I believe we had about 100 casualties on board ship because the weather was that bad. We still arrived within one hour of our schedule. It was important that we kept to the schedule because of the deep draught on the ship. Although Southampton has got four tides, we still had to allow for the deep draught. They were always dredging Southampton just so the two Queens could get up Southampton Water. Basically that should put to rest the idea of the great supremacy that the *United States* had over the Queens. If we are talking about supremacy then it was the two Queens that were supreme! We had a schedule and we kept to that schedule. The *United States* could never keep on schedule in the wintertime solely because of the way it was built.'

A Liner Built for War Duties

It is said that the United States Lines were very worried about their ships catching fire and avoided the use of wood. The only wood thought to be on board the *United States* was the piano and the butcher's chopping block!

The *United States* was designed by William Francis Gibbs, but the cost was largely put up by the US government. To gain the extra financing Gibbs said that the liner would be a great advantage in time of war. The liner would have two engine rooms for speed, useful for a troop ship and for avoiding torpedo attack, but he was also concerned about safety and had researched the loss of the *Titanic*, including ships that had caught fire. To that end he aimed to minimize the possibility of the liner catching fire.

With the introduction of the jet aircraft the *United States* began to lose passengers to the faster but not so luxurious airlines. A series of seamen's strikes caused the ship to be laid up during the busy summer months. The crew members were asking for more money, shorter working hours, improved pensions and more holidays. By 1969 further union strikes brought the problems to a head and the *United States* was taken out of service in late 1969. She was sold in 1992 to Turkish Interests and towed to Turkey before being returned to Philadelphia in 1996 and sold to Norwegian Cruise Lines in 2003.

Norwegian Cruise Lines, America, who own the *United States* and have been paying for the docking and maintenance, have now put the liner up for sale, which could mean that she could be bought for scrap. However, the SS *United States*

Christine Young travels back from New York in February on the *United States*. (Christine Young Collection)

Conservancy, whose president is Susan Gibbs, granddaughter of William Francis Gibbs, who designed the *United States*, is presently working hard to save the liner.

Passenger Views of the *United States*

Margaret Dines also sailed from New York to Southampton on the *United States* and compares her with the *Queen Mary*: 'I did travel home in July 1962 with my young baby on the *United States,* but it was nothing like as smooth as on the *Queen Mary*. If I tried to compare the Queens with the *United States* I would have to say the food was still very good, but the main thing we realised was it was not as luxurious. It was nothing like sailing on the *Queen Mary* and *Queen Elizabeth*, where there were impressive wooden staterooms with lovely wooden panelling.'

When the United States was built all the latest alloys were used. The superstructure was built of aluminium, which rattled when she travelled transatlantic. Margaret Dines remembers the rattling of the ship when at speed: 'The *United States* travelled so fast that everything in the cabin rattled. It is very funny but we clearly remember putting keys on the dressing table and they rattled the whole time. We couldn't really say tinny, but that was the impression we got.

'There were fewer people on board and many of them were Americans who were very sociable and made the crossing enjoyable.'

Christine Young stayed in Canada for a year and then travelled back on the *United States* in February 1966: 'The reason why I only intended staying a year was mother was on her own and I promised her I would come back after a year. I had met a boy in Canada who I promised I'd go back to, but it took me another two and half years before I returned.

'The reason I wanted to sail on the *United States* was when I was quite young my mother took me down to Southampton pier to see the *United States* come in when she won the Blue Riband. It was all very modern, fibreglass and things like that, and it was very nice that I had the chance to sail on the *United States*. It was February when we left New York, and we were dancing one night when the ship rolled and we all ended up in a heap at one end.

'While on the *United States* we had the anniversary of George Washington's birthday on 22 February and we had a special dinner and fancy hats. I still have the menu from that day.

The menu for George Washington's birthday on 22 February 1966. (Christine Young Collection)

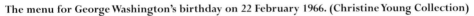

Chilled Fresh Jumbo Shrimp Cocktail   Suprême of Fresh Fruit, Kirschwasser
Fresh Crabmeat Cocktail   Pâté de Foie Gras, Melba Toast
Iced Table Celery   Queen Olives

•   •   •

Green Turtle "Windsor" en Tasse   Cream Martha Washington

•   •   •

Poached Gaspé Salmon, Sauce Hollandaise, Parsley Potatoes

•   •   •

Roast: Mount Vernon Turkey, American Stuffing, Giblet Sauce, Cranberry Jelly
Roast: Leg of Lamb au Jus, Mint Jelly

•   •   •

From the Grill: Bone-in Sirloin Steak, Fresh Mushrooms Sauté

•   •   •

Mashed Yellow Turnips
Petits Pois à la Française   Green Asparagus Spears
Potatoes: Boiled, Baked Idaho, French Fried or Candied Sweet

•   •   •

Chef's Salad Bowl, Special or Roquefort Dressing

•   •   •

Preserved Royal Anne Cherries

•   •   •

Vienna Mocha Layer Cake   French Ice Cream, Chocolate Sauce

•   •   •

Swiss, Gorgonzola or Camembert Cheese and Toasted Crackers

•   •   •

Crystallized Ginger   Assorted Nuts   After Dinner Mints
California Figs   Tunis Dates

•   •   •

Fresh Fruit in Season

•   •   •

Coffee   Tea   Fresh Milk

EB—TCD-444   Tuesday, February 22, 1966

'I remember meeting two men from Luxembourg and was up on the deck with them as we were coming into Southampton. I was pointing out the Isle of Wight and different places of Southampton such as the Civic Centre.

'However, the *United States* didn't have the old authenticity of the *Queen Elizabeth*, with the beautiful wood panelling. When I returned to Canada a few years later I went on the *Queen Elizabeth* again.'

The Final Years of the *Queen Elizabeth*.

Along with the gradual drop in passenger numbers through passengers turning to aircraft as a speedier method of travel, especially for transatlantic crossings, a decision was made to undertake cruises from New York to the Bahamas. In March 1965 the *Queen Elizabeth* had a major overhaul in Greenock, where she had air conditioning put in, was redecorated and had an outdoor swimming pool fitted. This work was finally completed in the spring of 1966, but another problem occurred which was to cause more potential passengers to turn to air travel. This was the seaman's strike in 1966, which caused a serious drain on Cunard's financial resources. Finally, by 8 May 1967, Cunard announced that the *Queen Mary* was being withdrawn from service and the *Queen Elizabeth* would also be withdrawn in the autumn of 1968.

The *Queen Elizabeth* made her final Atlantic crossing on 5 November 1968 and after being bought by some Philadelphia businessmen sailed to Port Everglades and opened to the public in February 1969. This was not a success due to losing money and the local authorities deeming it a fire hazard. In 1970 she was bought by C.Y. Tung of Hong Kong and it was planned for her to become a floating university. She was renamed *Seawise University* and sailed for Hong Kong in February 1971. However, due to machinery problems she did not arrive until July, when work began to refit her for her new role. The security on board was not up to standard and a number of fires were discovered that quickly spread, causing the ship to roll onto its side where it continued to burn. It was decided that the vessel was now only fit for scrap.

This was a sad end to what was once Cunard's flagship and one of the greatest liners. It was thought that the fires were started by an arsonist, who was never caught.

Other Cunarders
Saxonia on the Canadian Run

Pat Royl: 'I joined the *Saxonia* on the Canadian run, and that was where I met my wife, Ann. She was emigrating with her friend for a better life in Canada.'

Ann takes up the story: 'I come from a village background, where it was a very quiet life, and had this chance to emigrate to Canada in 1960 and began to save up for it. My parents agreed that I could go providing I saved enough to pay for a fare home if I didn't like it.

'I shall never forget getting on that ship that day because it was like a big city to me, a big city on water. The cabins were lovely, small, but nice, with two in the cabin. I enjoyed everything, the food, the entertainment, the library. There were so many books, and it was a "proper library". The meals were absolutely wonderful. Just to have good food and be waited on, to take part in events, to go to the cinema, to go on deck was wonderful, something I wasn't used to. There was always someone to help you when you needed help. I remember we all rushed up on deck to see an iceberg. Probably to the youngsters of today it would not mean much at all, but to me it was wonderful.

'We sailed from Southampton to Montréal and my friend who shared the cabin with me had her brother-in-law come down to pick us up. I registered with the personnel pool and had all kinds of jobs, but after seven months I came back on the *Saxonia*. It was on the *Saxonia* that I met my future husband, Pat Royl, who was a member of the crew.'

Pat Royl: 'In the summer we went from Southampton to Le Havre, Montréal and Quebec. The *Saxonia* was strictly the Canada route, and in the winter when the St Lawrence River was frozen, we would change to Halifax, Nova Scotia, St John, New Brunswick, but it was always a beautiful trip when we went up the St Lawrence River. I was deck steward and in those days we used to hire out deckchairs, cushions and blankets. The North Atlantic in the summer is not really terribly warm anyway and passengers used to want to get cushions and blankets. It was a great job because there were just two of us in the cabin, but it was a long day. We used to get up early and get the chairs ready. The deckchairs would still be lashed down from the night before. You couldn't leave loose deckchairs on deck during the night. Each evening they would all have to be

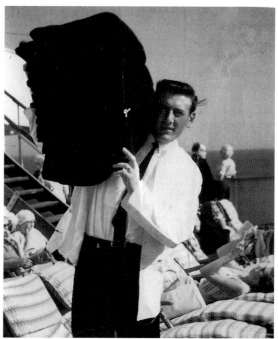

Pat Royl, deck steward, hiring out deckchairs for passengers. (Pat Royl Collection)

stacked up and lashed down. The cushions had to be stacked up and covered and blankets had to be stowed away. While we were getting ready the deck staff used to come along scrubbing the decks and spraying them down with hoses. You had to be careful not to slip on the wet surface. Once you had got everything ready you would go down to the cabin and get changed for the day's work.

'We used to serve beef tea on deck in the mornings and afternoons. Ships in those days had promenade decks, which were covered-in decks. It was a different type of people that travelled on the ships in those days than there are today. The boat trains used to come in and the ladies used to get off with long dresses, hats and gloves. The men had suits and ties and that was it.'

Pat Royl remembers the time when they transferred army personnel and their families between Germany and Canada: 'One of our trips on the *Saxonia* in the 1950s was to Bremerhaven to pick up the Canadian Black Watch and their families and take them back to Canada to St John's. I think we then picked up the 1st Battalion and took them back to Bremerhaven.'

Caronia

The *Caronia* was known as the 'Green Goddess' because she was painted in a pale green livery, and was a purpose-built cruise ship. At the beginning it was intended to use her for transatlantic travel and cruising, but she became a very popular ship, especially in the United States, for her world cruises.

The maiden voyage left Southampton on 4 January 1949 for New York, calling at Cherbourg, and then started her cruising season, at first to the Caribbean, and in the summer to the Mediterranean, Black Sea and Scandinavia, including the Norwegian fjords and the Baltic. During the winter there were cruises to the West Indies and South America, and then later came the world cruises. The *Caronia* even brought Americans over to see the Queen's Coronation in June 1953.

The *Caronia's* world cruises became very popular with the Americans who mainly made up the passengers for the annual cruises. To make it more comfortable on board in hot climates she received complete air-conditioning during her 1956 annual overhaul.

During her annual world cruise in 1958 the *Caronia* had a serious accident in Japan. She was sailing out of Yokohama harbour in high winds and had six tugs to escort her to the breakwater, but the Japanese pilot had released some of the tugs just after they had left the quayside. At that time the *Caronia* had one of the largest funnels, which would almost act as a large sail if hit by a gust of wind. A crew member was at the bow of the *Caronia* and saw a large American tank-landing craft sailing towards the harbour entrance from the sea to the US Naval Base on the port side of the ship. The landing craft kept on the same course, heading towards the *Caronia*. The officers on the bridge had to reduce power if another vessel was entering the harbour entrance and, with a combination of the strong wind, reduction in power and too few tugs to pull her back, the *Caronia* swung round to the starboard and into the breakwater, damaging the bows of the ship and demolishing a lighthouse in the process.

Gordon Brown was working on board as a butcher and remembers the event: 'I was in the bunk on my afternoon break when there was an almighty crack.' The damage had to be repaired, but fortunately the United States Navy allowed *Caronia* to use their Yokosuka dry dock in the naval base for repairs. However, the *Caronia's* crew were not allowed to go through

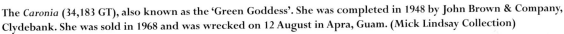

The *Caronia* (34,183 GT), also known as the 'Green Goddess'. She was completed in 1948 by John Brown & Company, Clydebank. She was sold in 1968 and was wrecked on 12 August in Apra, Guam. (Mick Lindsay Collection)

the naval base because of security. Gordon Brown: 'They wired out the keel shape from Southampton so she could sit down properly on the blocks. The whole bow was covered in bamboo and lashings of scaffolding all the way up.'

Barbara Pedan, assistant lady purser, was also on board the *Caronia* when the Yokohama accident occurred. She describes life on board during the time the repairs were being conducted in the USN dry dock: 'We left Japan with the bands playing and started to prepare for the next port but we were still within sight of land when there was a big crash and we had hit one of the small lighthouses that was on the outer edges of the harbour. We had a great gash in the ship and had to steam back again to Yokohama. There was no ship yard really big enough to take the *Caronia* except the American Fleet base at a place called Yokosuka. They agreed to take the ship there so that she could be repaired. The trouble was that there were 300 passengers on board and as the hotels were all full they couldn't be accommodated ashore. So the passengers had to stay on the ship while the repairs were carried out. All the services stop when the ship is in dry dock so things weren't too easy and the complaining passengers, of whom you always get a few, were in their element with complaints at every turn. It was nearly three weeks before the repairs were finished so I feel I know Japan better than some of the other countries. Of course, we were pretty busy during the time in dry dock as there were so many arrangements to be made, cables to be sent and passengers to be pacified.

'But we had some time off every day and time in the evenings. The US Navy had a couple of battleships in and they entertained us very well, and we were asked out several times to Japanese homes, which was very interesting.'

After the bow had been replaced the *Caronia* continued across the Pacific to Honolulu and then onto San Francisco on the west coast of America, through the Panama Canal and back to New York. The passengers disembarked at New York and the new passengers embarked for a Mediterranean Cruise lasting six weeks, then back to New York and finally to Southampton.

The *Caronia* continued with her world cruises and one year later engineer David Main, who had just joined the Cunard Steamship Company in early 1959, was on standby for the *Caronia* in Southampton when the ship was due to leave on her annual world cruise. David Main: 'I think there were four ships, the *Mauretania*, *Saxonia*, *Caronia* and *Ivernia*, and I was on standby for the *Caronia* just before she set out on a world cruise but was rather disappointed, because at the last minute the engineer who was missing turned up. They 'chucked' me on the dockside, still in my boiler suit with a suitcase by my side, pulled up the gangway and disappeared. I missed that trip and I would have enjoyed going around the world'.

Later on Gus Shanahan was much luckier than David Main. He joined the *Caronia* at Southampton as a relief carpenter and went on the world tour: 'I joined the *Caronia* as a relief for the chippie and had a nice cabin with the time on board made better by the crew members who were a pleasure to work with.'

Gus Shanahan remembers one lady who came from America and travelled every year on the *Caronia* using the ship as a floating hotel: 'I spoke to her one day at the gangway and she told me she sailed every year, had the same cabin and never left the ship the whole world tour.'

One of the stewards told Gus Shanahan that each year they would have the same group of American millionaires who would start the world tour, but after a month they would get fed up with each other's company and would leave the *Caronia* and fly back to the States.

Gus Shanahan: 'When we left Southampton we crossed the North Atlantic to New York, where the American passengers, including the millionaires, would join the ship. We would leave New York and spend some time in the West Indies and then continue on the world tour. Other ports of call included ports in Japan, Singapore and Hong Kong, then crossing the Pacific and finally ending up in Los Angeles on the west coast of America. When we left Los Angeles we came back through the Panama Canal and into the Atlantic, West Indies and had three days in America and then set off for the Mediterranean for six weeks. On the way back we came through the Gibraltar Straits to Lisbon and then back to Southampton. We were away for about five months, and it was quite a pleasant time. However, apart from the American millionaires, who, as the steward predicted, would leave the *Caronia* after a month, there were no other notable incidents that I can remember.'

Jim Taylor joined the *Caronia* on 22 September and signed for trips until 29 August 1959. These trips were mainly transatlantic, Southampton to New York and return, but also included three Caribbean cruises starting and ending at New York. Jim Taylor: 'New York was one of the places I always wanted to go to and I found it an amazing experience.

'Of all the ships I had been on I truly fell in love with the *Caronia*. She was built like a yacht and had that lovely raked bow, like some of the sailing yachts today. I spent two years on there, thoroughly enjoyed it, and made lots and lots of friends on board.'

The *Caronia* left New York in 1959 for her autumn Mediterranean cruise, which had been extended into the Black Sea. This was the first time the ports of Odessa and Yalta were opened to cruise ships after the Cold War. Jim Taylor remembers this very well: 'The *Caronia* was the first ship to cruise in the Black Sea after the Russians had opened up the ports of Odessa and Yalta. We were approaching the Port of Odessa when there was this turbulence of the sea alongside the ship, and an enormous Russian submarine surfaced alongside of us. About 50 uniformed and smartly dressed crew lined up on the deck of the submarine to welcome us'.

By the late 1960s there was an increase in air travel and a decrease in sea travel, so with a diminishing market Cunard decided that the *Caronia*, *Carinthia* and *Sylvania* would be taken out of service. The *Caronia's* last trip left New York, arriving back at Southampton on 24 November 1967.

There was a series of purchases of the ship and failures to get a regular cruising service in operation, and the vessel was sent for scrap in 1974. However, she did not reach the breakers' yard: while being towed in the Pacific she struck the breakwater at Guam, broke up and sank.

CHAPTER 7
OCEAN LINER VERSUS JET AIRCRAFT

Although in the 1950s the transatlantic liner was the popular means of travel between Europe and America, there was a gradual introduction of the jet airliner and with it a came a gradual change in the attitude of passengers. The ocean liner would take five days to cross the Atlantic and this would be a time of leisure and entertainment as well as relaxation for the passenger. However, the airliner would cross the Atlantic in five to six hours, and for the businessman this was ideal because they could attend meetings on the same day or the next day after leaving their home country instead of taking a number of weeks out of their business calendar.

However, from the early 1950s the Epirotiki Line, a shipping line that had operated from the mid-1850s, started to focus on the cruise market by operating cruises to the Greek Islands. This was at the time when the transatlantic liners were coming under increasing pressure from the introduction of jet aircraft.

Swan Hellenic also started to offer cruises to the Greek Islands in 1954, as did the Sun Line in 1958. By 1961 the first fly-cruise holidays for British passengers commenced, and as the cruise industry grew in the 1970s Epirotiki increased its fleet and became the largest cruise ship operator in Greece and the Eastern Mediterranean. However, during the 1980s and early 1990s the threat of terrorism in the air and at sea caused a drop in the numbers of cruise passengers, and in 1995 Epirotiki merged with Sun Line. A new line, Royal Olympic Cruise Lines, was born.

Those passengers flying to their holiday destination would be able to avoid the number of days getting there by ship and have more days on holiday because they would not have to worry about the time taken on a voyage home. They could also travel to places like Australia in just 24 hours and to exotic places, often within a day.

By the late 1950s and into the 1960s air travel began to put more pressure on the shipping companies. With the start of jet air travel and the introduction of the de Havilland Comet in 1958 there was a concern over more passengers changing to flying. However, the Comet did not have enough passenger capacity, and a number of air accidents did not help passenger confidence in the aircraft. It was first the introduction of the Boeing 707 and finally the Boeing 747 in 1970, with a carrying capacity of over 450 passengers, that made a huge impact on the shipping companies. Along with the competition from jet airliners, there were the rising fuel costs and introduction of the container trade which caused a serious decline in the use of the passenger/cargo ships. By 1958 there were more than a million passengers flying the Atlantic, surpassing the total of Atlantic Ocean liner passengers for the first time.

The passenger ships were kept in business through voyages as part of the assisted passages scheme to Australia. This was the 'Ten Pound Poms,' a colloquial name used in Australia for the British subjects emigrating from Britain to Australia. The assisted passage scheme was funded by the Australian government and ran from 1945 to 1972, costing each passenger £10. From 1955 to 1970 the Sitmar Line also carried thousands of British migrants to Australia, but then the contract was transferred to the Greek-owned Chandris Line.

There were also trooping and school educational cruises that kept a number of ships in work. The shipping companies had to make difficult decisions and many vessels were taken out of service, laid up, and some were even scrapped.

From 1946 to 1952 the *Asturias* returned to the commercial trade as an emigrant ship between Southampton and Sydney, Australia. The assisted passages scheme, whereby adults travelled to Australia for £10 and children travelled free, ran at this time. The voyage would take approximately five to six weeks, all for £10. Some of the migrants started their new life in Australia on arrival at Freemantle and others went to Melbourne and Sydney.

The *Asturias* was refitted in 1952 for peacetime trooping and during this time was managed for the Minister of Transport by the Royal Mail Lines. Her trooping colours were a white hull with a blue band around and a yellow funnel, and in 1953 the *Asturias* was used to bring British troops home from Korea.

John Fahy joined the *Asturias* in her last year before she was scrapped: 'The next ship I went on was the *Asturias* in 1957. She was one of two sisters, the *Alcantara* and *Asturias,* built of the same design. I was a steward serving on the officers' tables in the dining saloon. She was a lovely ship and I enjoyed my time on her. The *Asturias* was a Royal Mail ship and she was in dressed in her trooping colours with a white hull and a blue band around the hull.

'We used to do a lot of runs to trouble spots like Cyprus. We were taking troops there at the time of the EOKA (Ethniki Organosis Kyprion Agoniston, or Greek for National Organisation of Cypriot Fighters).'

In September 1957 the *Asturias* was sold for breaking up, but before she was eventually scrapped she played the part of the *Titanic* in the film *A Night to Remember.*

Ted Arison – Pioneer of Modern Day Cruising
Cruises to the Caribbean from Florida in the 1960s

Ted Arison is known as the pioneer of the modern-day cruise industry. The industry began in the 1960s, when Knut Kloster, a Norwegian ship-owner, operated a newly built passenger ferry, *Sunward*, sailing from Southampton to Vigo, Lisbon and

Gibraltar. However, it was not a very successful venture. Ted Arison invited Knut Kloster to relocate the *Sunward* to Miami to operate cruises to the Caribbean and so the Norwegian Caribbean Line was founded in 1966 as a joint venture between Ted Arison and Knut Kloster. This was a very successful venture and generated a great demand for cruise holidays. In 1972 Kloster and Arison parted company, with Arison forming a new company, Carnival Cruise Lines, which is today the world's biggest cruise company. The company started with one vessel, TSS *Mardi Gras*, but all was not 'plain sailing' because on her maiden voyage out of Miami the *Mardi Gras* ran aground on a sandbar. After Ted Arison retired, his son, Micky Arison, became CEO for the Carnival Corporation in 1979. The Norwegian Caribbean Line was renamed Norwegian Cruise Line in 1986 and has become well known today for introducing of freestyle cruising.

It was also in the late 1960s that another famous cruise line was formed, also based in Miami, Florida. Arne Wilhelmsen and Edwin Stephan came up with the idea that there were a lot of very wealthy Americans living in Florida who would be interested in luxurious, relaxing cruises to the Caribbean. They sold their idea to a group of shipping companies in Norway and so Royal Caribbean Cruises was founded in 1969. Their first ship was the *Song of Norway,* followed by *Nordic Prince* and then *Sun Viking* in 1972. Interestingly, it was the *Song of Norway* that was their first vessel to be 'jumboised' by inserting an 85ft (26m) section in the centre of the vessel, creating more passenger accommodation.

Government Restrictions Help the Cruise Industry

In post-war Britain over two-thirds of the British public had never left the country for holidays. However, the foreign package holidays changed all that by offering a 'fly out, hotel/resort, fly back' package to places such as Spain. The British government, for economic reasons, decided in the 1960s to impose currency restrictions on British passport holders to discourage travel abroad. However, just as prohibition and the booze cruises in America helped the shipping companies because there were no restrictions on selling alcohol at sea, so did the currency restriction in Britain help the cruise industry. British registered ships were exempt from these regulations and the cruise passengers were allowed to spend sterling on board, leaving them the opportunity to use their £50 foreign currency allowance when they went ashore. This was a boon for the shipping companies, who could then divert some of their vessels to the cruise industry, especially those ships that had been designed for the assisted passages scheme to Australia.

Despite the opportunity for some shipping lines to convert their ocean liners to cruise ships, the increasing price of fuel in the 1970s was the main reason that a number of shipping lines ceased operating, and it was the end of a number of well-known shipping companies. These included the Royal Mail Line, which closed by the early 1970s, the Union-Castle Line in 1978 and Shaw Savill Line in 1985. Both Shaw Savill and Royal Mail vessels were absorbed into Furness Withy & Company.

The liner services had taken quite a blow and this left just P&O, Cunard and the Fred. Olsen Cruise Line to service the mainstream British cruise market.

The 1966 Seamen's Strike

The 1966 Seamen's Strike did not help the problems hitting the British shipping companies. This was brought about by the period of gradual economic decline during the 1960s, and with it came increasing industrial disputes. When the NUS (National Union of Seamen) brought its members out on 16 May 1966. The strike was nationwide and the seamen were determined to see it through.

The strike had a devastating effect on the country due to many ports being closed and shipping lines unable to operate. However, Southampton was not closed to foreign shipping, which regularly called at the port. Many ships were tied up in Southampton Docks, some tied up three abreast, with most of Cunard's fleet out of action. When the *Queen Mary* arrived at Southampton from New York with 850 passengers on board, including Dr Billy Graham, about to begin a tour of Britain, the 900 crew members walked off the ship. There had never been so many ships stranded in the eastern and western docks at one time.

The reason for the strike was the number of hours the seamen worked and the pay they received. Before the strike a seaman would work a 56-hour week and their wages would be less than £15 per week. They wanted a 40-hour week and an increase in pay. However, the ship owners were only prepared to offer reducing the hours worked over a period of three years, and so the seamen came out on strike.

Finally, on 1 July, the strike ended and the seaman had won the battle. The outcome was nine extra days of annual leave and the introduction of a 40-hour week over 12 months.

The strike had a devastating effect on Cunard and their transatlantic service as the other shipping lines capitalised on it. The ocean liners from the French

The *Queen Elizabeth 2* (70,327 GT) leaving Berth 38–39 in Southampton Docks at night. (Richard de Jong Collection)

Line, Holland–America Line, Norddeutscher Lloyd Line and the United States Line continued the transatlantic service and so gained increased prestige and passengers, which did not help Cunard finances.

It was not much later when some of the famous ocean liners, like the Cunard *Queen Mary* and *Queen Elizabeth*, were taken out of service and many other liners scrapped, and it appeared to be the end of ocean travel as we knew it. However, it was also the time when the *Queen Elizabeth 2* came on the scene and was to be in the forefront of the Cunard transatlantic and cruising operations for the next 40 years.

Queen Elizabeth 2

The decision was made by Cunard to build a new ship that would cope with a dual-purpose role of transatlantic liner and cruise ship, and that was how the Q3 project came about, better known as the *QE2* (*Queen Elizabeth 2*).

Douglas Ward remembers the final transatlantic crossing to Southampton on the *Queen Elizabeth*: 'I remember it well because we arrived at Southampton on my birthday, which was in November. After that I had three weeks at home before I was sent up to Gourock, Scotland, to join the new *QE2*.'

While in Gourock, Douglas Ward was shown the plans for the *QE2* and was asked where he thought the musicians' accommodation should be put: 'That was rather nice for the contractor to ask my opinion. However, my agent was Geraldo and we negotiated passenger cabins for the 22 musicians in a very nice location.

'Suddenly we were to change from the ocean liner role to a dual role with a liner for transatlantic service and cruising, and it was completely different. There were not so many woods in the *QE2* because the designers were all using the latest materials of the time, such as Formica and some laminating finishes which were all the rage. The ship was very colourful, trendy and modern for the time.'

The keel of the *QE2* was laid on 5 July 1965 in the John Brown's shipyard on Clydebank and was launched on 20 September 1967 by Queen Elizabeth II, who used a pair of gold scissors that had been used by her grandmother to launch the *Queen Mary* and her mother to launch the *Queen Elizabeth*.

Gus Shanahan: 'When the new *QE2* was being built I was sent as standby assistant to the naval architect from 1965–67 until she was completed.'

It was on 9 November 1968 that the *QE2* set sail from the fitting-out berth at John Brown's shipyard under the command of William (Bil) Warwick, who was her first captain.

Gus Shanahan: 'When we did the trial run on the *QE2* I had to check that the anchor was alright. As the ship's carpenter on board you had to drop the anchor and sometimes you had to break the cable to detach the anchor, 'hang it' as they called it, so that you could moor to a buoy. This depended on what the port people wanted. The chippie gets involved in all sorts!

'We went from there to the measured mile at Skelmore and then down to Southampton. At first the *QE2* had some engine problems and was in Southampton for three months before she sailed for New York on her maiden voyage.'

Douglas Ward: 'When the *QE2* was brought into service in 1968 we did a Christmas cruise, which was the charity cruise from Southampton down to the Canary Islands. We had a lot of John Brown workmen on board as the ship wasn't finished, but she broke down off Las Palmas with broken turbine blades. Cunard refused delivery of the ship and she was then sent for repairs. Eventually she was given back to Cunard in April 1969 and we did two big charity functions in Southampton on 28 and 29 April. On 2 May 1969 the *QE2* left on her first maiden transatlantic crossing to New York, which took four days, 16 hours and 35 minutes, and was a fantastic, wonderful experience.

'I still remember arriving in New York and standing outside on deck, close to the bridge, and as we were passing the Statue of Liberty, all of a sudden, there was this tremendous roar! There were many vessels around the *QE2* escorting us into the maiden arrival in New York when two British RAF Harrier jets came down close to the bridge wing, and the captain and the pilots were able to wave to each other. That was a fantastic time and it was wonderful being there.'

A Carpenter's Life at Sea

Gus Shanahan: 'At sea the carpenter is not a watch keeper, he is on day work, but because of the different times of docking sometimes early morning the carpenter has to be ready to drop the anchor. There were the late night sailings, of course, when you were cruising. The actual day was 7am to 5pm, and outside of that was overtime.

'On the *QE2* my cabin was large, not like the bathroom size on the *Bantria*. It was luxury compared to that. When taking on water it could be from barges or the quayside. When on cruises there were some late sailings at 10pm which I had to be available for.

'The bridge officer, deck crew and engine department were on watches of four-hours on, eight-hours off throughout the 24 hour period. In most liners the crew had the Pig and Whistle where you could let your hair down and have a yarn with the boys.

'As carpenter I was on day work, starting at 7am. I would do an hour taking the soundings of all the tanks in the ship. That would be with a 'rod and line' as we called it, chain and line and dip it in the tanks and see how much water had been used in the previous 24 hours and enter it in a book. From 8–9am I would have breakfast and start work again on any jobs that cropped up as carpenter/handyman. Greasing on deck, such as the cargo blocks used on the cranes or 'derricks', as we called them, 'til 12–1, which was lunchtime, and after lunch continue with any other maintenance jobs, finishing work at 5pm. The evenings were your own.

'When we arrived in port I would stand by the anchor in case it was needed and when arriving at the dock a gang would be waiting to unload the cargo. I would have to knock all the wedges out of the hatch covers that were covered with thick canvas and get it ready for the dockers to move in and unload the cargo. By the time you had gone round all the ports the cargo holds would be empty and the deck sailors would sweep out all the holds ready to take in the homeward-bound cargo.

'I would take in the water when in the port, filling all the tanks up again. We might do three or four ports a week around the Italian coast. That was when I was on the new Cunard motor ships *Media* and *Parthia*.

'I used to see a lot of passengers because of us, the chippies, being all around the cabins doing repairs. Quite nice people, some were business people and used to use the week at sea as free time to catch up on the book work.

'On the *QE2* in 1970 we picked up an injured engineer off a tanker when we were cruising down off East Africa. We put the launch down and picked him up and the doctor looked after him. He had a blowlamp explode in his face.'

In 1971 the *QE2* took part in the rescue of passengers from the French Line vessel *Antilles* when she struck an uncharted reef off the island of Mustique. The leaking oil from the ship caught fire and she was eventually scrapped.

In May 1972 Cunard had received a message that there was a bomb on board the *QE2* while on a transatlantic crossing and a demand for $350,000 in cash. RAF bomb disposal experts were flown in and parachuted into the sea. Commodore Warwick: 'When the RAF flew a bomb disposal squad out they were parachuted into the ocean, and I was second officer in the lifeboat that picked them up and took them back to the ship. After a search of the ship no bomb was discovered and the *QE2* was able to continue on her voyage.'

Gus Shanahan: 'In really heavy weather the portholes were covered and you got very little fresh air coming in. In the small ships you had to rough it but in the *QE2* it used to ride the storm out. Life went on as usual, people got seasick. I was seasick quite often, I must admit. Some people never get over it. I never got over it and I used to feel really groggy at times.'

Gus Shanahan left the *QE2* in 1973: 'I eventually "swallowed the hook", as they called it, and came ashore.'

Family Connections with the *QE2* and *QM2*
Sam Warwick comes from a seafaring family and although he did not follow on with the family tradition he has a deep interest in the Cunard Line. His grandfather, William (Bil) Warwick, was commodore of the Cunard Line and first master of *Queen Elizabeth 2*. His father, Ronald Warwick, was also a Cunard commodore and was the master of the *Queen Elizabeth 2* in 1990, making Cunard history as the first time that a father and son had commanded the same liner. Commodore Ron Warwick was also the first master of *Queen Mary 2*.

Sam has travelled on ships with his father since an early age, but his interest in the sea doesn't lie in sailing on the surface but diving below it. He has been diving since 1992 as a hobby and has logged over 900 dives. His interest in the Cunard Line has led him to research and dive on the wrecks of Cunard ships: 'One of my main passions is scuba diving, so there's definitely a connection to the sea.'

Sam remembers his first trip aboard *QE2* in the 1970s with his father. He was a very inquisitive lad and had gone on the quayside to watch bananas being loaded by conveyor belt and could not be found. He still remembers the bananas, but not the consequences afterwards!

One event that has become a family story was when Commodore Warwick was battling with a hurricane and Sam was below deck in the nightclub, dancing the night away. *Queen Elizabeth 2* had left Southampton on 7 September 1995 for New York, but the officers on watch were aware of Hurricane Luis and had been plotting its movement since it had left the Caribbean. It became clear that the hurricane would pass close to the *Queen Elizabeth 2* and the captain warned the passengers of this possibility, and the crew were told to prepare for unfavourable weather conditions.

With the winds between 50–100 knots the *Queen Elizabeth 2* hove to and was riding out 30–50ft waves. Commodore Warwick describes the conditions: 'It was a dark night and the visibility was considerably affected by the storm conditions. The sea was nearly white in appearance with foam and driving spray lashing the ship. Waves were continuously breaking over the fore deck, leaving it awash for minutes at a time. At 02.10am the rogue wave was sighted right ahead looming out of the darkness and it looked as though we were heading straight for the white cliffs of Dover. The wave seemed to take ages to reach us, but it was probably less than a minute before it broke with tremendous force over the bow of the *QE2*. An incredible shudder went through the ship, followed a few moments later by two smaller shudders. At the same time the sea was cascading all over the fore part of the ship, including the bridge, and it was several seconds before the water had drained away from the wheelhouse windows and the vision ahead was restored.'

The height of the wave was described by Commodore Warwick as 'more-or-less level with our line of sight on the bridge, which has a height of eye of 95 feet above the sea surface. The presence of the rogue wave was also recorded by Canadian weather buoys moored in the vicinity, which measured the height as 98 feet. No passengers or crew were injured. Whilst most slept, there was, however, a 'Hurricane Party' in full swing in the Yacht Club.'

Commodore Warwick: 'In my 38 years at sea this was the largest wave that I have ever encountered and I cannot begin to imagine what effect it would have had on a smaller vessel – all I can say is that I was glad that I was on board the *Queen Elizabeth 2!*'

Sam has good memories of *QE2* when his sister got married on board. However, it was not straightforward, as the plan was to have the wedding on board the *QE2* in New York in October 2001, but the ship was diverted to Boston because of the 9/11 terrorist attacks on the city.

One of the most frequent questions from passengers to Commodore Warwick has been 'Can the captain perform marriages?' The answer has always been no, because since 1877 it has been illegal for captains on British ships to perform a marriage; however, Commodore Warwick found after research on the internet that he could perform the ceremony by getting special permission from the Governor of Massachusetts. The Governor's office explained that it could take six to eight weeks to get permission, but when it was explained to the Governor's aide the reason for the urgency of the request, he arranged for immediate granting of the document.

It was a very proud moment for Sam when he walked his sister up the aisle to give her away and a proud moment for Commodore Warwick to marry his daughter. This became Cunard history because it was the first legal marriage in living memory carried out by any master on board any of the Cunard fleet.

Sam used to live in Whiteley, Hampshire, but now lives in Sydney, Australia, where he has his own IT consultancy. His interest in the Cunard Line and especially his family connection with the line has led him to develop two websites, one on the *QE2* (www.qe2.org.uk) and the other on the *QM2* (www.qm2.org.uk).

QE2 and the Falklands War

At the start of the Falklands War the British government requisitioned the *QE2* and *Canberra* for service as troop transport vessels. However, when the *QE2* and the *Canberra* were recalled to Southampton all the Filipino and Indian crew were sent home because their governments did not want them taking part in a war. Cunard and P&O then had to advertise for ex-British merchant seamen to make up the crews for the ships to sail to the Falklands.

John Fahy was disappointed because his application was rejected by the Board of Trade because they said his job on Port Security was very important: 'That was despite me having done all the gunnery courses for Armed Merchant Cruisers, which were Oerlikons and 4.5 guns, but they eventually got enough volunteer crew to sail to the Falklands'.

The *QE2* was fitted out in Southampton for her war service in the Falklands. This included adding three helicopter pads, laying hardboard over all the carpeting to protect it from wear and tear and public areas were changed into dormitories for the 3,000 troops she would be carrying to the South Atlantic. Great care was taken on the voyage to South Georgia to avoid the *QE2* being attacked while at sea. Once the troops had disembarked at South Georgia other vessels, including the *Canberra*, transported the troops to the Falklands.

John Fahy: At the time *Sea Princess* was in dry dock getting new port bow thrusters. An officer warned me that two or three people would be visiting the ship at 12 noon and could I man the gangway? They arrived in suits and were accompanied by naval officers and the chief officer met them at the top of the gangway. They went to the wardroom and then inspected the whole ship. I found out later that the *Sea Princess* would have been the next ship to be sent to the Falklands, but this did not happen.

'We had three ammunition ships in at the time and an officer from the Marchwood Military Port was on board one of them. There were servicemen on board and on the quayside with machine guns and guarding the area. The officer told me that they had enough arms on board one ship to fight a war for the next two years, but the chance of one or two of the ships being sunk by torpedoes was very real and they couldn't risk just sending one ship and that is why they sent three ships.'

CHAPTER 8

CRUISING AND CRUISE SHIPS FROM THE 1960S

In May 1960 P&O Line and Orient Line merged, and with a combination of 16 passenger ships they had the largest fleet, with Cunard having five fewer ships in their fleet. At the same time the P&O and Orient Lines each had a ship being built that was the largest since the *Queen Elizabeth* was built in 1940. The Orient Line had the *Oriana* (41,923 GT) under construction at Barrow-in-Furness, and P&O had the *Canberra* (44,807 GT) at Harland & Wolff, Belfast.

The *Oriana* made her maiden voyage in November 1960 from Southampton to Australia, New Zealand, across the Pacific to Canada and then to the United States. After a cruise to Canada she went to Sydney as a full-time cruise ship.

The *Canberra* was 820ft (249.9m), with a beam of 102ft (31.1m), and had accommodation for 548 first-class and 1,600 tourist-class passengers, with a crew of 960. She was built originally for the Australian service as well as for cruising and her maiden voyage was in June 1961 to Australia and on to Canada and the USA. With the decreasing market the *Canberra* did several cruises, but from 1972 she became a one-class ship sailing out of Southampton. It was in 1982 that the *Canberra* was requisitioned for the Falklands War, and afterwards she was refitted and returned to passenger service. After her last cruise she returned to Southampton in 1997 and was finally scrapped in Pakistan.

Life as passengers on the *Canberra*

It was in the middle 1970s when Jim Brown and his wife got bitten by the 'cruising bug' and he talks about their first experiences on the P&O *Canberra*: 'My wife, Marion, and I are really enthusiastic cruisers now, and it all started in the mid-1970s when I was Health & Safety Officer for Solent Container Services. We found out that we were eligible for staff-discounted cruises. There were only two ships available for cruises then, and they were the *Canberra* and the *Sea Princess*. However, the *Sea Princess* was a bit more upper class as she was a smaller ship, and some of our senior managers went on her.

The *Oriana* (41,923 GT) was completed in 1960 by Vickers-Armstrong, Barrow-in-Furness. In 1986 she was sold and became a tourist centre in Beppu Bay, Kyushu Island. In 1995 she was sold again to Chinese owners. She was broken up in China in 2005. (Bert Moody Collection)

Relaxing in the sun and the pool on a *Canberra* cruise. (Jim Brown Collection)

The system at the time was for staff to take up last-minute vacancies. It was possible that there might only be two or three days, or even 24 hours notice. Jim Brown: 'There were only two ships cruising and, of course, to us cruising was for rich and wealthy people who could afford to go cruising. However, we put in our forms to go on a cruise and our first cruise was on the *Canberra*. We were very excited because the thought of having a cruise was out of this world. The cruise was 14 days to the Canary Islands. It was fantastic and the food was tremendous, and the menu on the *Canberra* had more courses than they have today. I think they have cut the courses back a bit now.

'The *Canberra*, with hindsight, was fairly small compared to some of the mega-cruise ships today, but to us at the time she was massive. We were used to the Isle of Wight or Hythe ferry boats, and sometimes cross-Channel boats, but the *Canberra* was big compared with those.

'The one thing that was great about the *Canberra* was that she was a very intimate ship and everyone was very friendly. The cruise director would be walking around all day long chatting to people on deck and you had a personal connection with him.

'On our very first cruise our cabin was in an alleyway along with a couple of other cabins. There was a big picture window at the bottom of the alleyway, and our cabin had a small window in one corner. When you walked on deck on every cruise you would see the crew always chipping away at the deck and resurfacing a section at a time.

'Looking back to the *Canberra* now, it appears so primitive. You didn't have showers in your cabin. On some cruises there was no toilet in the cabin, no en-suite and we had to walk down the corridor if we wanted a bath or go to the loo. If I wanted to go to the bathroom at 2am I had to get up and walk down the corridor. That depended what cabin you had, of course, as that would have been the lower grade cabins, but all cabins had a sink in them.

'However, it was a lovely ship, but one drawback was if you were at the stern sunbathing you would get oily flecks from the funnel blowing down and it would be on the deckchairs when you sat down. They couldn't stop it and it was a problem you had to put up with, but they did have a system in place to clean your clothes if you got oil on them. Sometimes they would have a little burn-out when big black smoke would come out of the funnel, and it could be a bit mucky and dirty on occasions like that.

'We enjoyed the cruises, which included the Mediterranean, and I remember when the *Canberra* was tying up in Port Said there would be the local Egyptian traders looking up and saying, "Hello Mrs Miniver" or "Hello Mrs Simpson!" They would think you were American.

'The beauty of cruising for us was that it was quite economical, what with the food and the entertainment. The shows were marvellous, and I think the company was about half a dozen, including the dancers and entertainers. In those days the entertainment staff were the equivalent to the Butlins Redcoats. They would put on bingo sessions and teach you line

A children's fancy dress competition on the Canberra. (Jim Brown Collection)

dancing, and the children would have fancy-dress competitions. The staff would also take part in the shows and so would the cruise director, who would be dancing on the stage and telling jokes. Today it is different altogether because the entertainment is run by professional entertainment companies on board, and the entertainment staff no longer take part in the shows. Today the cruise director doesn't have time to get involved in the entertainment because of the size of the cruise ships and increased administrative work. You will probably see the cruise director at the entrance to the theatre welcoming you when you enter the theatre. The shows today are truly professional and the dancers are truly amazing, they are so hard-working.

'One of the nice staff ones we had was when we flew to Singapore and joined the *Canberra*. We then came back through the Indian Ocean, Red Sea, Suez Canal, and Mediterranean and back to Southampton. It was nearly a month and was a matter of a few hundred pounds. I was lucky as a senior manager, because I could take the time off and leave my deputy to run things while I was away.

'On the *Canberra* you had different lounges, a quiet lounge where you listened to classical music in the evenings. Today you would still have the same, but there would be more lounges and more bars.

'The only difference there is between the bigger ships and the smaller ships is that bigger ones are steadier. We had the experience of coming back through the Bay of Biscay on the *Canberra* with a Force 11 gale and 40ft waves. We had an outside cabin and we stayed in our cabin for 24 hours and just drank water. We didn't feel like eating. We weren't seasick, but we weren't full of the joys of spring! I can see it now. We had a porthole in our cabin and you could look out and look down 40ft to the water below and looking ahead of you was a solid 40ft wall of water coming towards you. Next thing you were under water and looking through the sea.

'On that particular trip the waves smashed away about 20 yards off the handrail on the promenade deck. We weren't allowed on deck and they blocked off the access doors from the lounges. You couldn't go on deck or you would have been washed overboard because there was no handrail. On that trip the waves were breaking over the bow and over the crow's-nest bar on top.

'The *Canberra* had stabilisers and was one of the few ships that kept going and moving through the storm. We have been in Force 9 and Force 10 storms on the bigger ships and you wouldn't really know it, perhaps a slight swaying.

The *Canberra* (44,807 GT) appears from the mist on her return from the Falklands. (Roger Joyce Collection)

'We waved and the whole ship waved back!' (Roger Joyce Collection)

'We were on the penultimate cruise of the *Canberra* when we heard she was going to be scrapped, which we thought was tragic.

'We have been to the Holy Land, the Indian Ocean and the Caribbean several times, but we don't normally like flying, it's too much hassle! However, we did fly for our golden wedding, which was in 2003, for a cruise up to Alaska. That was something special.'

Canberra Arrives Home after the Falklands War

On 11 July 1982 Roger Joyce and Tony Lane were fishing from Tony's 13ft dory off Calshot Castle and this was the very morning that the *Canberra* was due to return to Southampton from the Falklands.

They had no luck and had not caught anything, when out of the mist appeared the *Canberra*. They decided to join the many boats and launches that were surrounding the *Canberra* and sailed up Southampton Water to the docks. There was a lot of waving and cheering from the accompanying craft, but it all died down, so Roger and Tony decided to wave to the troops, and to their surprise everyone on board the *Canberra* joined in, cheering and waving back at them.

Ron Hancock remembers the day well: 'One cloudy, misty morning I was sent to the Mayflower Terminal at 106 Berth, and my job was keeping the

A helicopter hovers above the *Canberra*. (Roger Joyce Collection)

crowds back the day the *Canberra* came home from the Falklands. To me this is one of my highlights from my time in port, and I got paid for it!

'We first saw this helicopter circling through the mist and then the *Canberra* appeared with a couple of tugs and a large flotilla of boats accompanying her. As she came alongside everybody started cheering and what an emotional welcome it was. I saw the dockies and the foremen, all grown men, weeping openly.

'You could see all the slogans hanging over the side of the ship. It made me smile and I still think about one of the slogans: "*Canberra* cruises while *QE2* refuses."'

This was the reference to the *Canberra* sailing in San Carlos Water, otherwise known as 'Bomb Alley', in the Falklands, while the *QE2* sailed to South Georgia which was 800 miles (1,290km) from the Falkland Islands. One reason for this was that the size of the *QE2* made it unable to manoeuvre effectively in the confined Falkland waters, and another was the submarine attack that sank the Argentine cruiser *Belgrano*. There was serious concern that, to avenge the sinking, the Argentine Air Force would fly long-range aircraft to attack and sink the most famous British ship, the *QE2*. Therefore, it was arranged that the *QE2* would sail to South Georgia and her troops would disembark and embark on the *Canberra*, which would sail to the Falklands. The *QE2* would take on survivors from HMS *Coventry*, *Antelope* and *Ardent* and bring them home.

Working on the *Canberra* After her Return from the Falklands War
Joining *Canberra* as a Trainee Electro-Technical Officer.
Chris Wright: 'When I joined *Canberra* in November 1986 I started as a trainee electro-technical officer, and at that time there was a very large deck and technical officer department. All the electrical officers on board were time-served shipyard electricians or from other industries, but the new breed of P&O electrical technical trainees were all from college and qualified to HND (Higher National Diploma) standard.

'From my perspective it was the first ship I had sailed on and it was a baptism of fire in what life at sea was about. To be honest my initial impression was that it wasn't very friendly, but that was more because nobody offered much in the way of help for what you had to do, where you had to be, and traditionally you either sank or swam.

'P&O started building ships such as the *Royal Princess* in 1984 that were advanced electrically and electronically and were looking to train electrical and technical officers that would fit the needs of the new ships coming on line. My background was electrical and electronic engineering, specialising in control engineering. The reduction in numbers of engineer officers today is the result of automation, and no longer is there the telegraph from the bridge to the engine room; it is all controlled from the bridge. The present-day cruise ships only need a senior watch keeper, who generally stays in the control room, a junior watch keeper, who is in the engine room keeping an eye on things and generally one motor man, who goes around topping up, cleaning and tidying up.

'When *Oriana* came out there were a lot of the passengers who had sailed on *Canberra* saying that it was not the same and how much they enjoyed cruising on the old *Canberra*. She was not the same as *Oriana* because *Canberra* was built with the materials of the day, Formica bulkheads and linoleum on the floors, yet when you walk on the *Oriana* you are walking on carpets with lots of wood in the décor.

'When the ships were built it was effectively a snapshot in time by using what materials that were available at the time. When the original *Queen Mary* made her first transatlantic crossing in 1936 they thought they had built a ship that was big and stable, but she rolled and pitched so much that it became necessary to fit handrails in every passenger alleyway. They used the most expensive and exclusive material of the time, which was plastic, but they looked like ivory!

'*Canberra* was originally built as a two-class ship, so at the forward end of the ship you had the first-class en-suites and at the aft end there was the second class where there were shared facilities. I noticed in the aft second-class area there were some large rooms that had a shower room. I wondered why there were two lights in those shower rooms. I discovered later that on the line voyages to Australia the whole family could all crowd into the cabin and there was a bunk that would slide into the shower room. When it came to bedtime the bedroom steward would come in and set up the bunk in the shower room.

'I believe in the 1970s they considered scrapping *Canberra* because of the competition from the jumbo jet, but cruising started to take off and that saved her.

'Every year we would go off on a world voyage and when I joined the majority of passengers on the world cruises would do the whole world cruise or get off in Australia. Then, after a few years, when cruising became more of a thing they started selling legs of the voyage and when someone left the ship, another passenger would join for the next leg, and so on.'

Joining *Canberra* as a Nurse
Ann Wright: 'I was trained as a nurse at the Warsgrave Hospital, Coventry, and then went to Worcester to train as a

Chris Wright working in the engine room on the *Canberra*.
(Ann Wright Collection)

Ann and Chris Wright met on the *Canberra* and were later married. Today they live at Dibden Purlieu, near Southampton, and have two boys, James, aged 14, and Alexander, aged 9. (Ann Wright Collection)

midwife. A midwife friend who had already done her midwifery had joined the *Canberra* and I went to see her on board. She showed me around and I saw the hospital and her cabin, and after hearing all the stories of life on board I decided that I wanted to join, so I applied. I was two years on the waiting list before I got an interview, was successful and was also sent to *Canberra*, which I joined on 15 April 1988.

'As I walked up the gangway of the *Canberra* on my first day I was greeted by the ship's surgeon and nurses with a bottle of champagne because some nurses were leaving and I was joining. I found out that my first cruise was to the Caribbean, and it was a dream come true as I'd wanted to go there all my life.

'Afterwards, a nurse colleague showed me around the ship and as we walked into the laundry room Chris Wright was at the washing machine with one of his colleagues. We just said hello and that was it, the spark shot across the room and after that everywhere I went he seemed to be there!

'The *Canberra* sailed and on the second night out the captain would always have his "Welcome Aboard" cocktail parties. There were two sittings for dinner, so there were two cocktail parties. One was at 6.30 and the other at 8.30, just before each sitting. Officers were expected to go to both parties, but quite often the nurses only went to the second sitting as the evening surgery would still be going on.

'There were two surgeries, one for the crew and one for the passengers. We also ran a hospital and if we didn't go to the cocktail parties after we had finished work it was noticed and commented on. It was like being in school!'

Chris: 'When I first started the junior officers would line up at the entrance to the party, usually a large lounge area. There would be one line with the captain on one door and another line with the chief engineer on the other door. As the cruise passengers came in you would escort them into the room and ensure they had a drink. It was a very practical way because it meant you would move everybody into the room and you would kick off the conversation. Once they got going you would then go back to pick up the next group from the door.

'The junior officers had a table at the end of the restaurant and the nurses used to join them. There were two doctors, three nurses, and a pharmacist at the time. The surgeon noticed that since Ann had joined *Canberra* a lot of light bulbs were changed in the hospital, but Ann confirmed that every afternoon they would have tea and cakes and it was then that the electrical officers would arrive and check the equipment at the same time!'

Ann: 'The nurses on *Canberra* shared a bathroom between four and there were sinks in the cabins. We had a cabin because we were all trained nurses with officer status and also worked nights. We were on call 24 hours per day, every day, but every afternoon we would have a sleep because we didn't know what was going to happen during the night.

'There was always one nurse on call, except the senior nurse who worked for the doctor with the passengers. You worked very hard but you also played very hard as well. We would have parties, but didn't call them that, we called them "pour-outs".

'In those days when you were in your cabin, other than when you were asleep, the cabin door was always open. You had a curtain across the door when it was open, but that all changed because of the introduction of new fire regulations, and then you had to have an automatic closing door.

'We used to have to go down below to get to know the engine room, but if you went into the boiler room it was so hot that the sweat used to pour off the men. However, it was to practice how to get there quickly if there was an accident and we had to get a stretcher down there.

'One man actually broke his ankle. We got him on to a Neil Robertson (a special stretcher used on ships and small spaces)

The medical team celebrating a birthday on the *Canberra*. (Ann Wright Collection)

and had to take him up a vertical ladder. My job was to be by his head the whole time, talking to him and keeping him calm. He was a very big man and I had to hold his hands because he was in a lot of pain. He has never forgotten me and always refers to it and offers me a drink.'

P&O – The American Market and Caribbean Cruises

In 1972 P&O launched a vessel that had originally been ordered by Norwegian Caribbean Line before they pulled out. This vessel was named *Spirit of London* (17,370 GT) and renamed *Sun Princess* after P&O had acquired the Canadian Company Princess Cruises in 1974. The aim at that time was to get into the American market for Caribbean cruises. Two other vessels were purchased in 1974 and they were the *Island Venture* and her sister ship, *Sea Venture*, bought from Flagship Cruises. They were renamed *Island Princess* (19,907 GT) and *Pacific Princess* (20,186 GT) respectively and became famous for their part in the 1970s sitcom *The Love Boat*.

Sea Princess (1), originally named *Kungsholm*, was built in 1966 by John Brown, Clydebank, essentially for the transatlantic service for the Swedish American Line. When launched she was 26,678 GT and was powered by diesel engines, giving a service speed of 21 knots. The *Kungsholm* was sold in 1975 to Norwegian Flagship Cruises and was ideal for cruising, with her two pools, a promenade deck that was both indoors and outdoors and a sheltered glass-covered sports area. The cabins were comfortable and air conditioned. In 1978 she was bought by P&O Cruises to replace the older *Arcadia*, which had been built in 1954 and was being taken out of service. Extensive conversion was undertaken at the Vulkan yard at Bremen, Germany, adding 86 cabins, extending decks, adding a third pool and extra public rooms, increasing the gross tonnage to 27,670. Of the two funnels, the forward dummy funnel was taken out and the aft funnel extended, mainly to avoid causing discomfort to passengers from smoke and dust particles dropping onto the rear passenger areas. She was renamed *Sea Princess*, joining Princess Cruises in early 1979, and by 1980 she and the *Canberra* and *Oriana* were the only cruising ships out of Southampton. In 1995 she was renamed *Victoria*, in keeping with the names of the UK Fleet, *Oriana* and *Aurora*. However, in 2002 she was replaced in the UK Fleet by *Ocean Princess*, who was renamed *Oceana*, and sails regularly out of Southampton today. The *Victoria* was then sold on and chartered by various shipping companies, and from 2008 she was sailing as the *Mona Lisa* (28,891 GT). However, as she does not comply with the 2010 SOLAS (Safety of Life at Sea) regulations that are coming into force, her future is uncertain.

It was the arrival of the new P&O *Oriana* in 1995, the first custom-built cruise ship for the British market, that created so much excitement in 'Maritime Southampton', and from then on increasing numbers of cruise ships have been visiting the Port of Southampton.

The *Pacific Princess* (20,186 GT) was built in 1971 and sold in 2002. She was renamed *Pacific*. (Ann Wright Collection)

Princess Cruises

Princess Cruises was formed by Stanley MacDonald in 1965 and its first ship was *Princess Patricia* (6,000 GT), which had previously been a ferryboat. The company was acquired by P&O in 1974 and by 1984 *Royal Princess* was the first purpose-built cruise ship to join the fleet. She was christened by the late Princess of Wales and was the first cruise ship to have all outside cabins, giving passengers a view of the sea.

When P&O Princess Cruises acquired the Sitmar Line in 1988, Sitmar *Fairwind* was renamed *Dawn Princess*, *Fairsea* became *Fair Princess* and *Fairsky* became *Sky Princess*.

In 1998 *Grand Princess* (109,000 GT) introduced the Princess Cruises Grand Class, and the same year *Sea Princess* (77,000 GT) of the Sun Class was in service. Both these cruise ships have sailed from Southampton, and *Grand Princess* still maintains a cruise service from the port today.

Cunard Builds its Cruising Fleet

In the early 1970s Cunard started building its cruise fleet, starting with the *Cunard Adventurer* (14,110 GT), and the *Cunard Ambassador* (14,110 GT) followed. Unfortunately, the Cunard *Ambassador* caught fire when she was on a positioning cruise and was declared a constructive total loss as a cruise ship. She was sold and converted to a livestock carrier. However, after a second fire the decision was made to have her scrapped.

Cunard continued with two more vessels entering the cruise market. They were the *Cunard Countess* (17,495 GT), which had her maiden voyage in 1976, and the *Cunard Princess* (17,495 GT), which had her maiden voyage a year later. The hulls of both ships were built by Burmeister Wain, Copenhagen, and then they were sailed to La Spezia, Italy, for fitting out. At the time Cunard said that *Cunard Princess* would be the last-ever cruise ship.

Before Commodore Ron Warwick was appointed relief command of *QE2* from 20 July 1990 to 1 October 1997 he had spent time in command of other Cunard vessels. From 16 August 1986 he was in command of the *Cunard Princess*, cruising in Alaska during the summer and the Caribbean and Central America in the winter. Later *Cunard Princess* served in the Gulf War in 1991 as a rest centre for US troops. The vessel was sold in 1995 to the Mediterranean Shipping Company (MSC) of Italy and is now named *Rhapsody*. On 30 January 1988 Commodore Warwick took command of *Cunard Countess*, operating from San Juan, Puerto Rico, and the Caribbean during her service with Cunard. By 1998 *Cunard Countess* had moved to Royal Olympic Cruises and been renamed *Olympic Countess*.

It was in 1994 that Cunard added the *Royal Viking Sun* (37,845 GT) to its fleet and one year later agreed with Crown Cruise Line to use three of their ships, *Crown Dynasty* (19,089 GT), *Crown Jewel* (19,089 GT) and *Crown Monarch* (19,089 GT). Commodore Warwick took command of *Crown Dynasty* on 9 December 1995, cruising Alaska in the summer and western Caribbean in the winter. *Crown Dynasty* had also been known as *Norwegian Dynasty* and *Crown Majesty*, but is perhaps better known today as the *Braemar* of the Fred. Olsen Cruises.

When Cunard bought the Norwegian American Line in 1983 they also took on the first purpose-built cruise ships, *Sagafjord* (20,147 GT) and *Vistafjord* (24,292 GT). Both these vessels are well known as the *Saga Rose* and the *Saga Ruby* (previously known as the Cunard *Caronia* (3)). However, *Saga Rose* has now been withdrawn from service. While under the Cunard flag they were very popular with the passengers and also were always given star ratings in cruise reviews. Both these vessels were sold to Saga, which caters for the 'over 50s' market, and maintain high standards of luxury and are very popular with experienced cruisers.

QE2-Concorde Partnership

The 1950–1960s was the time of great competition between the transatlantic ocean liner and jet aircraft, which caused the demise of many famous liners. However, in 1983 a partnership with air travel was created with a *QE2*-Concorde package, a joint agreement between British Airways and Cunard.

Although Concorde was used for flights to meet *QE2* while on her world tour in various parts of the world, it became the ultimate experience for transatlantic passengers to sail one way on the *QE2* and return on Concorde. However, in 2003 British Airways and Air France decided to take Concorde out of service, mainly because of the increased costs of maintenance and a fall in passenger numbers, and the partnership ceased.

Further Cruise Ships Added to the Fleet

When Cunard was acquired by the Carnival Corporation in 1998 both the two cruising yachts *Sea Goddess 1* (4,253 GT) and *Sea Goddess 2* (4,253 GT) were transferred to Seabourn, another company within Carnival that concentrated on the smaller ship luxury cruises. *Sea Goddess 1* was renamed *Seabourn Goddess 1* and *Sea Goddess 2* as *Seabourn Goddess 2*.

Royal Viking Sun was at first transferred to Seabourn and renamed *Seabourn Sun* but was then transferred to the Holland–America Line, also in the Carnival group, and was renamed *Prinsendam*.

Between 1994 and 1997 *Crown Monarch*, *Cunard Princess*, *Crown Jewel*, *Cunard Countess* and *Crown Dynasty* left the Cunard fleet, leaving Cunard with just two ships, the *QE2* and *Vistafjord*, which was to be renamed *Caronia* in 1999.

France becomes *Norway*

Just at the time that P&O took over the Canadian Princess Cruises in 1974, the French Line *France* (66,348 GT) sailed on her final voyage from New York to Le Havre via Southampton.

The *Norway* (76,049 GT) was originally called *France*. She was broken up in Alang, India, between 2006–07. (Richard de Jong Collection)

On 11 May 1960 the *France* (66,348 GT) was launched. She was 1035.2ft (315.5m) long with a beam of 110.9ft (33.8m) and had two funnels and one mast. Her engines were steam turbines powering four screws at a service speed of 30 knots. The *France* was built by Chantiers de l'Atlantique, St Nazaire, for the French Line (Compagnie Générale Transatlantique). There was accommodation for 500 first-class and 1,550 tourist-class passengers.

Originally the two wings on either side of the funnel were used to filter the exhausts from the engine room. However, this was later changed when the funnels were modified for the smoke to vent from the top instead of through the wings.

The *France* left Le Havre on her maiden voyage for Southampton and New York on 3 February 1962. However, later in 1962, the four-bladed propellers were replaced by five-bladed propellers, which increased the service speed.

Bill O'Brien remembers the *France* when she called at Southampton and tells the story about how one of the Southampton dockers finished up in New York instead of finishing his shift in the docks: 'There was a stevedore working the 5–9 shift on the SS *France* who became friendly with one of the passengers and was invited for a drink. During the time they were having their drink the ship had left its berth and had sailed down Southampton Water, and the first they knew that the ship was outward bound was when it was in the Solent. There was no possibility of the *France* turning back and the stevedore was arrested and had to sail all the way to New York. When the stevedore arrived back from New York to the Ocean Terminal on 43 Berth the superintendent said he would stop all his wages.'

Bill O'Brien, who had come ashore from his days at sea and was working in the docks, was also a shop steward: 'I was a bit of a militant shop steward and promptly told the superintendent that he could not do that as it was the responsibility of the foreman to see that all stevedores were off the ship before it sailed, and in this case that hadn't happened.' The stevedore did not lose his wages.

By July 1967 the *France* was sailing from Le Havre-Southampton-Quebec-New York for just three round voyages, and then in October 1971 she sailed from Bremen-Le Havre-Southampton-New York. On 5 September 1974 she sailed from New York-Southampton-Le Havre on her final voyage. The crew were not happy that the ship was being taken out of service and refused to enter Le Havre and anchored outside the port. On 10 October she finally sailed into Le Havre and was laid up in December 1974.

In June 1979 the *France* was purchased by the Klosters organisation and in August she finally left Le Havre for Bremerhaven. There she was converted from an ocean liner built for transatlantic travel to a cruise ship to be used in warmer climates by adding a new lido deck at her stern and two outdoor pools, and she became a one-class ship for the Norwegian Caribbean Line. Other work included removing the two outer propellers, which gave a service speed of 20 knots. After

The bridge on the *Norway*. (Richard de Jong Collection)

The engine room on the *Norway*. (Richard de Jong Collection)

The *Norway*'s stern. (Richard de Jong Collection)

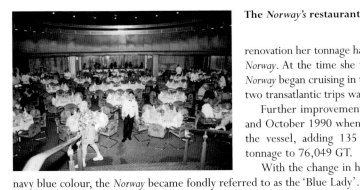

The *Norway's* restaurant. (Richard de Jong Collection)

renovation her tonnage had increased to 70,202 GT and she was renamed *Norway*. At the time she was the largest passenger ship in existence. The *Norway* began cruising in the Caribbean out of the Port of Miami and after two transatlantic trips was seen in Southampton in 1980 and 1984.

Further improvements were made to the *Norway* during September and October 1990 when two additional decks were added at the top of the vessel, adding 135 luxury cabins and suites and increasing her tonnage to 76,049 GT.

With the change in hull colour from the French Line black hull to a navy blue colour, the *Norway* became fondly referred to as the 'Blue Lady'.

1996 was also a memorable year because the Norwegian Cruise Line celebrated its 30-year anniversary with a transatlantic crossing of the *Norway* in August of that year.

The *Norway* departed from Miami on a 16-day cruise on 16 August 1997, heading for New York and then on to Halifax, Nova Scotia; St John's, Newfoundland; Cork, Ireland; and Southampton, England, with an overnight in Le Havre, France. This transatlantic crossing was sold out and as a result Norwegian Cruise Line planned two further transatlantic crossings in 1997.

Norway Visits Southampton in 1997

When the *Norway* arrived in Southampton in August 1997 David and Sharon Ellery and Richard de Jong visited the vessel to film for a future quality DVD. Richard de Jong: 'We managed to get a fair amount of footage of the inside of the vessel, including the bridge, engine rooms, restaurants, decks and captain's quarters, and were guided round the ship by a senior officer.

'Further footage was shot during a voyage from Southampton to Le Havre. However, I remember we were "right royally treated" during our stay on board and this included a lovely lunch in the superb Windward restaurant.'

The *Norway* left Le Havre on 1 September 1997 for her transatlantic crossing to New York, calling first at Southampton. From New York she was to return to Miami.

On 25 May 2003 a boiler room explosion occurred just after the *Norway* had docked in Miami at 5am. There was no injury to the passengers, but eight of the crew died, some of them later as a result of their injuries. It was later claimed that the explosion was an accident and the June cruises were cancelled. At the end of June the *Norway* left Miami, under tow for a transatlantic crossing, to be laid up at the Lloyd Werft yard in Bremerhaven, Germany, on 21 July 2003.

Norwegian Cruise Lines decided that the *Norway* would not return to cruising from Miami, but various options were considered and finally the *Norway* was towed to Port Klang, Malaysia, and then to Alang, India, where she arrived and beached in 2007 to be scrapped.

The Introduction of the 'Mega Cruise Ships'

From 1980 onwards there were a small number of cruise ships sailing in and out of Southampton, including Cunard, P&O and the Fred. Olsen Line, but over time there was to be a gradual introduction of cruise ships from other shipping lines.

It was in 1988 that Royal Caribbean introduced their first mega cruise ship, *Sovereign of the Seas* (73,192 GT). By today's standards she would only be considered a medium-size vessel, but she was the first ship ever to have an open atrium area. The second in the Sovereign class was the *Monarch of the Seas* (73,941 GT), which entered service in 1991, and she was followed by the *Majesty of the Seas* (73,941 GT), which entered service in 1992. However, in November 2008 *Sovereign of the Seas* was transferred to the Pullmantur fleet and renamed MS *Sovereign*. The next class of ships to be introduced by Royal Caribbean was the Vision Class. The first ship was the *Legend of the Seas*, which entered service in 1995.

When the P&O *Oriana* (69,000 GT) arrived at Southampton she was considered to be the first purpose-built mega cruise ship for the British cruise market. The *Oriana* was launched by Her Majesty The Queen and entered service in 1995. *Oriana* has been highly successful in the cruise market and is regularly seen sailing in and out of Southampton.

In 1998 Royal Caribbean International's *Vision of the Seas* was named in Southampton, and by 1999 Saga Shipping and Norwegian Cruise Line began cruising from the port. Festival Cruises' *Mistral* called in at Southampton on 27 June 1999 for travel agents and journalists to tour the vessel prior to leaving on her cruise season. The vessel was built for the European cruise market and her service started with her first cruise from Venice to the Greek Islands on 17 July 1999. She has eight hotel decks named after the European cities of Paris, Rome, London, Berlin, Brussels, Athens, Cannes and Madrid. She spent the next four months in the Mediterranean prior to spending the winter season in the Caribbean.

As the new Millennium approached a number of ships were launched in 1999, including the *Voyager of the Seas*, *Carnival Triumph* and *Disney Wonder*.

It was after her October delivery to Royal Caribbean International that the *Voyager of the Seas* called in at Southampton to be introduced to travel agents before sailing first to New York and then down to Miami for her naming ceremony.

Carnival Cruise Lines launched *Carnival Triumph*, one of their Triumph Class ships in 1999. *Carnival Triumph* had the theme of 'Great Cities of the World' and this was emphasised in the Paris Dining Room, the London Dining Room and the Rome Lounge. She operated from New Orleans to the Caribbean.

The *Oriana* (69,153 GT) was built in 1995 by J. Meyer, Papenburg. (Author's Collection)

Disney Wonder in Southampton

On 21 July 1999 the new *Disney Wonder* called in at Southampton while sailing from Fincantieri shipyard in Italy to America. Her restaurants keep the Disney tradition with Palo's, Triton's, Animator's Palate, and Parrot Cay. The pools are named Quiet Cove, Mickey's Pool and Goofy's Family Pool.

Disney Wonder left Southampton for the Art Deco-style Disney Cruise Line Terminal at Port Canaveral in Florida. The design of the terminal was inspired by Southampton's Ocean Terminal, built in the early 1950s for many of the world's great passenger ships when they called at Southampton. The Disney Cruise Line Terminal was opened in 1997 in readiness for the *Disney Magic* maiden voyage in July 1998. Both Disney vessels, *Disney Magic* and *Disney Wonder*, sail from there on cruises to the Caribbean and the Disney private island, Castaway Cay.

The author remembers *Disney Wonder* arriving in Southampton on her voyage from Italy to Port Canaveral, Florida: 'For those people who have had the experience of visiting the Walt Disney theme parks, there is always something magical for everyone, young and old, and I believe this would also apply to their ships. As she came into Southampton there was a bit of 'Disney magic' when the ships horn sounded the first seven notes of *When you wish upon a star*. However, for some of the Southampton marine pilots the magic soon disappeared because of the number of times they had to hear the tune!'

Cunard Sails into the New Millennium

In November 1999 it was announced that the Cunard Line would continue using Southampton as the home port for its flagship *Queen Elizabeth 2* and *Caronia* (formerly *Vistafjord*). This would increase Cunard calls to Southampton in 2000 to 23.

Vistafjord had been cruising for Cunard after they had taken over Norwegian America Cruises in 1983, but when the Carnival Corporation bought Cunard in 1998 it was decided that the *Vistafjord* would be sent to Germany for a refit. After her refit it was planned that she would be renamed *Caronia* as a tribute to the first voyage of the *Caronia* ('Green Goddess') 50 years before. It was in December 1999 that she was renamed in Liverpool. *Caronia* left Liverpool at midnight for Southampton and berthed behind the *QE2*, which had also just arrived from Germany after her refit.

On 18 December 1999 the new *Caronia* sailed from Southampton on the Caribbean Millennium voyage until 11 January 2000.

ABP Port of Southampton-UK Principal Cruise Port 1999

In December 1999 the ABP (Associated British Ports) Port of Southampton was considered the UK's principal cruise port after announcing a record growth in cruise bookings (up 37 per cent) and passenger turnover of over a quarter of a million. It was predicted that there would be 145 cruise ship calls in 2000.

One of the reasons the Port of Southampton had been chosen by many of the cruise lines was because it is close to Europe, has excellent road and rail links, and the international airport is nearby. Combined with deep waters, sheltered harbours and excellent port facilities, in all it makes the Port of Southampton an excellent choice for a growing cruise market.

Chapter 9

THE PORT OF SOUTHAMPTON IN THE NEW MILLENNIUM

The Old Docks and the New Docks

The two docks in the Port of Southampton are known as the Eastern Docks and the Western Docks. The Eastern Docks are also known as the 'Old Docks' because it was there that the foundation stone for Southampton Docks was laid in 1838 when the building of the docks began. The Western Docks are known as the 'New Docks' because they were completed in the early 1930s.

Family History of Working in the Docks

As we look at the work of Southampton Docks in the 21st century there are families that have a long history of working in the docks, and they have stories to tell.

Ron Hancock has worked in the Port of Southampton for almost 40 years and has seen the changes from ocean liner travel to cruising. Although he does not claim to be one of the oldest families that have worked in the port, he has been tracing his family history with another family member and can claim a long-standing relationship with the docks: 'We checked through the 1861 census and discovered that John Hancock, who was my great-great-great-grandfather, was a dock foreman. He was about 40 years old then, and possibly first joined the docks as a general labourer before becoming a foreman. However, it is my ultimate ambition to establish beyond doubt that someone from my family was working in the docks from day one. I'm not yet back to 1842 but not far off'.

The family history reveals that Ron Hancock's grandfather, Charles Luther Hancock, was born in 1895, and when he was old enough to go to sea he got a job on the White Star Line: 'He was actually on the *Olympic* when she sailed into the port on 30 March 1912. My grandfather was aged 17 and tried to transfer to the *Titanic* for her maiden voyage, but there was a long waiting list and he was not successful in gaining a place on the crew. However, he had been paid off from the *Olympic* and was ashore all the time the *Titanic* was in dock.

'History unfolded and the *Titanic* left and my grandfather never went back to sea again, but he survived World War One and when he returned he worked on the railway traffic side.

'My father, Charles William Hancock, was born in 1922 and he joined the docks in 1937 as a junior clerk. He became one of the first container port managers in 1968 when it became fully operational. I was very fortunate for the very good advice my dad gave me that has helped me in my work and stood me in good stead ever since.

'The only one of the family who actually went to sea was my great uncle, Robert, who was a master mariner for Union-Castle. However, in 1901 he had the experience of being a harbour commissioner, working for the harbour board.'

Ron Hancock's interest in the port and ships started early because he would spend most weekends in the docks: 'I might have only started work at the Port of Southampton in August 1971, but I have vivid memories of coming into the docks before that as a schoolboy with either my father or grandfather. I used to sit in the foreman's office and draw pictures of the big liners as they came in. I would see the *Queen Mary*, *Queen Elizabeth* and the *United States*, and I just took it for granted. When I went to school on the Monday morning they didn't believe that I had been on the *Queen Mary*.'

At that time you could enter the docks and look at the big ocean liners, and many people would fish from the quayside, something you cannot do today. As a young lad Ron Hancock was keen on canoeing, and some potentially dangerous antics took place near the liners: 'I used to canoe a lot on Southampton Water as a lad and one of our great games for this was cutting in behind a great liner and surfing the waves.

'It was a hive of industry, especially at the Union-Castle berths, but even at that tender age I could see that the writing was on the wall for ocean-going liners such as the *Queen Elizabeth*, *Queen Mary*, *United States* and much of the older P&O fleet. It seemed like the end of an era. At the same time I remember the *Canberra* coming into the port when I was about 10 and also the *Northern Star*. They seemed to be making the crossover into the cruising market, whereas the others were not.

'By the time I joined ABP the cruise market was beginning to open up, although the passengers still seemed to be regular ship-goers of the "old school", but within a few years it all seemed to change. Passengers stopped "going somewhere" in favour of "going on holiday" and shipowners seemed to be bowing to the inevitable, what with fuel hikes and mass air travel, and they were forced to broaden their customer base. Ships such as the *Canberra*, *Arcadia*, and *Oriana* had begun to cruise in the summer and voyage to Australia in the winter – the beginnings of the world cruise, perhaps.

'I have a clear memory of a change in marketing strategy during the late 1970s and early 1980s. P&O in particular seemed to tap into a wider market and attracted many first-time cruisers. The shift seemed quite subtle at first, but became more apparent as the '80s drew on. I recall the *Canberra* once leaving practically full of Welsh miners and their families, who had decided to spend their redundancy money on a "once-in-a-lifetime" cruise. Rumour had it at the time that the *Canberra* needed to restock their bars in Gibraltar!

'I think it would be fair to say that cruising from Southampton has become a much more serious business, with several new players entering the market place. Passenger fares have fallen in real terms as expectations have grown. Back in the late '70s and early '80s there always seemed to be more time. Even the *QE2* used to come into port in the afternoon and stay overnight, but now 12 hours alongside is the norm – even allowing for the increase in passenger throughput.

'Ironically, in the mid-to-late 1970s the Dock Company was closing old Passenger Waiting Halls such as 30 Berth, 46 Berth, 104 Berth and 107 Berth, just as the market was starting to pick up. The port now has four modern Cruise Terminals with a fifth under active consideration.

'One of my first jobs on operations was being in the passenger sheds and acting as an interface between passengers and their shipping company by helping and guiding them when they arrived. Today this job is big time with the "meet and greet" staff helping passengers at the cruise terminals.'

Increasing Numbers of Cruise Ships Visit the Port of Southampton

Cruising from Southampton had a big boost in May 2000 when four cruise ships called at the port in one day. They were Cunard's *Caronia*, P&O's *Oriana* and *Victoria,* and Phoenix Reisen's *Albatros.* In August the new Hapag-Lloyd's cruise ship, *Europa*, made her maiden call to the Port of Southampton.

There was a further boost when, on the first weekend in January 2002, six ocean liners with over 6,000 passengers arrived at Southampton and turned around in less than 72 hours. These ships were the *Aurora, Saga Rose* and *Black Prince* on the Friday, *Black Watch* and *Oriana* on the Saturday and the *Caronia* on the Sunday.

On 23 April 2006 five cruise ships berthed, the first time this had occurred in any UK port since 1966. They were Cunard's *Queen Mary 2* and *Queen Elizabeth 2*, P&O's *Oceana* and Saga Cruises' *Saga Rose* and *Saga Ruby.*

As the port became busier there were increasing numbers of cruise ship calls, and starting on 21 April 2007 26 cruise ships berthed in Southampton Docks, including *Navigator of the Seas, Oriana, Oceana, Aurora, Arcadia, Artemis, Saga Ruby, Saga Rose, Boudicca, Constellation* and *Sea Princess.*

Another busy weekend was the three-day period from Friday 31 August to Sunday 2 September 2007, when seven vessels of the Carnival fleet were in port. They were the Cunard *QE2* on the Friday, P&O Cruises' *Oceana and Oriana* and Princess Cruises' *Sea Princess* on the Saturday, and Princess Cruises *Grand Princess* and P&O Cruises *Arcadia* and *Aurora* on the Sunday. In total there were 28,319 passengers disembarking and embarking on the cruise ships during this period.

Holland–America Line's new 2,104-passenger cruise ship *Eurodam* sailed into Southampton for two days in June 2008 before she was formally named by Queen Beatrix of Holland on 1 July in Rotterdam.

The 2009 August bank holiday was very busy for the Port of Southampton when nine luxury liners sailed into the port. On the Saturday five ships arrived and they were Cunard's flagship, *Queen Mary 2,* Royal Caribbean's *Independence of the Seas,* P&O Cruises' *Oceana,* Princess Cruises' *Grand Princess* and Fred. Olsen Cruise Lines' *Black Watch.* On the Sunday there were P&O Cruises' *Aurora, Oriana* and *Ventura* and Cunard's *Queen Victoria.* Over 45,500 passengers disembarked and embarked during that weekend.

Other cruise ships that have sailed in and out of Southampton include *Ocean Majesty* (Majestic International Cruises), *Albatros* (Phoenix Reisen), *Millennium* (Celebrity Cruises), *Silver Shadow* (Silversea Cruises), *Constellation* (Celebrity Cruises), *Crystal Serenity* (Crystal Cruises), *Asuka* (Asuka Cruises), *Ocean Village 2* (Ocean Village Holiday), *Thomson Celebration* and *Thomson Spirit* (Thomson Cruises) and *AIDAaura* (Aida Cruises).

Awards for the Port of Southampton

Following on from 1999, when the ABP Port of Southampton was considered to be the UK's Principal Cruise Port, other awards were forthcoming. In 2002 the Port of Southampton won two further awards, Northern Europe's Most Efficient Terminal Operator and Northern Europe's Best Turnaround Port at the annual cruise conference, held in Miami. Another award was won in 2006 for Best Turnaround Port Operations.

In 2009 the Port of Southampton came runner-up in the Best Turnaround Port Operations at the award ceremony held in Hamburg, Germany. The winning port was Venice, Italy.

Carnival Group UK Home Port

Southampton is now the Carnival Group's UK home port. The Carnival Group includes Aida, P&O Cruises, Princess Cruises, Cunard, Carnival, Ocean Village, Costa, Seabourn and Holland–America Line. The new Carnival UK headquarters was officially opened in Southampton in June 2009. (Information courtesy of ABP Southampton.)

The Four Cruise Terminals of 2010

With the opening of the new Ocean Terminal in 2009 there are now four cruise terminals in the Port of Southampton. Two cruise terminals are in the Western Docks and they are the Mayflower Cruise Terminal at Berth 106 and the City Cruise Terminal at Berth 101, close to Mayflower Park. In the Eastern Docks there is the Queen Elizabeth II Cruise Terminal on

Southampton Docks today, pictured in 2009. The *Queen Mary 2* is in the foreground. (Courtesy of ABP Southampton)

Berths 38–39 and the new Ocean Terminal on Berths 46–47. The new Ocean Terminal is situated in the Ocean Dock opposite Berths 43–44, where the *Titanic* sailed from in April 1912 and where the Art Deco-style Southampton Ocean Terminal stood from its opening on 31 July 1950 by the Prime Minister the Rt Hon Clement Atlee MP until it was finally demolished in 1983.

The Cruise Terminals in the Western Docks
Mayflower Terminal

Work originally started on a new passenger terminal in 1959 at Berths 105 and 106 in Southampton Western Docks to serve the new P&O service to Australia.

The new terminal was officially opened by Field Marshall the Rt Hon Viscount Slim on 29 November 1960. There was a railway platform just outside the terminal where a boat-train service would operate to and from London for the arrival and departure from the docks.

It was announced in 2000 that major reconstruction would take place on the site of the existing Mayflower Cruise Terminal, which is P&O Cruises' home berth. The Mayflower Terminal project at Berth 106, costing £6.5 million, included a refurbished lounge area, new reception, check-in area and a baggage hall. Facilities for arrivals included a Customs Hall leading to the Arrivals Hall. It was

Mayflower Cruise Terminal in Western Docks (New Docks) at Berth 106. (Courtesy of ABP Southampton)

intended that the completion of the Mayflower Terminal was to be in time for the arrival of the P&O *Oceana* and *Adonia* for their naming ceremonies on 21 May 2003. The new ships would then join the remainder of the P&O fleet, *Aurora* and *Oriana*, in sailing from their home port of Southampton. However, the refurbishment also included the removal of the railway platform and is no longer is served by boat-trains from London.

Today the Mayflower Cruise Terminal at Berth 106 is home to P&O Cruises' fleet of ships that includes the *Artemis, Arcadia, Oceana, Oriana, Aurora, Ventura* and *Azura*. However, *Artemis* has now been sold by P&O Cruises to MS Artania Shipping. She will still sail under the P&O flag until her final cruise to the Mediterranean from 12 April 2011–26 April 2011, departing Southampton, when she leaves the fleet.

City Cruise Terminal, Western Docks

In November 2002 ABP announced that it was to provide a third cruise terminal at Berth 101, the Western Docks, adjacent to the Mayflower Park. It aimed to develop a terminal that would be capable of berthing the largest cruise ships in the world.

At a cost of £1.5 million, the new terminal was constructed on the site of the former Windward Terminal, the dedicated Geest Bananas terminal that was opened on Berth 101 in 1992. The banana import trade was eventually transferred to Portsmouth, and the opportunity arose for ABP to make good use of this facility.

On 14 August 2003 the City Cruise Terminal was officially opened by the Lord-Lieutenant of

City Cruise Terminal in Western Docks (New Docks), with *QM2* at Berth 101. (Courtesy of ABP Southampton)

Hampshire, Mrs Mary Fagan. By April 2005 further extension was completed on the terminal. This work included putting in more check-in desks, doubling the baggage hall area and increasing car parking space and coach bays.

The City Cruise Terminal had a further £9 million upgrade to accommodate the largest cruise ships of the day. This included a wider entrance lobby, enlarged reception, enhanced security facilities and increasing the check-in desks from 28 to 50. However, the City Cruise Terminal is different than the other three cruise terminals because passengers go through the x-ray screening first and then will be directed to check-in. At the other terminals check-in is undertaken before the x-ray screening.

The upgraded City Cruise Terminal was officially opened by Ms Susan Hooper, Senior VP (International) & Managing Director (EMEA), Royal Caribbean (International) and Celebrity Cruises on 27 April 2007, coinciding with the arrival of Royal Caribbean's *Navigator of the Seas*, which arrived at the terminal that morning and was based at Southampton during 2007.

The Cruise Terminals in the Eastern Docks
Queen Elizabeth II Terminal, Eastern Docks

The Queen Elizabeth II Cruise Terminal is situated at Berths 38–39 and replaced the old Art Deco-style Southampton Ocean Terminal on Berths 43 and 44 in the Ocean Dock. The Queen Elizabeth II Cruise Terminal was officially opened in 1966 by HM Queen Elizabeth II. It was principally built for the Cunard Line, although other shipping lines use it.

In 2003 the QEII Terminal had an extensive refurbishment programme carried out to provide an extra 50 per cent passenger capacity required for the new Cunard ocean liner, *Queen Mary 2*, when she started her regular sailings from the port in 2004. The work carried out included the construction of a new overhead gangway, refurbishment of the waiting lounge, enhanced baggage hall facilities and improvements to the embarkation lounge, which doubled the number of check-in desks.

On 3 October 2003 Pauline Prescott, wife of the Rt Hon John Prescott, opened the newly modernised Queen Elizabeth II Cruise Terminal.

QEII Ocean Terminal at Berth 38–39 with the *Queen Mary 2* (148,528 GT). (Courtesy of ABP Southampton)

New Ocean Terminal with the *Ventura* at Berth 46. (Courtesy of ABP Southampton)

The New Ocean Terminal

After ABP Southampton and Carnival UK signed a major 20-year contract on 7 December 2007 it was announced that a fourth cruise terminal was to be constructed in Ocean Dock at a cost of £19 million.

The new Ocean Terminal was designed to handle the largest cruise ships afloat and has been built on Berths 46–47 in the Ocean Dock. Ocean Terminal was officially opened on 29 May 2009 by David Dingle, Chief Executive of Carnival UK, and P&O Cruises' *Ventura* was the first cruise ship to sail from the terminal.

Cruise Ships Sailing Regularly from the Port of Southampton
P&O Cruises

P&O Cruises vessels sailing today from their home port of Southampton are the *Arcadia, Artemis, Aurora, Oceana, Oriana, Ventura* and *Azura*. When *Oriana* (69,000 GT) arrived at Southampton in 1995 she was considered to be the first purpose-built mega cruise ship for the British cruise market. The facilities include two restaurants, a casino, gym, theatre, three outside swimming pools, self-service laundry and eight cabins for disabled passengers. *Oriana* has been highly successful in the cruise market and is regularly seen sailing in and out of Southampton.

Aurora (76,000 GT) is a family-friendly ship with a wide range of facilities for all ages, including a gym, three swimming pools, health and fitness facilities, West End-style theatre, night club and casino, cinema, three dance floors, two

The *Arcadia* (83,781 GT) was completed in 2005 by Fincantieri at Monfalcone. (Author's Collection)

restaurants, pizzeria, patisserie, and children and teenage centres. Cruises include the Mediterranean, Canary Islands, the Baltic and the Caribbean.

Sea Princess and *Ocean Princess* were originally with Princess Cruises before they transferred to the P&O Cruises fleet in 2003. *Sea Princess* was delivered to Princess Cruises from the builders in Fincantieri, Italy, in 1998, and *Ocean Princess* joined the Princess Cruises fleet in 2000. After a refit *Ocean Princess* joined P&O Cruises as the *Oceana* and *Sea Princess* as the *Adonia* in the first-ever double naming ceremony. The vessels were named by HRH the Princess Royal and her daughter, Zara Phillips. However, the *Adonia* returned to Princess Cruises in 2005 and was given her original name of *Sea Princess*.

Oceana is a family ship and offers holidays for passengers of all ages to the Caribbean in the winter and to the Mediterranean, Norwegian Fjords and Atlantic Islands during the summer. She also offers a selection of week-long cruise breaks.

Arcadia (83,781 GT) is a child-free ship that gives passengers a spacious and flexible holiday environment and includes a three-tier theatre; a main restaurant that spans two decks; an extensive spa, which comprises a thermal suite and hydrotherapy pool; and a restaurant created by masterchef Gary Rhodes.

Arcadia was christened by Dame Kelly Holmes in a spectacular naming ceremony in Southampton in April 2005 and set sail on her maiden voyage on 14 April. During the winter the *Arcadia* travels the world visiting ports in the Mediterranean, Middle East, India, the Orient and Australia, and for the rest of the year she visits various cruise destinations across Europe and the Mediterranean.

Artemis (45,588 GT), previously named *Royal Princess*, was the first P&O Cruises purpose-built cruise ship and the first to have all outside cabins. She was christened by Diana, Princess of Wales, in Southampton in 1984. *Artemis* has sailed to most parts of the world, including the Mediterranean, Norwegian Fjords and up the River Amazon in South America. She is a child-free ship offering a traditional style of cruising.

In 2009 *Artemis* was sold to Artania Shipping and will be leaving the P&O fleet in April 2011. Her replacement will be the *Royal Princess* (30,277 GT), one of the smaller ships of Princess Cruises, and will be renamed *Adonia*. She will be the smallest cruise ship in the P&O fleet, carrying just 710 passengers, and will be based in the Mediterranean for fly-cruising from the UK. The size of the *Adonia* will enable her to visit ports of call not possible for the larger cruise ships. The *Adonia* will remain as a child-free ship.

Ventura (115,000 GT) sailed into her home port of Southampton for the very first time on 6 April 2008. Dame Helen Mirren became the ship's godmother and christened her on 16 April 2008. *Ventura's* 14-night maiden voyage departed from Southampton on 18 April 2008.

On board there are a wide range of interesting activities including a circus school; theatre; nightclub and casino; children's clubs for all ages, including Noddy and Mr Bump; a spa and hair and beauty salon; shops and a gymnasium.

Princess Cruises

Grand Princess (109,000 GT) is 951ft (289.9m) in length with a beam of 118ft (36m). She has 18 passenger decks and carries 2,600 passengers with a crew of 1,200. Built by Fincantieri, she entered service in 1998. *Grand Princess* regularly visits

The *Independence of the Seas* (154,417 GT) passing *Queen Mary 2* in Southampton Docks. (Richard de Jong Collection)

The *Independence of the Seas*' royal promenade. (Richard de Jong Collection)

The royal suite on the *Independence of the Seas*. (Richard de Jong Collection)

Southampton and is a popular family ship. One of her features is the 'Hearts and Minds', where couples can be married at sea by the ship's captain. *Crown Princess* (113,000 GT) is sailing with *Grand Princess* in the 2010 cruising season.

Royal Caribbean International Cruise Ships that Have Visited and Sail from Southampton

Royal Caribbean International cruise ships have been regular visitors to the Port of Southampton. These have included *Adventure of the Seas* (137,276 GT), *Legend of the Seas* (70,000 GT), *Jewel of the Seas* (90,090 GT), *Freedom of the Seas* (160,000 GT), *Navigator of the Seas* (138,000 GT), *Liberty of the Seas* (160,000 GT) and, since 2008, *Independence of the Seas* (160,000 GT) has been sailing from her home port of Southampton. From April 2010 Royal Caribbean International will be offering year-round cruises from Southampton on the *Independence of the Seas*.

It was in 2001 that *Adventure of the Seas* visited Southampton, the year she entered service. *Jewel of the Seas* was named in Southampton in May 2004 and left on her maiden voyage to the Baltic. On 29 April 2006 *Freedom of the Seas* arrived at Southampton and, with her tonnage, became the world's biggest cruise ship. Also in 2006 *Legend of the Seas* was sailing from Southampton for the summer cruise season. *Liberty of the Seas* entered service in 2007 and visited Southampton on 24 April that year, a memorable day for city as two of the world's largest cruise liners, *Queen Mary 2* and *Liberty of the Seas*, were in port, and it was also the day *Ocean Village 2* was named.

Independence of the Seas was built at the Aker Yards, Finland. She was named and based in Southampton from April 2008, sailing from Berth 101, City Cruise Terminal.

There are different kinds of cruises that passengers can choose from, which cater for different cruise markets. A potential passenger would need to consider what kind of holiday they want. There are the boutique ships which are for 50–200 passengers (1,000–5,000 GT), the small size ships that are for 200–600 passengers (5,000–25,000GT), the mid-size ships for 600–1,600 passengers (25,000–50,000 GT) and the large resort ships for over 1,600 passengers (50,000–220,000 GT). (Information from the Berlitz *Complete Guide to Cruising & Cruise Ships*, author Douglas Ward.)

Independence of the Seas is one of the large resort ships and is more of a Las Vegas 'glitzy' style of holiday. The cruises are for people who just want fun, sun and luxury living. The cruises to the Caribbean or other such holiday destinations enable people the opportunity of just relaxing; walking the Royal Promenade; going shopping; taking part in more physical exercises such as surfing, climbing, ice skating; or just watching a show or dining in the three-tiered dining room.

Public rooms include the Viking Crown Lounge, the Dog & Badger Pub, Boleros, Vintages, the Plaza main pool, solarium, library and the Skylight Wedding Chapel.

H$_2$O Zone on the *Independence of the Seas*. (Richard de Jong Collection)

Dining on the *Independence of the Seas*. (Richard de Jong Collection)

The *Independence of the Seas'* Skylight wedding chapel. (Richard de Jong Collection)

The *Black Prince* (9,499 GT) on her final cruise from
Southampton in October 2009. (Keith Mullard Collection)

Fred. Olsen Cruise Line

Fred. Olsen cruise ships have regularly sailed from Southampton as
well as other ports. The fleet consists of *Black Prince, Black Watch,
Balmoral, Boudicca* and *Braemar*. However, the *Black Prince* had her last
voyage with the company in 2009 and has been sold to a South
American shipping company.

Although established as ship owners from the middle of the 19th
century, gradually developing a trade in passenger/cargo routes,
Fred. Olsen entered the British cruise market in the 1960s with a
ferry-passenger service. They combined with the Bergen Line,
introducing the ferries *Black Prince* and *Black Watch*, sailing from Norway to the UK and also from the UK to the Canary
Islands, a route that had become very popular with the company. During the winter *Black Prince* and *Black Watch* operated
from London to the Canaries and in the summer they operated as the *Venus* and *Jupiter* for the Bergen Line on their summer
service across the North Sea.

The *Black Prince* was built in 1966 and the Bergen Line and Fred. Olsen Cruise Lines joined in joint ownership of it, an
agreement which lasted until 1986. The *Black Watch* was sold to the Norway Line, also in 1986.

Although the ferry service was well established from the UK to the Canary Islands, passengers were offered cruises as
well. This became very popular, and the company decided to refit the *Black Prince* as a full-time cruise ship and joined the
small number of cruise ships that were operating out of Southampton at the time.

Black Watch was built originally as the *Royal Viking Star* (22,000 GT), but when the Norwegian Cruise Line bought the
Royal Viking Line in 1984 she was renamed *Westward* in 1990. Then in 1994 she became the *Star Odyssey* of the Royal Cruise
Line, and she was finally bought by Fred. Olsen in 1995.

Balmoral was built as *Crown Odyssey*, but when operating for the Norwegian Cruise Lines she was known as the *Norwegian
Crown*. The present shipping line is Fred. Olsen Cruise Lines, who bought her in 2006 and lengthened her by fitting a new
centre section. She eventually entered service in 2008 as the largest vessel in the Fred. Olsen fleet.

Boudicca (28,338 GT), originally *Royal Viking Sky*, was first launched in 1973 and refitted in 2006.

The *Black Watch* (28,492 GT) arriving at Southampton Docks early in the morning. Built in 1972 as the *Royal Viking
Star*, she was renamed in 1990 as *Westward* and again in 1994 as *Star Odyssey*. In 1996 she was given her final name of
Black Watch. (Author's Collection)

Cunard's *Caronia* (24,492 GT), formerly *Vistafjord*, was built in 1973 by Swan Hunter, Wallsend on Tyne. In 2004 she was sold to Saga Cruises and renamed *Saga Ruby*. (Author's Collection)

Braemar was first purchased by Fred. Olsen as the *Crown Dynasty* from the Crown Cruise Line in 2001. She was renamed *Braemar* and sailed from Southampton. The vessel was lengthened for the 2008 season, adding 80 passenger cabins and suites with balconies.

Black Prince became a very popular choice for passengers and in October 2009 made her final cruise for Fred. Olsen before being sold to Venezuela.

Fred. Olsen cruise ships sailing from Southampton in 2010 are *Black Watch* and *Balmoral*.

Saga Cruise Line 2009

Saga Cruise Line sails regularly from Southampton and caters for the over 50s, sailing all over the world. The three ships are *Saga Ruby*, *Saga Rose* and *Saga Pearl II*. The advantage of the smaller cruise ships is that they can visit the ports that the larger cruise vessels cannot reach.

Saga Ruby (24,492 GT), previously called *Vistafjord* (1973) and *Caronia III* (1999), is 627ft (191.1m) in length with a beam of 82ft (24.9m) The vessel caters for 587 passengers, with a crew of 380, and has eight passenger decks. Although *Saga Ruby* is not a twin to *Saga Rose* they both sailed for the Norwegian American Line. After a three-month refit in Malta she joined Saga Cruises as *Saga Ruby* in 2005.

Saga Ruby at the Queen Elizabeth II Terminal. (Richard de Jong Collection)

Saga Pearl II (18,591 GT) was built in 1981 by Howaldtswerke-Deutsche Werft, Hamburg, as *Astor*. In 1995 she was renamed *Arkona* and then in 2002 she was renamed *Astoria*. In 2009 she was renamed *Saga Pearl II*. (Richard de Jong Collection)

The *Norwegian Jade* (93,558 GT) was completed in 2006 by Meyer, Papenburg, as *Pride of Hawaii*. She was renamed *Norwegian Jade* in 2008. (Keith Mullard Collection)

Saga Rose (24,474 GT), previously called *Gripsholm* and *Sagafjord,* is 619.6ft (188.8m) long with a beam of 80.3ft (24.5m). The engines are diesel. The vessel was originally built by Forges et Chantiers de la Mediteranée in 1965. There are 328 passenger cabins for 587–620 passengers. The ship carries a crew of 350. There are seven passenger decks. *Saga Rose* was retired in 2009 because she did not meet the new 2010 SOLAS regulations. She has been replaced by *Saga Pearl* II, originally built in 1981 in Germany and named *Astor*. She was renamed *Arkona* in 1985 and again renamed *Astoria* in 2002.

Norwegian Cruise Line 2009

With the arrival of Norwegian Cruise Line's (NCL) *Norwegian Jade* (93,502 GT) in Southampton on 30 May 2008 came the introduction of 'freestyle' cruising from the port. Freestyle cruising offered by NCL is aimed at giving the passenger more freedom in dining, fun and accommodation. The freedom in dining involves being able to choose whether to dress up or go casual; the freedom in fun gives the choice of being active or just relaxing; and the freedom of accommodation allows passengers different options, including being able to stay in the cabin on day of disembarkation instead of queueing up. However, *Norwegian Jade* will be relocating to Barcelona for the 2010 cruising season.

Another of the NCL cruise ships made a brief call at Southampton. This was the *Norwegian Pearl* (93,500 GT), which was built in 2006 and on 1 December 2006 called at Southampton from Rotterdam, departing again the next day on her maiden Atlantic crossing to Miami, her home port.

CHAPTER 10
THE CUNARD FLEET

The Cunard fleet sailing from their home port of Southampton in 2009 are *Queen Mary 2* and *Queen Victoria*. They will be joined by the new *Queen Elizabeth* in October 2010.

Queen Mary 2

Queen Mary 2 (148,528 GT) is 1,132ft (345m) in length with a beam of 135ft (41m) She has four diesel engines and two gas turbines propelling four pods of 21.5 MW each (two fixed and two azimuth – see below), powering the vessel at a maximum speed of 30 knots. *QM2* can carry 2,620 passengers and has a crew of 1,254. She has an extra thick steel hull for strength for Atlantic crossings and two stabilisers. She was built by ALSTOM Chantiers de l'Atlantique, France, at a cost of £550 million and entered service in 2004.

The Pod System

The Mermaid Pod System is used now on most new builds and consists of electrically-driven azimuth thrusters where the ship's propellers are in pods that stick down below the ship. The pods can be rotated 360° in any horizontal direction, making a rudder unnecessary. This allows the ship to have better manoeuvrability than with the fixed propeller and rudder system and also does away with the need for tugs, unless extreme weather conditions make tugs necessary for docking.

The system was developed by ABB, Kvaerner-Masa Yards, in the late 1980s, mainly for ice-breaking ships, but has resulted in replacing the rudder system on cruise ships. This gives the cruise ships the advantage of being able to dock on their own, especially in some of the ports of call.

QM2 has two fixed-pod outboard pods and two azimuth thrusters that can move and act as the rudder. This avoids the need for tugs for docking or turning, except where the wind speed is too strong for safe manoeuvring when in port.

Queen Victoria

It was on 7 December 2007 that the *Queen Victoria* arrived in Southampton and was named on 10 December by the Duchess of Cornwall, accompanied by the Prince of Wales. The next day *Queen Victoria* left on her maiden voyage around Northern Europe. Built by Fincantieri, she is 90,049 GT and 964ft (293.8m) in length with a beam of 106ft (32.3m). There are 12 passenger decks and she carries 2,014 passengers and a crew of 900.

The *Queen Mary 2* (148,528 GT) arriving at QEII Terminal early in the morning. (Author's Collection)

The *Queen Victoria* (90,049 GT) sailing from Southampton. She was completed in 2007 by Fincantieri, Monfalcone. (Richard de Jong Collection)

Stephen Payne: 'The *Queen Victoria* is based on a stretched Vista Class hull of the Holland–America Line. Doing this stretch for the *Queen Victoria* enabled them to incorporate several rooms that have been found a great success on the *Queen Mary 2*, such as the Queen's room, the ballroom and the like. The *Queen Elizabeth* has a few more cabins than the *Queen Victoria*, mostly because the price of the ship inflation increased and the aim was to get the cost per bed the same as the *Queen Victoria*.'

Queen Elizabeth

The third Cunard cruise ship is the *Queen Elizabeth*, arriving in October 2010. Although the Cunard Line was founded in 1839, the fleet today will consist of three vessels: *Queen Mary 2*, which entered service in 2004, *Queen Victoria* in 2007, and *Queen Elizabeth* in 2010, making the Cunard fleet one of the youngest fleets in the 21st century.

Queen Elizabeth is second-largest Cunard ship ever built and will maintain Cunard traditions, but will also have her own personality and style. She is the sister ship to the *Queen Victoria* and she is going to be decorated in a more Art Deco form than the Victorian decor of the *Queen Victoria*.

The 90th Anniversary of the Cunard Connection with the Port of Southampton

It was on 11 November 2008 that the *Queen Elizabeth 2* left Southampton for the last time and one year later, on 11 November 2009, there was a celebration at the Ocean Terminal and on board the *Queen Mary 2* to mark the 90th anniversary of the Cunard Line's connection with Southampton as their home port for their famous ocean liners. It was in 1919 that Cunard transferred its Express Transatlantic Service from Liverpool to Southampton.

APB Chief Executive Peter Jones and Port Director Doug Morrison invited Cunard's Chief Executive, David Dingle, and Shadow Secretary of State for Transport, Theresa Villiers MP, to join them to cut a special anniversary cake to mark the occasion.

Project Queen Mary

The aim of Project Queen Mary was to design and build the biggest passenger ocean liner ever, a liner that could cross the North Atlantic at speed in any weather. When in service the new *Queen Mary 2* was to operate the transatlantic crossings from Southampton to New York that had been the traditional route of the only other purpose-built ocean liner, *Queen Elizabeth 2*, since 1969.

In 1998 Cunard released details of Project Queen Mary and the first plans for the new liner were prepared. A number of well-known yards were invited to tender for the contract, including Harland & Wolff, Belfast, Fincantieri of Italy and Meyer Werft of Germany. It was ALSTOM Marine that was finally chosen to build the new *Queen Mary 2* at the Chantiers l'Atlantique shipyard, St Nazaire, France.

The contract was signed on 6 November 2000. Interestingly, this was the same yard that had built the *Normandie* and *France*, previous challengers to the Cunard ocean liners. However, the construction methods today contrast significantly with the earlier shipbuilding techniques, where ships were built from the keel up with the steel sheets of the hull and the superstructure riveted together with hot rivets by an army of workmen, and later, from approximately the 1940s, welding the steel sheets instead of riveting.

Modern shipbuilding uses a method called block construction, where prefabricated sections are built in advance in other areas in the yard. When needed, the blocks are taken to the building dock, where they are lifted into place and then welded to the hull and superstructure. In addition, sections such as electrical wiring and plumbing that in the past would have been fitted after the hull and superstructure had been completed are now preinstalled in the prefabricated sections, thus saving time and effort later.

On 16 January 2000 the first sheets of steel were cut and the building of the blocks began. Modern technology was used to cut sheets from computer-designed templates, which ensured precision cutting and shaping of each sheet.

The ceremony of the keel laying was held in St Nazaire, France, with the hull number G3 on 4 July 2002. Until then the first Master Designate of the new *Queen Mary 2* was a closely guarded secret. However, on the day, with the media present, it was announced that Captain Ron Warwick had been appointed Master Designate of the *Queen Mary 2* and the news was quickly reported to press and television worldwide.

The hull of the *Queen Mary 2* was constructed from 98 prefabricated blocks, which were lifted into position and welded together to complete the hull and superstructure. It was essential to ensure that the hull was strong enough to enable the vessel to plough through the roughest Atlantic conditions at speed, and it was necessary to use steel twice as thick as that used on cruise ships.

On 1 December 2002 *Queen Mary 2* was floated out and the work continued until the sea trials were conducted between 25–29 September, and the second sea trials from 7–11 November 2003, during which speeds of 30 knots were achieved.

Sadly, on 15 November 2003 a gangway collapsed while a number of shipyard workers and their families were crossing it on a visit to the ship. They fell 15m (49.21ft) down into the dry dock, killing 16 and injuring 32.

Construction was completed on schedule and *Queen Mary 2* was formally handed over to Cunard on 22 December 2003. The plan was for her to sail to Southampton, but Captain Warwick felt it was important to carry out trials with the ship's company and arranged to sail to Vigo, where they carried out a series of routines and tests. Christmas Day 2003 was spent at sea in the Bay of Biscay where Christmas dinner was served to the crew, enabling the hotel staff to practice food preparation and restaurant procedures. *Queen Mary 2* arrived in Southampton on 26 December on a dull and misty day. On arrival at Southampton Captain Warwick was promoted to Commodore.

Her Majesty Queen Elizabeth II named *Queen Mary 2* on 8 January 2004 and four days later she departed from Southampton on her maiden voyage to Fort Lauderdale, Florida.

The maiden westbound transatlantic crossing left Southampton for New York on 16 April, and on 25 April both *Queen Mary 2* and *Queen Elizabeth 2* sailed in tandem on an historic eastbound transatlantic voyage from New York to Southampton.

Queen Mary 2, with a gross tonnage of 148,528 GT, entered service in 2004 as the largest, longest, tallest and most expensive passenger ship in the world. She held this record for two years until Royal Caribbean International's *Freedom of the Seas* entered service in 2006 when, at 160,000 GT, she took over the honour of being the largest passenger ship ever built. However, although the gross tonnage of the *Freedom of the Seas* is greater, she is still 20ft (6.1m) shorter in length and 8.3ft (2.5m) narrower at the beam than the *Queen Mary 2*. Not only that, *Freedom of the Seas*, at 209ft (63.7m) in height, is shorter than the 237ft (72m) *Queen Mary 2*, and her cruising speed of 21.6 knots is 8.4 knots slower.

Queen Mary 2 was constructed for transatlantic travel in the summer months and for world cruises in the winter and, therefore, has been built with greater speed and a stronger hull for crossing the North Atlantic. To sail on the *Queen Mary 2* is to experience the Cunard tradition of elegance and luxury and to be able to relive the glory days of the 1920s and 1930s when royalty, famous film stars and politicians travelled transatlantic.

Stephen Payne OBE Senior Naval Architect for the Carnival Corporation
Chief Designer of the *Queen Mary 2*
Living a Dream

Walt Disney once said: 'It may be those who do most, dream most'. A young Stephen Payne realised his dream early when at the age of seven he said, 'When I grow up I am going to design and build a great ocean liner'. These were the words of a determined young boy whose passion for passenger ships was first ignited by visiting the *Queen Elizabeth 2* at Southampton in 1969 and by watching *Blue Peter* programmes. Today Stephen is living his dream as the designer of the greatest ocean liner of the 21st century, *Queen Mary 2*.

It was in December 2009 that the author interviewed Stephen Payne OBE RDI FREng at the Carnival UK centre in Southampton. He was very welcoming and his enthusiasm for his work and determination to succeed in his profession are truly inspirational; furthermore, he is keen to pass this on to the engineers of the future, especially for the pupils aged between nine and 16 at the junior age and secondary age who have the opportunity of visiting the *Queen Mary 2*. From my previous experience in education, especially with the junior age group, I know the value of catching and stimulating their interests at a young age. Children of junior age are far more forward-thinking about their future and future career interests than many people think.

Stephen Payne's Story

'My name is Stephen Payne and I became interested in passenger ships when I was seven years old. I remember coming home from school and switching on the television to watch *Blue Peter*. On one programme there was a feature with the presenters Valerie Singleton and Chris Searle crossing between Cherbourg and Southampton on the old ocean liner *Queen Elizabeth*. Although in those days we only had grainy black-and-white television, the sight of the *Queen Elizabeth* sailing captured my imagination, and I thought it would be fantastic to grow up to design and build ships like that.'

Two years later Stephen was on a family holiday at Bournemouth and felt very lucky that his parents took him on a coach trip to see the *Queen Elizabeth 2* berthed in Southampton Docks: 'There was a coach trip to Southampton Docks and in the port was the QE2, just one month into her

Stephen Payne with a model of *Queen Mary 2*. (Courtesy of Stephen Payne)

service. It was June 1969 and in those days (before the port security we have now) coach parties were allowed to look around the ships, and so with mum and dad and two of my brothers we toured the ship. My father took his Cine 8 film camera. He also filmed the *United States* coming into Southampton on one of her last trips. That was a tremendous day all round and, of course, it increased my interest in great ships.'

Stephen continued to watch *Blue Peter* programmes and remembers that in January 1972 a planned programme was interrupted to bring a live link to Hong Kong Harbour where the *Queen Elizabeth* was on fire: 'The *Queen Elizabeth* was being rebuilt as the university cruise ship, *Seawise University*, but was now on fire and sinking in the harbour. It was a sad fact that she was destroyed by arson.'

Later that year *Blue Peter* published their Christmas annual for 1972, and within the book there was an article featuring the *Queen Elizabeth*. It was this that stirred 12-year-old Stephen into action to write a letter of complaint: 'It stated in the last paragraph that it was a sad day for everybody who loves great ships and that the *Queen Elizabeth* was a superliner and nothing like her would ever be built again!

'It just so happened that in school in London we were learning how to write letters and my English teacher, Pat Boutle, said that the most important letter that you could learn to write was a letter of complaint. So we were asked to write letters for homework complaining about something. So I wrote off to *Blue Peter* complaining that their statement that the *Queen Elizabeth* would be the last great liner was going to be proven wrong, because when I grew up I intended to design and build such a ship.

'Of course, I received a letter back from *Blue Peter*, which I still have, saying that the presenters enjoyed reading my letter and that I should not be disappointed if it never happened. With the letter came a blue *Blue Peter* badge, which I must admit at the time I was very disappointed with because I thought I should have received a silver or gold badge for putting forward my ideas for such a wonderful new ship.'

It was many years later that Stephen finally did get his gold *Blue Peter* badge, at the naming ceremony of the *Queen Mary 2* in 2004. It is *Blue Peter's* highest award for individual achievement.

University, but the Burning Dream was still There!

Stephen: 'In 1978, when I finished my schooling, I was directed by my school to forget about becoming a naval architect because they said that engineering and shipbuilding was dead in the UK. They said I should pursue another one of my interests such as chemistry. As I was the first person in my family ever to go to university I obviously needed the advice of my school and various people to help me make such important decisions.

'I started at Imperial College in London reading chemistry for a year, and during that time I met my former physics teacher, Justin Johnson. He said to me, "You're making a very big mistake; because you are so interested in passenger shipping you should really try and follow that for your career. You will never be happy doing chemistry, even if you're good at it because you will always wonder what you could have done if you'd been a ship designer." With his help I was able to switch from chemistry to study ship science, which is naval architecture at Southampton University. I studied that between 1981 and 1984.'

'However, the studies were mainly theoretical and to gain first-hand experience of working on ships and shipping I joined the university's Royal Naval Unit, which was part of the Royal Naval Reserve based in Southampton Docks.'

After Graduation

'When I graduated I wrote off to various shipping companies and one was a consultancy in London called Technical Marine Planning Ltd. They had no immediate vacancies but I found a job with Marconi Radar in Chelmsford working on the specifications for new Royal Fleet Auxiliaries.

'After nine months Technical Marine Planning wrote back to say that they now had a vacancy for a young naval architect and that they were engaged in passenger ship building on behalf of Carnival Cruise Lines. So I left Marconi and joined Technical Marine Planning, which became absorbed into Carnival as the new ship building division in the mid-1990s.

'The first ships I worked on for Carnival were the *Holiday*, *Jubilee* and *Celebration*; subsequently I've had a part to play in all the follow-on ships since then. I've always been very conscious of the difference between a liner and a cruise ship because all the ships we were building for Carnival up until that time were purely cruise ships. The big difference, of course, between a liner and a cruise ship is that the liner has deeper draught, which is very good to sea-keeping in rough weather. The liner generally has a higher speed than the cruise ship, and for that she needs a much more pointed bow to cut through the water. It is because the liners are on tight schedules that they need more power to go faster and have to be driven hard in rough weather. To achieve this the liner needs a stronger hull and that means thicker plating and thicker beams, which we call scantlings.'

Appointed to Design a New Transatlantic Liner
'It was after being involved in the design of many cruise ships that I was actually sailing on board *QE2* in 1998 when word came through to the *QE2* that Cunard had been bought by Carnival and that there were plans afoot to design and build a new transatlantic liner, and that I was going to be appointed to design the ship.

'I remember coming back from that *QE2* trip and having first meetings with the Carnival management, Micky Arison and Howard Frank. It was not really clear at that moment in which direction the company wanted to go, whether or not to build a proper liner or to build a cheaper cruise ship that could be used mainly in the summer months on the Atlantic.'

Disney Magic
'At that time Disney had just built their first two ships, the *Disney Wonder* and the *Disney Magic*. From the outside, to the uninitiated, they looked like liners because they had long, black hulls with white superstructures and two red and black funnels. That was all part of the Disney theme in trying to make the ships look like liners. I had to explain to my management that they were definitely not liners, but just cruise ships in disguise, and if we operated such ships on the Atlantic and the Atlantic cut up rough, the ships would not fare very well. It would be very uncomfortable and if they were driven hard to keep to schedule it could be very dangerous.

'There was a lot of debate and a lot of consideration, looking at the price differential between a true liner and a cruise ship that looked like a liner. When you take into consideration the extra power, the extra speed, the extra strength and the shape of the liner, and the fact you cannot carry as many passengers on a liner as you can on the same size cruise ship, the liner price differential of 40 per cent is a very big price increase to convince the accountants that it is necessary if you want to do this crazy thing and build a true liner.

'In the end everybody agreed that we should do it and I was given the task first of all of designing a ship with a few colleagues from Carnival Shipbuilding office in London, which took us two years. Then there were negotiations with five shipyards to see whether it was possible to build such a ship that would be economical to run with a good return on investment.'

Problems to be Resolved
'The biggest problem I had was that the *Queen Elizabeth 2* was the last true liner built prior to the new ship. She had relatively few balcony cabins, but things had moved on since she was built and most passengers now demand balcony cabins. The problem to be solved was "How on earth do you put balcony cabins on a transatlantic liner which will sometimes have to go through very rough weather?"

'I really had to start from scratch. Something that helped me was the philosophy that I firmly believe in – that you can only move forward with any real chance of success if you have a real appreciation of what has been a success and failure in the past.

'Thankfully I am very keen on the historical aspect of passenger shipping and I have collected a library full of deck plans of all the old ships. I tried to analyse them to find out which arrangements within the general schemes could work on a new ship. I had a fair idea of the different features I wanted to duplicate – those from the *Normandie*, such as her split uptakes where the main passageways to the public rooms are on the centre line rather than on the side of the ship. And the breakwater at the bow, positioned in order to protect the superstructure from waves in rough weather. But most importantly a wrap-around promenade where the forward end was protected so that you could walk right around the ship as on *Rotterdam* (1959), something you couldn't do on the *QE2*.'

The Initial Design Process
'I started off with a blank sheet of paper and a pencil and drew a line representing around 350 metres in length and from that the whole ship really evolved. I didn't use a computer because I wasn't, and still am not, proficient enough for computer drafting. Of course, the big thing to do was to get the balcony cabins on the ship, and to do that they would have to be a certain height above the waterline. I got around that problem by deciding to bring the public rooms down from the top part of the ship, where they would have been traditionally positioned, and I relocated them immediately above the crew accommodation on the lower decks. I also decided to make the public room decks higher than normal for two reasons: firstly to enable the public rooms to have the grandeur of height – much more than you have on cruise ships. Instead of 3½ metres between the decks they are 4½ metres, giving an extra 1 metre (3½ feet) of height on the *Queen Mary 2*.

'This made the public rooms very special, but it also meant that there were two public room decks before the balcony cabins. That gave sufficient height above the waterline to protect the balcony cabins from the elements. As an additional safety measure the three balcony cabin decks that are in the hull have steel bulwarks and are integrated into the hull rather than being constructed of glass.

'Another interesting aspect was the positioning of the lifeboats. The latest rules and recommendations in SOLAS require that the boats have to be positioned low down on a cruise ship so they're easy to launch if the ship is heeling over.

'I was well aware that on occasions the lifeboats on the *QE2* had suffered damage, even though they were positioned relatively high up at nearly 100 feet above the waterline. I asked the British Coastguard Authority (MCA) their opinion and whether they would be happy for the lifeboats on the *Queen Mary 2* to be positioned at the same height as on the *QE2*. They agreed but said that the people I would have to get an agreement with would be the US Coastguards.

'I flew out to Washington to meet the head of the American Coastguards and explained the situation on the *QE2*, and I said that I wanted the lifeboats on the new ship in the same position. They told me that it was totally logical and that they had no objections. So the *Queen Mary 2* has her lifeboats as high as the *Queen Elizabeth 2*.'

Priorities to Concentrate On

'The most important priority was to provide the ship with a liner pyramid shape rather than a squared off cruise ship box shape. When you look at *Queen Mary 2* you see that she is pyramid-shaped and most of the weight is concentrated in the middle of the ship, and she also has a fairly long foredeck.

'There are two reasons for the long foredeck. The first one is that when water does go over the bow it's not going to damage anything because there is a fair distance before the main superstructure. Secondly, it means that there's not a weight concentration at the forward end of the ship so that when the ship is riding across the Atlantic waves and the ship bends and twists, she's not stressed too much because the weight is in the middle where the buoyancy can support it. If you have a lot of weight at each end, as waves travel along the length of the ship you can set up very high forces that in the end will cause fatigue and cracks, necessitating expensive ship repairs.'

The Building Begins

'The ship was built from 98 blocks, which were constructed in big sheds at the builders and placed in the building dock one by one. The yard started to put the blocks in the dock in July 2002 and by March 2003 the 98 blocks, weighing about 50,000 tons, were in the dock.

'The ship is powered by four diesel engines and two gas turbines. The original plan was to just have diesel engines within two large engine rooms, but the French Chantiers l'Atlantique yard, who were building the ship, suggested that by removing one of the diesel engine rooms it would give more space inside the ship, and because we did not need the uptakes it would make more room available for other machinery. They suggested that by having two gas turbines, which were relatively light, and placing them up behind the funnel they would be able to provide a lot of boost power for the fast transatlantic run when needed. The gas turbines are light enough that they don't affect the stability too much. We agreed to adopt that idea and with four diesel engines and two gas turbines the engines produce roughly 120 MW (which is more power than the whole of Southampton and the surrounding area requires). Of course, we only use part of that on normal transatlantic service. It's only when the weather gets really rough that all the power is needed for the ship to remain on schedule.'

The Pod System

'We have four Mermaid pods: two are fixed and two of them rotate and actually steer the ship as well as propel it. We had a lot of experience prior to *Queen Mary 2* with pods on various Carnival and Holland America Line ships. The *Queen Mary 2* is the first ship to have four pods, which are the largest pods built so far. They weigh about 320 tonnes each, which is the weight of a 747 jumbo jet on take off.

'The reason we used pods instead of propeller shafts with a supporting 'A' brackets is that shafts disturb the water before the water enters into the propeller. As a propeller rotates if it encounters water that is not steady the disturbance sets up vibrations in the propeller. The vibrations get transmitted to the ship and that's what makes a ship vibrate and be noisy. About seven per cent loss of efficiency results by having that disturbed water. With a pod the propeller is facing forward and the pods are behind the propeller. The propeller is actually encountering undisturbed water all the time, so you get improved efficiency and less noise and vibration.

'This is very important for the *Queen Mary 2* with the amount of power she needs when going at high speed. In total she has about 85 MW of power to actually drive the ship forward at 29.62 knots, which was a speed she achieved on trials.

'On a six-day crossing of the Atlantic the ship runs at around 25 knots. However, in future Cunard is going to start running seven-day transatlantic crossings in order to reduce the fuel bill. In those circumstances the ship will be running at about 21 to 22 knots, so she'll have a very big margin, which means she should never be late arriving at Southampton or New York.'

The Interior Design

The interior design architects usually have a fair amount of freedom on cruise ships to adapt the structure of the ship to suit their design ideas. However, with an ocean liner that could cause serious safety issues, Stephen was quite firm about any structural alterations requested by the interior design architects: 'I didn't have any direct input on the interior design of the ship apart from being asked my opinion. I gave the interior architects the volumetric space within the ship, many of the rooms running up through two, sometimes three decks. At 11 metres high from the deck to the top of the glass skylight, the Britannia restaurant runs up through three decks. I insisted that the interior architects could not delete any of the structure. This was not always popular but the structural integrity of the ship was paramount.

'It is usual on cruise ships for the interior architects to take great liberties, taking away pillars or moving beams and structure. On a cruise ship that is not going to be stressed too much by rough weather you can do that, but not on a liner that has to cross the Atlantic! So I was very firm with the architects; however, the rooms were big enough that they were able to do some fantastic design schemes and the structure did not impact too much. I must say I was very pleased with the outcome.'

The Bow and Stern

'The bow is actually modelled on the bow of the *QE2*, although it is considerably higher. The *QM2* is also wider than the *QE2* so it had to be adapted for the new dimensions, but the curves started off from the shape of the *QE2* and were adapted to suit. There is also the breakwater, which is like a snowplough and comes from the French Line *Normandie* of 1935.

'The stern of *Queen Mary 2* is very curious as well. Most great liners of the past had a cruiser stern, but it has been shown that they are not as efficient as the more modern transom-type stern. However, the big problem for a liner crossing the Atlantic in heavy seas is that the ship can pitch. If the ship has a large transom stern, as the stern comes up out of the water and then sinks down into it, which creates a tremendous amount of pressure underneath the hull and a lot of noise, and could lead to potential damage.

'A cruiser stern is nice and rounded. It will sink back into the water with a less devastating effect. I remembered in the 1960s that there were a number of Italian ships built with a combination of transom stern and cruiser stern (known as the Constanzi Stern). The Italian naval architect Constanzi designed that and I suggested to the French yard that we should do the same for the *Queen Mary 2*. We model tested it and found a compromise between the two designs which worked fairly well. We decided to adopt it on the ship. However, there has been some criticism that it doesn't look right on the *Queen Mary 2*, but in my opinion from many angles it looks as though she's got the cruiser stern, and we do gain a little bit of efficiency having the squared off bit at the bottom. Sea-keeping wise, it works well and there's not too much banging and thumping when the ship is pitching.'

When asked if he was proud of the *Queen Mary 2* Stephen relied, 'Yes, she's my baby.'

Future Engineers

From Stephen Payne's experiences, first as a young seven-year-old who became intensely interested in ships and shipping, and then as a 12-year-old writing to *Blue Peter* to complain that, contrary to what they said, ocean liners would still be built in the future, to designing and building a great ocean liner, naval architecture has been a rewarding profession.

Looking back it is amazing that his school should have advised Stephen not to become a naval architect as in their opinion engineering and ship building was dead and chemistry would be a better career choice. It all seemed to go against what he really wanted to do, but luckily he followed his young, forward-thinking teacher's advice to go for what he wanted to study in his heart. With his experiences so vivid in his mind Stephen Payne has aimed to show youngsters who are interested in a career in engineering that there are the opportunities for young people to take it up as a career. This is despite hearing from today's youth that they are still finding some teachers are trying to put them off their ambitions.

So what has Stephen done about this? With the support of Brian Ansell, a physics teacher who is keen on youngsters taking engineering as a future career, he set up Future Engineers to encourage youngsters to live their dream by arranging for 9–16-year-olds, with the support of Cunard, to visit *Queen Mary 2* and other engineering sites. The aim is to show them what captured his imagination on his visits to the *Queen Elizabeth 2* and the *Blue Peter* programmes. Maybe their visits will spark a bit of Disney magic and encourage them to dream their dreams, which may lead them to a fulfilling career in engineering in the future.

Commodore R.W. Warwick OBE FNI LLD MNM

At the age of 15 a young Ron Warwick was not sure what job he wanted to do, despite having a father who was at sea: 'I was one of those youngsters not sure what they wanted to do for a job. My father was at sea, and he used to come home and ask me what I would like to do when I left school and I never had an answer. In the end I told him I thought of going away to sea. He said it was not a bad job and that was it.

I was sent to HMS Conway, a college for preparing youngsters to go to sea, based in Anglesey, North Wales. I spent two years there and when I was 17 I had an apprenticeship with a company called Port Line, which was actually a subsidiary of Cunard Line, but the companies operated quite separately without the interchange of any personnel.

I served my apprenticeship there for three years and during that time visited many different countries. Port Line's main area of trade was Australia and New Zealand, but we would periodically call at ports in North America, South Africa and Japan. It was a very interesting apprenticeship and I remember the very first voyage I did. It took just over nine months, quite an amazing time to stay away from home for the first time.'

After leaving Port Line, Commodore Warwick spent a number of years sailing on different ships to gain experience, but it was his time on the RMS *Andes* as a junior officer that gave him a desire to concentrate on working on passenger ships. However, he was advised to obtain his Master's Certificate first.

Commodore Warwick then obtained a position as second mate on the *Jamaican Planter*, which was running from London to Jamaica. It was run by a Jamaican company, the Jamaican Banana Producer's Steamship Company. He remained with them for four and a half years and became chief officer on the *Jamaica Producer* and gained his master's ticket. Commodore Warwick: 'During that time in the 1960s they had started to build the *Queen Elizabeth 2*. I remember one day crossing the Atlantic to Jamaica when the radio officer came to the bridge while I was on watch and said that he had received a message in Morse code that my dad was to take over the new *QE2*. I went to the radio room and found that he had been appointed the Master Designate of the *QE2*, so that was quite exciting.

Commodore Ron Warwick. (Courtesy of Commodore Warwick)

'When the *QE2* went on trials, including a spell in the English Channel, I remember steaming along in the English Channel, outward bound to Jamaica in 1969 and the *QE2* was there. My dad knew I was around somewhere so the radio officers exchanged signals and we just maintained our course down the Channel when the *QE2* came along and turned round and steamed alongside us. We were all in only doing about 14 knots and it was very exciting to see a brand new ship go past at 30 knots.'

In April 1970 Commodore Warwick joined the *QE2* for a short time as junior officer to stand by while she was in port: 'I then joined the *Carmania* as fourth officer in 20 April 1970, which had just come back after having been in a serious accident in San Salvador when she ran aground, causing extensive damage to the hull. She had sailed back to Southampton without passengers and was going to Rotterdam for a refit. I sailed on the *Carmania* for about two years and then my father retired from Cunard and went ashore. I was then sent to the *QE2*. I joined as a second officer and then became first officer and was the navigator for the first world cruise in 1975.'

Commodore Warwick was chief officer on the *QE2* when she was requisitioned for the Falklands War in 1982. He then transferred to some of the Cunard smaller ships: 'I went to the *Cunard Adventurer* as chief officer then to the *Cunard Princess*, *Cunard Countess* and *Crown Dynasty*. At the end of the year I was given permanent command, moving between the *Cunard Princess*, *Cunard Countess* and *Crown Dynasty*. The *Cunard Princess* was located in the Caribbean and Central America in the winter and Alaska in the summer, and the *Cunard Countess* operated in the Caribbean. *Crown Dynasty* was also operating in Alaska in the summer and the Caribbean in the winter. I really enjoyed working on these different ships and stayed with them for quite a few years.'

It was in July 1990 that Commodore Warwick was appointed to the relief command of the *QE2* and was captain during the visit of Her Majesty Queen Elizabeth II and His Royal Highness the Duke of Edinburgh on the occasion of Cunard Line's 150th anniversary celebrations at Spithead. Commodore Warwick remained in relief command until 1 October 1997. His command of the *QE2* made Cunard history by commanding the same ship as his father, the late Commodore William E. Warwick CBE RD RNR.

In June 1996 Commodore Warwick was appointed to the new position of marine superintendent of the Cunard Line fleet: 'I didn't really want to stay ashore but agreed to the position. I did it for a year then handed over to one of the other captains. I went back to sea on the *QE2* as a senior master right through to 2003.'

Queen Mary 2

Commodore Warwick: 'In 1998 Carnival Corporation took Cunard over with the aim to develop the company, which appears to be what is happening in the industry all the time now.

'I was approached and told that they were going to build a new ship and was asked to delay my retirement to be the first master. I was retiring in 2001 and getting prepared for that emotionally, so it was quite a decision. However, it took me about half a microsecond to accept the position!'

The news that Commodore Warwick was to be appointed as Master Designate was kept secret and was not announced until the keel-laying ceremony on 4 July 2002. Commodore Warwick left the *QE2* and was invited to the keel-laying ceremony: 'A representative of the shipbuilders made a speech and Pamela Conover, Cunard's president, was asked to make a speech and perform the keel-laying. For this she would have a microphone and tell the crane driver to lift the keel into place. However, she felt that it was appropriate that the Master Designate of the *QM2* did it and handed the microphone to

The *Queen Mary 2* has 'beautiful wide walkways with high ceilings'. (Author's Collection)

me. That was how the official announcement came out because there were many press people there. That was a very proud moment in my life to do that.'

Commodore Warwick moved out to France and lived there while the ship was being built: 'My staff captain, Chris Wells, was already there by the time I got there, as was the chief engineer and the chief electrician. The shipyard people would come along and would talk about any necessary adjustments. Everything had to be checked, the systems, watertight doors, everything had to be approved and signed off. The staff captain and chief officer were moving around all the time, undertaking surveys and checking things off, but I was in overall charge of everything.

'I had to do a tremendous amount of PR work, but one of the most important things from my perspective was to train all my officers and myself, indeed, in understanding the new technology. There were a lot of things that we were not familiar with, the pod engines, control monitoring systems and electronic charts and so on.

'More engineers arrived, as did the hotel personnel, and the crew members had to be trained for familiarisation with the ship safety training and crowd control training. We had to do that as best as we could. Six weeks before the ship was handed over we had every crew member accommodated in holiday camps in the region that were closed for the winter.

'My own bridge team had to ensure that we really understood the control systems on the vessel. We had technical documents on the modern technology systems on board, especially the new pod propulsion, and needed to know if the ship would behave in the way it was predicted to do.

'To do this the whole team, including junior and senior offices, went over to Florida, where a simulator had been set up with the profile of the ship. We practiced docking, undocking, and importantly with all the new systems we needed to establish procedures, such as designated people who would be in charge of switching over when you went from one side of the bridge to the other, and what buttons to press in an emergency.

'We practiced control for the bridge to the engine room and vice versa. We had a consultant whose job was to draw up the manual of the bridge procedures and of the thousands of buttons and what they did.

'Back in France meetings were held in the dockyard when representatives from Miami and Cunard were present. Towards the end of the completion we went out on trials, including speed trials, when the ship performed extremely well.'

There were two trials, one between 25–29 September 2003 and another between 7–11 November 2003, and during these trials Commodore Warwick was an observer. It was 22 December 2003 when Commodore Warwick took over command of the *Queen Mary 2*: 'The moment we took over the ship the shipping company flag was taken down and the Cunard flag raised, and we sailed within the hour. The company said they wanted the ship to go directly to Southampton on 23 December 2003, but I wasn't too keen so I went over to Miami and made the case for having the ship to ourselves for a few days. They agreed and I contacted the harbour master of Vigo about using the port for further trials.

'We sailed across the Bay of Biscay to Vigo just before Christmas. The weather was brilliant and Vigo was an ideal harbour with deep water. There was only the crew on board and we practised docking the ship. We went in and rehearsed docking and practised tying up. The gangway went down and was immediately taken back up, and we went back out again and then did it in reverse on the other side. I had control but handed over to the captain who was going to be my relief and he also practised

The seven-metre bronze relief by John McKennain in the grand lobby of the *Queen Mary 2*. Ann and Chris Wright know John McKenna and saw the relief being made in his studio in Ayrshire, Scotland. Another John McKenna relief can be seen in the grand lobby of the *Queen Victoria*. (Ann Wright Collection)

the manoeuvres. We took the ship into the centre of the harbour and launched the lifeboats, and practised with the bow thrusters and various other routines, including anchors, boat drills and emergency drills.

'We set off for Southampton on Christmas Day and while sailing in the Bay of Biscay the hotel manager and chef agreed to serve Christmas dinner in the main restaurant to all the crew so that the kitchen and waiters could practise giving full service.

'We arrived in Southampton on Boxing Day, took the ship right up to the far end of the docks and turned around just to show the flag. It was very blustery and we had tugs in attendance just in case, but the ship behaved extremely well. If you can dock a great ship like that without tugs it is incredible. The ship was beyond all our expectations. The technology on the ship is just overwhelming, not the slightest hiccup or anything.

'After we had tied up Micky Arison and Pamela Conover were on the dock to meet us, and after I had got down to the dockside my promotion to Commodore was announced.

'The ship was stored up and we commenced the shakedown cruises and spent three days cruising around different parts of the English Channel. The crew were given the opportunity to invite friends or family for the shakedown cruises.'

The naming ceremony

'The monarch had agreed to name the ship. Cunard are noted for their meticulous planning and so is Buckingham Palace, so we spent quite a bit of time practising the route the Queen would take. The Duke of Edinburgh would go on a different route to see more of the technology and engine room. It was all well planned and went extremely well.

'I greeted the Queen at the top of the gangway and escorted her around throughout the time on board. The monarch was very generous with her time and the time she gave to the crew members, talking to them. It was a very special moment for the whole staff.

'We went ashore for the naming ceremony, for which a large marquee had been erected on the dockside with an enormous curtain. When the time came for the Queen to name the ship the curtain just opened and there was the bow of the ship with a piper on the foredeck. The whole naming ceremony, including the fireworks, was excellent and great credit must be given to the vision of the person who planned it all.

The Queen's Room on the *QM2*. (Author's Collection)

Britannia restaurant on the *Queen Mary 2*. (Ann Wright Collection)

Pictures of past famous passengers on the 'Queens'. (Author's Collection)

The Winter Gardens on the QM2. (Ann Wright Collection)

'There was a very exciting maiden voyage that called at Madeira, Las Palmas and across the Atlantic to Miami and then up to Fort Lauderdale.

'The actual maiden transatlantic crossing from Southampton to New York was for me, personally, an anti-climax. The one my father did with the QE2 was quite different. I have black-and-white photographs of the maiden cruise of the QE2 to New York and the water was alive with boats while the QE2 was going into New York. It would have been a spectacular occasion.

'I decided that the transatlantic crossing was what the ship was all about and both my children and their spouses came on board. When we arrived in New York we arrived early in the morning, but the coastguards kept all the small boats away and we had tied up by 7am. The Mayor of New York was on the dockside and it was a nice welcome. A couple of days later the QE2 came in and as I have a great affinity for that ship I went to the top deck above the bridge, but could not believe my eyes when I saw her. She was so tiny in comparison to the QM2. We came back in tandem from New York to Southampton.'

A further memorable but proud moment for Commodore Warwick was when his granddaughter, Elizabeth, was christened

in the Atlantic Room on board *Queen Mary 2* on 23 April 2006. There were also two very proud parents, Sam and Hilary Warwick, as not only was their daughter Elizabeth being christened, it was also the first christening service to be held on *Queen Mary 2*. The service was conducted by the Revd Andrew Huckett of the Mission to Seafarers, Southampton, with the ship's bell being used as the christening font.

Elizabeth Warwick was the first child to be christened on the QM2. From left to right: Kim Warwick (the Commodore's wife), Sam Warwick, Revd Andrew Huckett, Commodore Ron Warwick, Hilary Warwick holding Elizabeth Warwick. (Courtesy of Sam and Hilary Warwick)

Boat Trains from Southampton Docks

When the *Queen Elizabeth 2* escorted the new *Queen Mary 2* in tandem back from New York, arriving on 1 May 2004 at Southampton, VSOE provided a special Pullman boat train to take passengers from both vessels back to London. However, the VSOE British Pullman service ceased operations with its final train from London to Southampton Docks in October 2007 for the *Queen Mary 2*.

Before World War Two there were the 'Ocean Liner Specials' that brought passengers from London to Southampton Docks to meet the transatlantic liners arriving from New York. Once the passengers from New York had disembarked they would board the boat train for London, and the passengers that had arrived on the boat train would then embark for their transatlantic crossing to New York.

It was in July 1952 that the first post-war boat train service left Southampton Docks for London, and by then the boat trains had started to have different names. Perhaps the most famous was the *The Cunarder* that met the *Queen Mary*

and *Queen Elizabeth*. The Queen Elizabeth II Terminal at Berths 38–39 had a full-length platform and passengers could disembark from the liner and immediately board the boat train for London. These trains were part of the Luxury Pullman Ocean Liner Express boat train service, and as well as *The Cunarder* there was *The Statesman* that met the *United States* from New York.

A Holland America boat train, 34025 Whimple West Country Class, en route to Waterloo in summer 1965. (Richard de Jong Collection)

The *Orient Express*, seen at the Queen Elizabeth II Terminal on 30 April 2010, was hauled by the diesel locomotive *Royal Diamond*, not by a steam engine. The *Orient Express* left Victoria at 09.44 and arrived at Southampton Eastern Docks at 13.18. The return journey left Southampton Eastern Docks at 17.20 and arrived at Victoria at 20.43. (Author's Collection)

There was also the Ocean Liner Express service for the Holland America Line and the Greek Line transatlantic services. Other shipping companies had the express service too, including Royal Mail Line's South American service, Union-Castle Line's South African service, and Sitmar's Australian service. The *Oriana* and *Canberra* had an Ocean Liner Express service for their Australian service.

By the end of the 1960s both the *Queen Mary* and *Queen Elizabeth* had ceased the transatlantic service, but the VSOE (Venice Simplon Orient Express) British Pullman boat train service began operating for the *QE2* and later for the *QM2*.

VSOE (Venice Simplon Orient Express)

In February 2000 the famous locomotive the *Flying Scotsman* arrived in Southampton Docks hauling the world's most famous train, the *Orient Express*. At the time the *Flying Scotsman* was making over 25 calls to the port each year and trains were provided for special occasions. For example, the VSOE would take passengers to Southampton before beginning their voyage on vessels leaving the port. On the journey a champagne lunch

The locomotive was named by Her Majesty the Queen and His Royal Highness the Duke of Edinburgh at Rugeley station on 12 October 2007 in celebration of their diamond wedding anniversary. (Author's Collection)

Sir Lamiel pulling a boat train into QEII Terminal platform. (Richard de Jong Collection)

B4 Normandy pulling a boat train. (Richard de Jong Collection)

is served so passengers can really feel that their holiday has started even before they board their ship.

Queen Elizabeth II Terminal with *QE2*

The photographs of the Adams B4 Tank Engine at the Queen Elizabeth II terminal show the *QE2* in the background and the SR King Arthur Class 777 *Sir Lamiel* preparing to collect passengers for the boat train to London.

Adams B4 Tank Engines

When L&SWR (London & South Western Railway) took over Southampton Docks in 1892 it was not long before the Adams B4 tank engines were working in the docks. However, the B4s were scrapped in 1948 and replaced by American tank engines that had been used in the docks during the war. The Adams B4 0–4–0T No. 96 *Normandy* is owned by the B4 Loco Group, part of the Bulleid Society, and can be seen at the Bluebell Railway.

King Arthur Class *Sir Lamiel* at Southampton Docks. (Richard de Jong Collection)

Southern Railway King Arthur Class

Sir Lamiel was built in Glasgow in 1923 and was a L&SWR N15 Class 4–6–0 express passenger steam locomotive, designed by Robert Urie. When L&SWR became part of Southern Railway in 1923 the locomotives were then known as the 'King Arthur Class' and worked as express trains to the South Coast ports. *Sir Lamiel* had the Southern Railway number 777 and later the British Railway's number 30777. The locomotive was withdrawn in 1961 and is now part of the National Railway Museum Collection, York.

Pullman **train at QEII Terminal on 30 April 2010. (Author's Collection)**

35005 Canadian Pacific-Merchant Navy Class-Ropley in September 1995. (Richard de Jong Collection)

CHAPTER 11
CRUISING AND CRUISE SHIPS TODAY

Douglas Ward, author of the Berlitz *Complete Guide to Cruising & Cruise Ships*, talks about how he became interested in ocean liners and cruise ships and what led him to become the foremost authority on cruising and cruise ships in the world today.

Douglas's first experience at sea in 1965 was as a bandleader. After many years he ended up as a cruise director for the Cunard Line. He moved to Philadelphia in 1979 with a deep interest in ocean liners and cruise ships and wanted to find out more about the industry. He studied all aspects of the passenger/cruise industry, including safety codes, shipbuilding and onboard services, with the aim of creating a system of ratings to evaluate the standards on board passenger ships. He is today president of the Maritime Evaluations Group and spends much of each year travelling on cruise ships, evaluating standards and awarding ratings for the annual edition of the Berlitz *Complete Guide to Cruising and Cruise Ships*.

Douglas Ward: 'I started on the RMS *Queen Elizabeth* and RMS *Queen Mary* as a bandleader working in first class from July 1965, and this was my first acquaintance with Southampton Docks. After I had left the music side I became a tour manager then cruise director for Cunard, and at that time we had just three ships, the *QE2*, *Cunard Princess* and *Cunard Countess*. I did all of the maiden voyages on the *QE2* in her first year and spent about four years on her for transatlantic and world voyages. I was at sea for about 17 years, and as well as Cunard I also worked for seven other shipping lines including Union-Castle, Shaw Savill, Royal Mail and Fred. Olsen Cruise Lines.

'When I first went to sea I fell in love with ships and started to learn about how they were designed and constructed. I became fascinated by the transatlantic liners and when we were in New York I would visit other liners in the docks at the same time. As we had two and half days off in New York I had plenty of time to do that. It gave me the chance to look at vessels such as the *United States*, *Michelangelo* and *Raffaello* and other ships from well-known shipping lines.

'The International Association of Cruise Passengers was formed after I had finished work one night when we were crossing the Atlantic. I joined a group of passengers at 2am who were very fascinating, well-to-do and really interested in ships. After a long discussion in which I shared my deep interest in ships we decided to get together to form an association.

'I moved to America in 1979 and was living near Philadelphia. The International Association of Cruise Passengers was registered and it grew until we eventually had about 5,000 members. I was writing newsletters and cruise reports comparing the ships of the time for the association members, who loved being kept up to date about what was happening in the growing cruise industry. The magazine, called *Porthole*, grew in size and we eventually had to take advertising, but after about 20 years the International Association of Cruise Passengers was disbanded because it was too expensive to keep running. *Porthole* was sold and is still published in America today.

'In 1982 the managing director of Berlitz language books contacted me having seen a rating report which I compiled for all the members of the association. At the time I was not interested and declined the offer. However, he persisted in contacting me and after a further four telephone calls I eventually agreed to write a book and so the Berlitz *Complete Guide to Cruising and Cruise Ships* was born.

'The first book was finished in 1984, published in 1985, and has been going ever since. During that time we have established criteria for professionally rating and evaluating passenger ships and cruise ships, and the rating system is now accepted worldwide. It is a very extensive system. And we are now in the 25th anniversary edition in 2010 and hopefully will continue.

'My Berlitz *Complete Guide to Cruising and Cruise Ships* book has no sponsorship, no advertising and no connection with any cruise line. That is why we can undertake totally objective ratings and evaluations, which is very rare because very many travel guide books are supported by advertisers.

'We are totally self-sufficient, which is an enviable position to be in. It has

Douglas Ward looking out on to Southampton Water. (Photo Credit: Ayako Ward)

earned me respect and authority within the cruise industry and it is very useful for me to get around and see people and talk behind the scenes and make corrections. I do make recommendations and these are acted upon, and we actually keep the standards up. That is what people see as my role in the cruise industry, setting the standards and keeping them.'

The cruise vessels are judged by an evaluation tool that works on a system of ratings based on 400 individual items. These are assessed by Douglas Ward and his small team of testers, who join cruises and evaluate the standards on board. Each area has a maximum of 100 points and these are recorded in 20 major areas, giving a maximum of 2,000 points. There are five main sections: Ship, Accommodation, Food, Service and Cruise Operation.

Douglas Ward: 'I keep up with all current regulations and my ratings have to be accurate and objective. I talk to the lines regularly and I also send them private reports after I've been aboard a cruise just to let them know which items need attention.

'I sail aboard the cruise ships along with my team of testers, who report back to me, but I am the only one allowed to score each vessel. When we visit the cruise ships we look at the maintenance of the vessel, cleanliness of accommodation, service and hospitality, cuisine, entertainment and cruise experience. This includes noise level on board, such as insulation between cabins, which on some of the new ships could be better.'

'It is as detailed as whether there is a doily between a cup and saucer to reduce the noise of the cup clicking into the saucer, and whether the doilies are paper or linen. On some cruise ships passengers get plastic coffee cups with wooden stirrers, but on others there are china cups with silver teaspoons provided. There is also the matter of hygiene, and an example is where sugar tongs are provided to pick up sugar cubes from the bowl instead of picking them up with the fingers to stop the transmission of any infection.

'There has been a lot of publicity about norovirus on cruise ships, and one of the reasons is that health officials track illness on cruise ships and when outbreaks are found they are reported more quickly than on land. People can become infected with the virus by eating food, drinking liquids, touching surfaces or objects that have been infected by the virus and person to person contact, such as shaking hands and not washing hands after using the bathroom before preparing food. This is not a reporting requirement for airlines or even hospitals, and that is why cruise ships have been reported so much in the media.'

Today as passengers arrive to check-in they are required to sign a health form stating whether or not they have been ill prior to arriving at the cruise terminal. If there is any doubt the medical officer from the cruise ship will make the decision on whether or not the passenger may board.

The overall rating of a cruise ship is displayed within a star system, with five stars being the highest rating and one star the lowest. On a ship rated at five stars the passenger can expect outstanding luxury, but one star is a cruise experience that perhaps most potential passengers would like to avoid.

Douglas Ward: 'I am very seldom on land and am now spending up to 200 days at sea, which includes approximately 50 to 60 international flights a year. The aim of the Berlitz *Complete Guide to Cruising and Cruise Ships* is to keep people informed about cruising and cruise ships, and the book is updated annually and always eagerly anticipated.'

Where are we today?

'In the last 25 years cruising has changed and so have the needs of passengers. Luxury cruising in the past was aimed at the very rich, but today we see passengers from all kinds of social and economic backgrounds. Travel agents now provide low-cost package holidays for families and children especially, but there are also premium and luxury markets where people are demanding the best surroundings and food.

'The cruise industry carries approximately two million children a year which is amazing. We have specialized companies like Disney Cruise Lines with their own ships, and they are amazingly successful with such a good product on board and do a fantastic job with the kids.

'The cruise industry also caters for passengers who may be retired and can take longer cruises, and I also see the market for the short-term cruises for families and others who don't have a lot of time. Then there are the child-free ships and the Spanish, German and Japanese language ships and other niche markets. There are a lot of niche markets that the big operators do not really want to be involved in.

'When thinking about cruising, many people just have the 'resort' cruise ships in mind, but there are other types of ships that may be better choice for some than for others, depending on what kind of holiday they are seeking. There are specialist expedition/nature ships, sailing ship cruises, coastal cruises, river cruises and voyages on cargo ships, which are often very comfortable and call at some interesting ports not frequented by cruise ships.

'One thing that has become more and more popular is couples spending their honeymoon on board a cruise ship. Alternatively they have cruise ships that can officiate a wedding ceremony and they can then have their wedding and honeymoon while on the cruise of a lifetime. Arranging a wedding on board can have many benefits because the ship will offer all the things required, such as dining, flowers, entertainment, photographs. In fact the whole package is in one place.

At embarkation at the four cruise terminals in Southampton couples are regularly seen boarding for their honeymoon and at the City Terminal they can be seen boarding the *Independence of the Seas* carrying the wedding dress for their marriage on board in the Skylight Chapel.

'Now we have cruise ships just dedicated to warm-weather cruising. Sea-keeping practices have changed markedly. I think some of these high-sided cruise ships of today really catch the wind, and they do roll a bit. However, the *Queen Mary 2* doesn't roll and with her pod propulsion she just purrs along at speed. She is different because she is built as an ocean liner and has a lot more class. As a cruise ship I don't think she performs as well because it does take a long time to get people on and off the ship if you're not alongside the quayside. The balconies are not very useful on the North Atlantic because when you're going at 28½ knots it is not impossible to have wind speeds of 60 to 70 miles per hour against you, so you would not be very comfortable on a balcony. The balconies are better in the warmer climates when the ship is pursuing a slower cruising speed.

Most cruise ships today have a service speed of 20–21 knots, 23 maximum. Interestingly, the *QE2* could go backwards at 19 knots, and that was faster than many cruise ships could go forward. However, when at speed you could feel her vibrating, but today you have diesel propulsion or diesel electric propulsion and this has reduced the vibrations when at speed because of huge rubber insulating pads that the engines are mounted on.

The later ships coming online are really green and with the new environmentally friendly engines that has an ecological impact on the earth. We have the new Celebrity ships, *Celebrity Solstice* and *Celebrity Equinox*, where they have 216 solar panels, which boosts the ships' power supply and also powers the elevators. The new *Oasis of the Seas* is 15 to 20 per cent more efficient than the *Independence of the Seas* and the fuel savings are much greater in the latest generation of power plants.'

Douglas Ward sees a healthy advantage to cruising, and what he has observed is that people who suffer with allergies on land do not seem to suffer them when at sea. It appears that the ocean surrounded by nature has a very beneficial effect on the human body. This was recognised in an article in the *British Medical Journal* of 1880 on the health benefits of cruising with the 'fresh sea air' as having 'curative qualities'. However, there is a downside to the new ships being built, which is that many people suffer from the synthetic fibres and glues used during the outfitting stage.

Douglas Ward: 'One of my most memorable voyages was to the Antarctic Peninsula. We now have a tradition on Christmas Day when we have two German expedition cruise vessels meet in South Georgia where Shackleton is buried. We pour Aquavit on his grave at midday.'

New SOLAS Regulations

In 2010 new SOLAS (Safety of Life at Seas) regulations come into force. The first version was adopted in 1914 in response to the *Titanic* disaster.

Douglas Ward: 'We will lose about 15 to 16 ships, mostly smaller ships. The issues are the measurements and widths of the fire zones and position of fire doors. *Saga Rose* did not meet the new SOLAS 2010 requirements and was retired at the end of 2009, but *Saga Ruby* will be safe. It is such a shame because these wonderful ships have lovely traditional features, with a lot of wood panelling and glass in the interiors and beautiful teak promenade decks.

'New safety requirements do not take into account wonderful sailing ships like *Sea Cloud*. She uses only sail power, with the exception of a tiny engine for sailing in and out of port. She was built in 1931 and rebuilt in 1979 for cruising. She has fine wood panelling in the public rooms and still has her original cabins. However, I have just heard that an exemption has been granted for this beautiful ship'.

Mega Cruise Ships

'When you think, the first ship over 100,000 tons was *Carnival Destiny* in 1996, but by December 2010 there will be exactly 40 ships measuring over 100,000 tons or more. However, sailing from Southampton we do also have these large resort ships because that is what they are, floating resorts. The *Independence of the Seas* (160,000 GT) sails out of Southampton regularly and is a fun family experience with lots of activities and entertainment, but not a loss of places for relaxation. I sometimes wonder now if the ships are getting a little too big.

'However, I have sailed aboard the *Oasis of the Seas* (220,000 GT) which has a lot of entertainment and activities and is a great ship for families with children. It's a bit like Las Vegas or Coney Island all mixed into one, but noisy because there's always something happening. Not so quiet unless you have a balcony cabin facing the sea. I had one looking into the boardwalk and it was really noisy, but the Central Park area is essentially much quieter.

'With *Oasis of the Seas* at 360m with a beam of 47m, I don't think we should go much larger than this. I think for the safety handling, evacuation and the distribution point of view it's not feasible.

'I'm not sure how the ship will handle when she encounters high winds because she hasn't done so yet, and also what would happen with gusts of wind at the back of the ship going to Boardwalk-view cabins because they are in an open area. However, she is totally stable ship from my experience.'

Cruise companies with vessels sailing out of Southampton include Cunard, P&O Cruises, Royal Caribbean International, Fred. Olson, Saga, plus other companies and the numbers are increasing year on year. This is very practical for British passengers who can drive and leave their car in the port for the duration of their cruise or take a coach or train to embarkation, and you don't have to fly. However, those who do not mind flying can fly to Southampton International Airport, which is not too far from the docks.

Douglas Ward: 'When you consider the number of cruise passengers in 1970 was 500,000 worldwide, and now in 2009 it will be just over 20 million, plus about one million river cruise passengers. So Southampton Docks stands to benefit and I'm sure will be competing with some other ports in the UK who would like a slice of the action.'

Royal Caribbean International's *Oasis of the Seas* (220,000 GT) in the Solent on 2 November 2009. (Ron Hancock Collection)

With all his years of experience in the cruise industry, assessing and evaluating standards on cruise ships, Douglas Ward sees a buoyant future for the cruise industry: 'It is good to see all the different choices for holidays at sea because there are so many different aspects of the cruise industry. We have something for everyone. I see the market for longer cruises will expand quite a lot in the next few years, and ships sailing with longer itineraries will become more in demand. However, I think what has happened in the last few years, and what is happening now and into the future, is that the cruise industry will be slightly divided. There will be the large resort ships and in the other direction people who want to go for the smaller ships and the small niche markets. There is a huge range of cruise ships now and I hope that this will continue into the future, because I really feel that cruising is a wonderful high value money holiday.

'I am convinced that the consistent growth rate in cruising of seven per cent year on year since 1970 will continue as more people discover the benefits of cruising, and with the growth in the cruise industry I believe it is possible that demand will continue to exceed supply, particularly of niche market products.'

Oasis of the Seas

Having become used to the mega cruise ships of the day it was quite a surprise for cruising passengers when in 2009 *Oasis of the Seas*, the first of Royal Caribbean International's Oasis Class, entered service. At 220,000 GT *Oasis of the Seas* is 1,184ft (360.9m) in length with a beam of 184ft (56.1m) and a cruising speed of 22 knots. She is 16 decks high and has 2,700 staterooms and capacity for 5,400 passengers with a crew of 2,165. She had her naming ceremony on 30 November 2009 when she arrived from the builders, STX Europe shipyards in Turku, Finland, to her home port of Port Everglades in Fort Lauderdale, Florida.

Although the *Oasis of the Seas* is just 52ft (15.8m) longer and 49ft (14.9m) wider than the *Queen Mary 2*, it is important to remember that the *Oasis of the Seas* was built as a cruise ship. *Queen Mary 2* is built as an ocean liner, able to withstand the rigours of the North Atlantic, and although she also still undertakes cruises *Queen Mary 2* holds the record as the world's biggest ocean liner.

Senior Naval Architect for the Carnival Corporation Stephen Payne: 'The *Oasis of the Seas* is a tremendous ship. I can't fault her at all and from an engineering viewpoint she is totally a cruise ship. She is not designed to cross the Atlantic at high speed and she is not even a floating hotel city, she is a floating resort. Rather than having one superstructure she has two. She has a very wide beam with these two superstructures at the side of the ship which enables them to do various things on the centre line such as the Central Park and things like that. The big problem of ships like that is the sheer number of people, which could be up to 6,500, and that's an awful lot of people to process through security in the ports of call when you've only got say five hours ashore when they registered with a card that they've left the ship. From the engineering standpoint she has some amazing features which I'm sure will be a big success.'

Round-Trip Cruises or Fly-Cruising?

The fly-cruise, where passengers can fly to join their cruise ship, is popular with many holidaymakers. This could include flying to New York and returning transatlantic on *Queen Mary 2*, or flying to the Mediterranean or Florida where cruisers can embark on their relaxing vacation at sea. However, there are some cruisers who are tired of the 'rush and tear' of airline travel to destinations and have started to consider the more relaxing cruise from their nearest home port. For example, there are more ports in the UK where passengers can join their cruise ship and once on board their holiday starts, but they will return to the same port that they left. Southampton now has four cruise terminals with more and more cruise passengers arriving year on year.

Passengers can arrive at the port, have all their bags taken from them, board the cruise ship and from that moment their holiday starts. Once on board they have their comfortable cabins and staterooms and only have to unpack and pack once. There is time for relaxing in deckchairs or swimming in the pool, strolling along the promenade, evening dining and watching the entertaining shows in the ship's theatre.

Cruises can be for one week, two weeks or even longer, including world cruises. An added bonus is the fact that cruise ships do not just visit one holiday destination, but visit a number of different ports, and cruise passengers are able to take day trips on coaches or just visit the local towns or cities and sample the various experiences offered. However, with more and more cruise ships visiting the popular ports there are more visitors exploring the local sights, and some experienced cruisers like the smaller cruise ships that can go into ports that the larger ones cannot use. The following descriptions give a flavour of cruise holidays that some regular cruisers have experienced.

Cruise Passengers Talk about Cruising Today

Fay Bratcher compares the changes in cruising over time: 'Today people now realise that cruising is good value and I think there are some very good deals for families.

'We prefer the laid-back type of cruising where you share a table with other people and get to know each other well. We now have many friends that we first met on a cruise. The *Queen Mary 2* still has the traditional dining on the same table. However, today on most cruise ships there is free dining where passengers can choose where they eat and sit.

'We have done over 30 cruises since 1961, but the best service of all was the *Saga Rose*. We were looked after so well by the crew, the food was good and everything about it was good. It was organised at a reliable pace for people to enjoy it. However, today the bottom line is money and profit. Several things disappear on a ship that you don't notice, like nuts in a jar on the table. The Filipino crew are marvellous and if today you said, "Thank you very much", they would say, "You're welcome".

'Today there are more and more cruise ships arriving at the ports of call and I remember this year when we were on a cruise and called in at Grenada and we got a water taxi to the Grand Anse Beach. We arrived by 9am, and it was beautiful white sand and we settled down for a relaxing time on the beach. However, the *Ventura* and two Royal Caribbean cruise ships with approximately 10,000 people on board had also arrived at the island. By 11am you couldn't see the sea because the beach was so crowded and there were so many people in the water!'

Grenada is the most southerly of the Windward Islands in the Caribbean and is a tiny point on most world maps, with an area of only 133 square miles. Grenada has a population of about 100,000 and is 21 miles long and 12 miles wide. Grenada has a great deal to offer its visitors in terms of hiking, exploring, sailing, diving and much more.

Fay Bratcher: 'When we have cruised on the Holland America Line all announcements are in Dutch, English and German. If you play bingo they call out each number in the three languages!

'Today most lifeboat drills are held in the lounges and if you had left the ship on your return you have a swipe card to check back on board.'

Cruising with P&O

Keith Mullard and his wife Julie are now seasoned cruisers and talk about the cruises they have experienced: 'My wife and I have been cruising with P&O for 10 years. It all began with a seven-night cruise on the old *Arcadia*, now known as *Ocean Village*. We visited the Norwegian fjords, had a wonderful time and were hooked on cruising straightaway.

'The following year we went on the *Aurora* to the Canaries. This is our favourite ship, not least because of the lovely Andersons bar and the atrium area complete with waterfall. Our cabin did creak, though, but you soon get used to it! The Orchid Bar on *Arcadia* and Metropolis on *Ventura*, where the background is a different world city every night, are also not to be missed.

'We have now been on every one of the P&O ships and enjoy it very much. We like the very friendly crew who cannot do enough for you. It is pleasing that no compulsory tips are added, not even 15 per cent for bar services, so you are free to reward your individual cabin steward, waiters, restaurant waiter, and so on. The mix of formal and casual dining evenings is just about right and you can freely wander over all the ship; no areas are partitioned off for suite passengers.

'The best cabins we have experienced are the balconies at the stern on Egypt Deck on *Arcadia* and the same area on F Deck on *Ventura*. They are very spacious and it is just great to sit and watch the wake of the ship.

'We did one fly-cruise to the Caribbean to join *Oceana*, but although the cruise was superb, the flights were a nightmare. No, it's cruising from Southampton for us, especially as we live only five miles from the cruise terminals! Also, there are no restrictions on the amount of luggage you can bring as long as you can carry it all. P&O cruises, thoroughly recommended.'

Cruising in and out of Southampton in the 21st Century

Jim Brown compares his earlier experiences on the *Canberra* with today: 'We went to the Baltic and the Black Sea last year and did the maiden cruise of the *Ventura*. However, at my age of 77, we are trying to get two cruises a year in. What has been good for the last few cruises is the opportunity to have our family on board when our daughters and granddaughter came as well.

'What is so good today is just getting in your car or getting a taxi, arriving at the terminal, putting your cases on the ground, and the next time you see them they are in your cabin. You go and have some lunch and there is no hanging around like there is in an airport. We usually take three cases that pack inside each other to save space in the cabin.

'Today the *Aurora* is our favourite ship because it is more traditional. That was what we liked about the *Canberra* because she was also traditional. You dressed up formally on the formal nights, and there was the smart casual and it was British food.

'The whole atmosphere on the *Canberra* is matched today on the *Aurora*. The shows and the comedians, the whole ambience is pleasant and nice. You've got the formal nights, informal nights, semi-formal nights and they are all evenly spaced out.

'The *Ventura* is very nice and we also like the *Oceana*, which is our second favourite. Some cruise ships, like the *Artemis*, are child free, but we think it is nice to have children on board. It is great seeing the children going around and enjoying themselves. The *Ventura* is excellent for families with children. It has a big area for the kids and is broken down into different age groups. They have ample young crew to look after the children and they are great with the kids. You've got from the tiny little toddlers, who are safe and well looked after at the protected area at the stern, up to the teenagers who have their own video games, mini bar and their own room where they can sit and chat like youngsters do. They have all the computer games, skate boarding and all that.

'The *Ventura* has two swimming pools and you have the slide-off roof when there is good weather. The comparison with the *Canberra* was you had one smallish pool on deck and if it was cold or rough the water ran around and that was it. Today you have the open deck ones on the big ships like the *Oceana*, *Ventura* and the new *Azura*, and now you have weather protection on them as well.

'Even though you have more passengers you still have more space, and you've always got a deck chair. This wasn't the case on the *Canberra*, where I don't think there were as many deckchairs as passengers, so you had to fight to get a deckchair and even towels, which were sometimes in short supply.

Celebrity Cruises' *Celebrity Equinox* **(122,000 GT). (Keith Mullard Collection)**

Sindhu restaurant on the *Azura*. (Courtesy of P&O Cruises)

'On the *Canberra*, compared with today, it was not possible to phone home. Today on the cruise ships you have a phone in your cabin and any time of the day or night you can phone home because you've got the satellite communication. You can take your laptop on board and use the internet. On every ship now you have television and can watch all the programmes you get at home, and on one channel you can tune in to the camera on the bow of the ship and even see what the weather is like.

'The shopping was much more primitive on the *Canberra* where you had two or three little shops, but now you've got arcades of shops. You didn't have the spa treatments or luxury pampering, but now it is a big industry and there is a big area set aside for it. There are also massive gyms on board for fitness, and to get rid of some of the weight put on by the amount of food available on board ships today.

'You can even learn to be a circus performer on the *Ventura*, where they have a permanent travelling circus on the top deck where you can learn to walk the tightrope or trapeze.

'The big drawback today for the cruise ships is the ports they can use. *The Canberra* could go to a smallish port – sometimes she moored alongside – but more than often you went ashore by tender. If you go on a cruise ship today to a medium-size port you swamp it. You've got 3,000 people going ashore at once, and you are queueing up for a cup of coffee or a drink in the bar or in the shop.

The Playhouse on the *Azura*. (Courtesy of P&O Cruises)

'You can have two or three cruise ships in at the same time. In fact, on our last cruise they had to alter the itinerary. We were due in Barcelona on the Wednesday and they had to make a last-minute change because there were too many ships in Barcelona and there was no space. We went in there on the Sunday, but it was still crowded. You can have as many as four or five cruise ships with 3,000 passengers and you have about 15,000 people descending on the town. Just imagine 15,000 people coming up the shopping precinct in Southampton, as well as the usual shoppers.'

At the time of the interview Jim Brown was quite excited because he had won a competition in the *Daily Echo* that gave him a prize of going on board the new *Celebrity Equinox* for a short cruise: 'Tomorrow I will be a guest on the new *Celebrity Equinox* where I will be playing croquet on the grass.'

Jim and Marion Brown have also cruised on the

An outside single cabin on the *Azura*. (Courtesy of P&O Cruises)

The Beach Hut on the *Azura*. The Reef Children's Clubs include the Seabed for under 2s, the Beach Hut for ages 2–4, Frontiers for ages 5–8, the Hub for ages 9–12, and Apartment 16 for ages 13–17. (Courtesy of P&O Cruises)

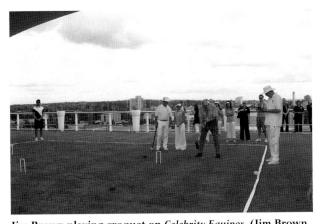

Jim Brown playing croquet on *Celebrity Equinox*. (Jim Brown Collection)

Cunard Countess and *Cunard Princess* and made a short trip on the *QE2* in 1991, but didn't care for that so much because 'Cunard appear more Americanised and not so traditionally British, which is what we prefer. I think P&O have cracked the cruise market and I would go with P&O anywhere. Our favourite cruise ships have been the *Aurora* and *Ventura*.'

However, for their 36th cruise in May 2010 Jim and Marion joined the *Queen Victoria* and now see Cunard in a different light: 'The furniture and fittings on the *Queen Victoria* are the most luxurious and comfortable that we have ever seen, and the library is the largest and most comprehensive, spreading over two decks. The theatre show on the last night was as good as *Sunday Night at the London Palladium* and the theatre is the more than equal to anything in London or elsewhere. In fact, just about everything surpasses what we have seen on other ships.

'The deck announcements on ships are normally similar to the old British Rail, which were muffled and hard to understand. On the *Queen Victoria* they are crisp and clear as a bell.

'The choice of food at the buffet has to be seen to believed; breakfast meant having to choose from whatever you could think of as every possible fruit and food was plentifully available. This is our 36th cruise and beyond question the ship is the best we have ever sailed on. It has now become our favourite cruise ship!'

Jim and Marion joined the *Queen Victoria* at the new Ocean Terminal and it was the first time they had used it: 'Even arriving at the new Ocean Terminal in the old docks was the best we have ever used. Their system of staggered embarkation times, as per our ticket, meant we arrived in a car driven by a friend, and, unlike the Mayflower Terminal, no long queue of cars was waiting to unload, we just drove straight up, dropped the suitcases and went into the arrival lounge. In the lounge there was the largest number of seats you could imagine, no waiting in a long snake, just sitting comfortably until called to have your photograph taken and go on board.'

John Harding was on the *Queen Victoria* for the same cruise as Jim Brown and talks about his experiences sailing on Cunard ships: 'This is our fourth cruise on *Queen Victoria* and we find it is always very relaxing. The crew are also very laid back, friendly and constantly communicating with their guests. We enjoy the food on board and have eaten in the two-tiered Britannia restaurant on decks 2 and 3, but have also enjoyed the Lido restaurant buffet, which is a very relaxed dining experience.

Queen Mary 2 Transatlantic Crossing from New York

John Harding: 'I felt very proud when I first stepped onto the *Queen Mary 2* in 2005 in New York to travel back to the UK. We had flown over to see our son, who lives in New York, and the idea was to fly one way and return by travelling transatlantic on the *Queen Mary 2*. The reason for this was my wife always likes to do a lot of shopping in New York and by coming back by sea we would not have the problem of the weight restrictions and excess baggage you have on the airlines. It was also basically a way of winding down and doing something relaxing.

'This was our first trip on the *Queen Mary 2* and we were very impressed with our balcony cabin and the service given to us by our cabin steward, who could not do enough for us. However, we found there was an air of formality on board where the service was very disciplined and certainly up to the Cunard high standards. The food and service was excellent in the Britannia restaurant, and overall it makes you feel important and special.

'We have now sailed transatlantic three times and even in November, with the Atlantic weather, the *Queen Mary 2* made the crossing feel comfortable.

'With both the *Queen Mary 2* and the *Queen Victoria* the food, accommodation, entertainment and service is second to none and is at the at the height of the Cunard status in the transatlantic service and cruising world.'

The Royal Court Theatre on the Queen Victoria

Jim Brown mentioned how impressed he was with the show he saw in the Royal Court Theatre and met *Queen Victoria's* entertainment director, Amanda Reid, who talked about the theatre. Amanda has worked with many of the Cunard ships, including *Cunard Countess* and *Cunard Princess*, and also for Celebrity Cruises and Silver Seas Cruises before rejoining Cunard on *Queen Mary 2* in May 2004 as social hostess. In June 2006 she was appointed assistant cruise director on *Queen Mary 2* and was transferred over to *Queen Victoria* for the inaugural season before becoming entertainment director.

Amanda Reid: 'The Royal Court Theatre on the *Queen Victoria* is a state-of-the-art theatre and the first one of its kind. It is very much like the old-style Victorian theatres in the West End of London in décor but, of course, the ship was built with the latest technology for the lighting, sound and backstage. So it is the first of its kind and has no restrictive viewing anywhere and is the most beautiful theatre afloat. We have the theatre box programme where guests can reserve a box at

The Royal Court Theatre on the *Queen Victoria*. (Courtesy of Cunard)

the purser's desk. It comes with a package where guests are shown into the theatre lounge by the bellboys in their red uniforms and invited to sit with a glass of champagne. Just before the show starts the guests are escorted to the box they have reserved, where there is more champagne and chocolates and then a photograph of the cast after the show. It's a lovely way to make an evening very special.

'The Royal Court Theatre on *Queen Mary 2* is a beautiful theatre and is also on two levels but doesn't have the boxes. However, the cast are a little bit closer to the audience when on stage.

ABP Southampton Port Director Doug Morrison. (Courtesy of ABP)

In October 2010 Cunard will name the new *Queen Elizabeth*. Tickets for the maiden voyage were sold out in a record 29 minutes, beating the previous record sales for the *QE2's* final voyage in June 2007 by seven minutes.

Since 1998, when there were 110 cruise calls in the Port of Southampton and 259,000 passengers, there has been an increase year on year to 271 cruise calls and 1,025,700 passengers in 2009.

The Future for Southampton's Cruise Industry

Doug Morrison, ABP Southampton Port Director, reflects on passenger travel in the past and the present, and his vision for the future of the cruise industry in Southampton: 'The heyday of passenger travel from Southampton was long thought to have been the early part of the 20th century, when record numbers of passengers were seen passing through the port. In reality the port has never in its cruise history been busier than it is today. Since 2005 (the year we officially broke the passenger record set in the 20th century) we have continued to break the previous year's record every year!

'This year over 1.2 million passengers will pass through the port's four dedicated cruise terminals. As the demand for cruising from the port has increased, it is now a regular occurrence that we see four cruise ships and at times even five cruise ships in the port on any one calendar day. In 2011 we are even expecting our first ever six cruise-ship day. As cruise ships have increased in size over the years, many of the cruise ships now calling at Southampton will carry as many as 4,000 passengers. This means in any one four cruise-ship day over 30,000 passengers can pass through our terminals, all within a 12 hour period.

'As an award-winning turnaround port a great deal of specialist services are required to turn these vessels around. These range from the stevedores to coach companies, taxis, check-in staff and various cruise vessel support services which are necessary to maintain the high standards of service that these vessels provide to their guests. In all it is estimated that every time one of these iconic cruise ship calls at the port over £1.25 million is generated in the regional and local economy.

'The ability to accommodate growth and such large vessels has been facilitated by ABP's substantial investment in our cruise facilities. In fact, in recent years we have spent over £42 million developing and upgrading our terminals, including the recent opening of our £19 million Ocean Terminal, based on a long-term contract with Carnival, the biggest cruise company in the world.

'The phenomenal success of cruising from Southampton is certainly something to be very proud of, however, of course, with growth there are new challenges for the port and the city. Looking forward, industry experts continue to predict growth in the UK cruise market, some suggesting as much as a doubling of cruise passengers through UK ports in the next five years.

'To accommodate the predicted industry growth we are now evaluating the case for a fifth terminal at the port. Accommodating this future growth is important for both the port and the local and regional community. As more jobs and support services become dependent on this industry it is imperative that we work with key stakeholders to ensure that we continue to maintain our market share. Whilst we can build more terminals to meet the anticipated demand, the challenge will be for the city to ensure the supportive infrastructure can accommodate the increase in passenger numbers. Southampton is the fastest growing cruise port in the UK, and as the cruise business continues to increase there will be the need to accommodate four, five and even six cruise vessels on certain days.

'Today Southampton remains the undisputed UK cruise capital, and we continue to be proud that iconic ships such as the *Queen Victoria* and *Queen Mary 2* carry around the name 'Southampton' on their stern. Competition from other ports to increase their stake in this lucrative cruise market continues to accelerate as they recognise the economic impact of even one cruise call to their city. If we are unable to accommodate this growth in Southampton it will no doubt be lost to other cities. We must, therefore, ensure that all the services and infrastructure can support growth to keep this industry in Southampton. This will ensure that future generations continue to benefit and Southampton retains its status as the UK's cruise capital.'

P&O *Azura*

P&O Cruises' new cruise ship *Azura*, commanded by her master Captain Keith Dowds, is one of their largest vessels, with similar accommodation to her sister ship, *Ventura*, but she will have her own individual personality and style. She will be family friendly, but there will be a focus on creating a peaceful and relaxing environment for adults. Whereas the aim for the *Ventura* was to attract those new to cruising, *Azura* will appeal to the more experienced cruisers who enjoy the traditional P&O high-quality service, but now within a modern and contemporary environment.

There are three silver service restaurants on board *Azura*, where passengers are able to choose between club dining and freedom dining. Club dining is for passengers who have the same table reserved for them and dine at the same time, with

P&O *Azura* (116,000 GT). (Richard de Jong Collection)

the same table companions each evening; but freedom dining is where passengers are free to dine at any time with whomever they choose.

Other dining venues include Sindhu, an Indian-style restaurant created by Michelin-rated chef Atul Kochhar, and the Glass House, where wine expert Olly Smith selects vintage wines recommended for each course.

There is an adults-only sun deck sanctuary called The Retreat, with a child-free pool, and for families there is a Nintendo Wii room and children's club facilities for different age groups. Noddy and Mr Bump will be on board. For those who like watching

The Retreat on the *Azura*. (Courtesy of P&O Cruises)

The atrium of the *Azura*. (Courtesy of P&O Cruises)

movies there is SeaScreen, an open-air movie screen positioned above the Aqua Pool where films are shown day and night. Other entertainment includes various venues for music and drinks, a casino, the Playhouse theatre and dancing in the Atrium.

There is a wide range of staterooms specifically designed for modern tastes and over 900 balcony cabins. Another new feature is the spa cabins, giving exclusive access to the Oasis Spa and Retreat. Yet another new feature is 18 single staterooms, which are a first in the P&O Cruises fleet.

The 14 Decks of P&O *Azura*

There are 14 decks on the new P&O *Azura* and starting from the top there is the Sky Deck, which has a sports court and golf nets, and the Ocean Deck that is located aft. On this deck there is the Planet Bar, which has an audiovisual wall showing worldwide footage filmed specifically for the *Azura*.

On the Sun Deck there is the Seventeen restaurant and The Retreat, an outdoor spa terrace specifically for adults. The Aqua Deck has children's clubs, the Oasis Spa, gym, and SeaScreen, the open-air cinema screen.

The Lido Deck has the Aqua and Coral Pool and areas for casual dining that include the Venezia, the *Azura*'s main self-service restaurant, where food is available all day. The Verona is also open throughout the day, serving pizzas, burgers and pasta, and there is a poolside pizzeria.

The Riviera Deck has the Terrace Pool and some staterooms, some with balconies and some inside; however, the main accommodation decks are A–E decks.

The Prom Deck has the Indian Sindu restaurant and the Glass House. Also on this deck are the Blue Bar, Malabar, Manhattan and the Playhouse theatre, which can seat 800.

Two of the main restaurants for club dining are on F Deck. There is also Brodie's Pub, the casino, shops and the 18 single staterooms. On P Deck there is the *Azura*'s Atrium with a dance floor, library, art gallery and the Amber restaurant, exclusively for those who want freedom dining.

P&O *Azura* was named on Saturday 10 April 2010 by the ship's godmother, Darcey Bussell, former Royal Ballet principal ballerina. On Monday 12 April 2010 *Azura* left Southampton for her 16-night maiden voyage cruise to the Mediterranean, with calls in Malaga, Corfu, Dubrovnik and Venice.

Celebrity Cruises

Celebrity Cruises have Millennium class and Solstice class, and of the two classes *Celebrity Constellation* and *Celebrity Millennium* of the Millennium Class have visited Southampton.

There is also *Celebrity Xpedition* (2,842 GT), an expedition cruise ship that runs year-round voyages around the Galapagos Islands, and has capacity for 90 passengers with 64 crew. The ship leaves Baltra (Galapagos) for seven nights around the Galapagos Islands and returns to the same place.

The *Celebrity Eclipse* (122,000 GT) at the Meyer Werft Shipyard. (Simon Brooke-Webb)

The first of the Solstice class, *Celebrity Solstice*, came into service in late November 2008 and the second, *Celebrity Equinox*, was named in Southampton in summer 2009. In April 2010 the third, *Celebrity Eclipse*, was named in Southampton and became the first Celebrity ship to be based in the port, cruising to the Mediterranean and Northern Europe.

Celebrity Cruises Began in 1988

Celebrity Cruises was founded by the Greek Chandris Line in 1988 and in 1997 became part of Royal Caribbean International. Due to the previous links with Greece, Celebrity Cruises often have Greek captains and officers on their cruise ships. Other links with the Chandris Line still remain: the Celebrity Cruises vessels have a large white X on their funnels. The X is the Greek Letter 'chi' and is a reminder of their previous connections with the Chandris Line.

Captain Panagiotis Skylogiannis, who is a Greek national, was the first master on the *Celebrity Solstice* when she was officially named by godmother Professor Sharon Smith on 14 November 2008 in Port Everglades, Florida. *Celebrity Solstice* was the first of the Solstice class ships.

The second vessel in the Solstice Class was the *Celebrity Equinox*, whose first master was Apostolos Bouzakis, also a Greek national. *Celebrity Equinox* was officially named by godmother and Walk the Walk breast cancer charity founder Nina Barough CBE in Southampton on 29 July 2009.

On 24 April 2010 the third vessel in the Solstice class, *Celebrity Eclipse* (122,000 GT), was officially named by godmother Hampshire yachtswomen and breast cancer survivor Emma Pontin. The first master of the new *Celebrity Eclipse* is Captain Panagiotis Skylogiannis, who lives in Norwich with his wife and three children.

Celebrity Eclipse Leaves the Mayer Werft Shipyard

In March 2010 the new Celebrity Cruises cruise ship *Celebrity Eclipse* left the inland Meyer Werft shipyard, Papenburg, Germany, to sail 42km down the River Ems to Emshaven in the Netherlands. The vessel was towed backwards with two tugs, one at the stern and one at the bow. However, the skill of Captain Panagiotis Skylogiannis came to the fore, first in squeezing through the narrow shipyard entrance and then the tricky manoeuvres in passing through narrow locks and bridges, a journey lasting up to 15 hours. The official name for this operation is 'conveyance' and Captain Skylogiannis emphasised that sea captains do not often experience the challenges that conveyance presents.

After reaching Emshaven *Celebrity Eclipse* started her sea trials before going to Hamburg and then Southampton in April for her naming ceremony.

Naming Day in Southampton

Captain Skylogiannis is a very popular captain with his passengers, who have commented about his friendly nature and willingness to share his knowledge and experience. This was exactly what the author found when he talked to Captain Skylogiannis on board the *Celebrity Eclipse* on the day the vessel was named in Southampton: 'I was walking along the promenade deck when I met this very smartly dressed ship's officer who was smiling and appeared very friendly. Not realising that it was the captain I asked what his job was. He replied, "I'm the Captain!" This was an ideal opportunity for

Captain Panagiotis Skylogiannis and the author. (Richard de Jong Collection)

me to talk to him and ask if he minded me asking a few questions.'

Captain Skylogiannis has been with the company for 22 years and has spent nine years as captain. He compares the changes during his time at sea: 'When I started the ships were much smaller, and we spent much more time at sea. You could be on board for seven, eight, or even nine months before getting time off, but today it is three months on, three months off.

'In the earlier days the captain did not have use of modern technology and perhaps had less to do, but it was a nice life at sea. Today, with the modern technology on board for the ship to function correctly, there is more studying of procedures. Things may seem easier, but to understand how the new systems work there is much more reading of the manuals.

'I work every day when at sea, but you can just pick up the phone and talk to your family and friends and deal with emails. It is a nice life and I have never regretted my time at sea.

'Without the new technology of today you could not manage a ship of 122,000 tons. The ship is very good, very manoeuvrable and much better to handle than the older ships.'

Celebrity Eclipse on a Rescue Mission

After *Celebrity Eclipse* arrived in Southampton on Tuesday 20 April 2010 a decision was made by Celebrity Cruises to send the ship to Bilbao, Spain, on a rescue mission. This was to bring back 2,200 holidaymakers from UK tour operators' package holidays, stranded due to the ash clouds from the Icelandic volcano that had grounded all aircraft.

Celebrity Eclipse was due to arrive at Bilbao in the early hours of Thursday morning and the stranded passengers would board and sail back to Southampton, arriving on Friday evening on 23 April.

In order to undertake the rescue mission the activities planned for a two-night celebration cruise on 22 April had to be cancelled; however, the activities and naming ceremony on 24 April went ahead as scheduled. Celebrity Cruises aimed to accommodate guests who had been disappointed by the cancelled launch celebration to join the *Celebrity Eclipse* on a two-night naming celebration cruise, leaving on 24 April after the official naming ceremony.

The author asked Captain Skylogiannis if the rescue trip to Bilbao was useful for the crew, practising their roles with 2,200 unexpected passengers. Captain Skylogiannis: 'Well, we had been practising before the trip to Bilbao, but this was very good practice for one day and everything was open for the passengers to experience.'

The *Celebrity Eclipse's* iLounge. (Richard de Jong Collection)

The decor on the *Celebrity Eclipse*. (Richard de Jong Collection)

The *Celebrity Eclipse's* Hot Glass Show. (Richard de Jong Collection)

The *Celebrity Eclipse's* pool area. (Richard de Jong Collection)

Celebrity Eclipse – Facilities On Board

Similar to her sisters, *Celebrity Eclipse* features a half-acre Lawn Club where passengers can enjoy a game of croquet, bowls or golf, have a picnic or just walk through the grass in bare feet.

There is the Hot Glass Show, a live glass-blowing studio at sea, where guests can observe hot molten glass being turned into objects of art. Other facilities include three swimming pools, one of which is indoors; the Celebrity iLounge, complete with 26 workstations; and the Eclipse theatre where guests can relax and watch a Broadway show.

AquaClass is a new accommodation class with 130 balcony staterooms and an exclusive restaurant, Blu, for guests choosing to stay in AquaClass. At least 1,286 cabins have a sea view, with 1,216 having a private balcony. Only 140 cabins do not have a sea view.

There are in total 10 different restaurants, including the two-tier main dining room and smaller dining options, from the casual dining at the Aqua Spa Café to speciality restaurants designed to offer guests a wide range of cuisine to please all tastes.

Stephen Payne: 'Since the *Celebrity Eclipse* follows on from the *Celebrity Solstice*, it is the aim on that class of ship to get more cabins. To do that they have got interlocking cabins, so the cabins are narrower and in a pair: one bed is near the window in the wide part and in the narrow part there are the wardrobes. The other cabin is opposite with the bed is near the door and the wardrobe near the window. By doing it this way they have been able to add 10 extra cabins per deck.

'There is very modern interior decoration on the Celebrity Ships. I visited the *Celebrity Solstice* in the yard and I must say I did like it. Regarding the sloping back, it has been realised that we have to move the weight back to the middle. This confirms that the way the old ships were built was right and the steep angle at the back of the ship moves the weight further forward.'

Queen Elizabeth

Cunard Line is one of the oldest shipping companies still operating and it could now be said that Cunard has one of the youngest fleets in the 21st century. With the new Millennium came the *Queen Mary 2*, which went into service from 2004, and then the *Queen Victoria* entered service in 2007. On 11 November 2008 *Queen Elizabeth 2* left Southampton for the last time on her final voyage to Dubai. This left just the *Queen Mary 2* and *Queen Victoria* as the only two Cunard ships in service. However, in October 2010 the new *Queen Elizabeth,* under the command of her master Captain Christopher Wells, will sail into Southampton for her naming before entering service and making the Cunard fleet up to three vessels.

Queen Elizabeth is the third new ocean liner to be introduced by Cunard in six years and will be the second-largest Cunard ship ever built. Although she will feature the unique Cunard traditions linking her with her sisters and their predecessors, *Queen Elizabeth* will also have her own personality and style, and also the modern innovations and luxuries that regular Cunard guests expect.

An illustration of the new *Queen Elizabeth* (90,400 GT). (Courtesy of Cunard)

Keel laying of the new *Queen Elizabeth* on 7 July 2009 at the Fincantieri shipyard, Monfalcone. (Courtesy of Cunard)

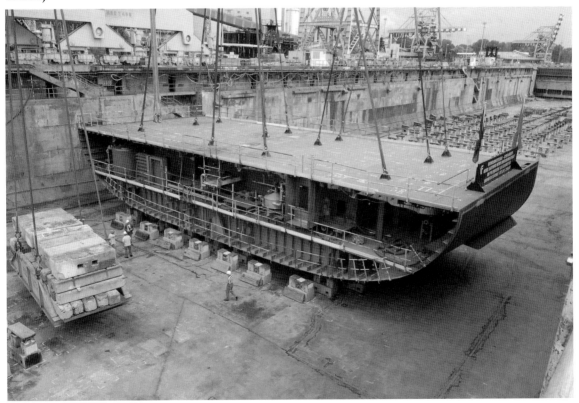

The *Queen Elizabeth* yacht club. (Courtesy of Cunard)

Queen Elizabeth is named after the first Cunard, launched in 1938 and at the time the world's largest liner. Her décor will reflect that of the period, with Art Deco features, wooden panelling and chandeliers, and she will offer guests experiences of that time. Her black and red livery will distinguish her as a Cunard vessel.

Queen Elizabeth will have its own 'Yacht Club', reminiscent of the aft lounge of the *Queen Elizabeth 2*, with a 270° view. As well as reflecting on the artwork and memorabilia of the *Queen Elizabeth 2* there will be photographs and memorabilia of the historic links Cunard has enjoyed with royalty over time. Other photographs can be seen of the famous people who have travelled on the Cunard liners in the Cunarders' Gallery.

Public rooms will include the Queen's Room, the traditional Cunard ballroom which will be used for grand balls and tea dances while at sea. There is a garden lounge where guests can dine and dance under the stars, and a time for afternoon tea served by white-gloved waiters.

The games deck is reminiscent of the same deck on the original *Queen Elizabeth*, where guests will be able to play paddle tennis, croquet and bowls. Memories of the first *Queen Elizabeth*'s era will be seen in the memorabilia displayed in the Midship's Bar.

The *Queen Elizabeth* Queen's Room. (Courtesy of Cunard)

The five restaurants, depending on the accommodation, include the Queen's Grill and Princess Grill, the Courtyard, Britannia Club, (a private dining room for guests in the top balcony staterooms) and the Britannia Restaurant, a two-tiered dining room with Art Deco features and cuisine served with Cunard's exclusive White Star Service. There are alternative dining venues, including the Lido Restaurants on deck 9, the Café Carinthia and the Golden Lion Pub, offering English pub food in a traditional pub setting.

For entertainment there is the Royal Court Theatre, with tiered seating for 832 guests, the Queen's Room ballroom and various bars and clubs, including the Commodore Club.

The Royal Arcade on decks two and three will feature shops representing famous brand names and there will be a two-tiered library with a collection of 6,000 books.

The Queen's Grill on the *Queen Elizabeth*. (Courtesy of Cunard)

On decks one and three there is the ConneXions Conference Centre and Internet Centre, which features classes in learning or updating computer skills and allows guests to surf the net. There are WiFi Internet connections within the staterooms for laptop users, and GSM mobile phone connections for guests to remain in contact with friends and family while on their journey.

Children of all ages are catered for with The Play Zone and The Zone, and for younger children there are trained British nannies. Other staff are available in the inside and outside play areas to supervise children aged 1–12.

For the health and fitness enthusiast there is the Royal Spa and Fitness Centre featuring the latest spa and beauty treatments and a hydro-pool and thermal suite. There is also a gymnasium and aerobics area with a range of fitness equipment. There are two outdoor swimming pools on deck nine, and the Pavilion pool has two whirlpools.

The *Queen Elizabeth's* Britannia restaurant. (Courtesy of Cunard)

The Royal Court Theatre on the *Queen Elizabeth*. (Courtesy of Cunard)

Staterooms and Suites

Of the 1,046 staterooms, 892 are outside staterooms with 738 having balconies, and 127 are Queen's Grill and Princess Grill suites with guests dining in the Grills restaurants. For the first time the six main Queen's Grill suites will be named after the six Cunard Commodores who have been knighted: Commodore Sir Arthur Rostron, Commodore Sir Edgar Britten,

The *Queen Elizabeth*'s pavilion pool. (Courtesy of Cunard)

Commodore Sir Ivan Thompson, Commodore Sir Cyril Illingworth, Commodore Sir James Bisset and Commodore Sir James Charles. Each suite will feature a portrait and biography of the Commodore after whom it is named.

The breakdown of the nine different types of suites and staterooms are as follows:

4	grand suites, named after Commodore Sir Arthur Rostron, Commodore Sir Edgar Britten, Commodore Sir Ivan Thompson and Commodore Sir James Bisset on decks six and seven
2	master suites, named after Commodore Sir James Charles and Commodore Sir Cyril Illingworth on deck seven
25	penthouses on decks four, five, six and eight
35	Queen's suites on decks four, five, seven and eight
61	Princess suites on decks four, five, six, seven and eight
39	Britannia Club on deck eight
572	Balcony rooms on decks four, five, six, seven and eight
146	Outside rooms on decks one, four and six
162	Inside rooms on decks one, four, five, six, seven and eight

This gives a total of 1,046 staterooms.

Cunard's Commitment to the Environment

Cunard are committed to environmental issues, especially the marine environment, and have developed their own environmental management system that aims for high standards of excellence and responsibility to global issues regarding preserving the planet for future generations.

To deal with the waste generated on board much of the general waste is recycled, thus reducing the amount of waste that is landed ashore. Waste water treatment is appropriately managed to reduce any impact on the oceans, and other measures are taken, such as fuel efficiency to help to reduce air emissions.

To meet the commitment of Cunard to the environment *Queen Elizabeth* has been designed as one of the most energy-efficient and environmentally-friendly ships in service today. Some of these efficiency saving systems have included energy efficient lighting, the introduction of key-card holders, ensuring that when guests leave their staterooms the TV and lights are switched off, and improved double glazing for staterooms and public areas. Other energy efficient measures have included having sensors that switch the deck lighting off at dawn and on again at dusk and time clocks to control the air-conditioning in public areas at night.

Queen Elizabeth will leave Southampton for her maiden voyage on 12 October, calling at Vigo, Lisbon, Seville, Las Palmas, Tenerife, La Palma and Madeira. After the maiden voyage *Queen Elizabeth* will sail on five more inaugural voyages, Mediterranean Premiere, Aegean Introduction, Gallic Debut, Iberian Discovery and Festive Debut. (Information courtesy of Cunard.)

As One Era Ends Another Begins

The author concluded his book *The Story of Southampton Docks* with the sad, but memorable day that *Queen Elizabeth 2* left Southampton for the last time for her final journey to Dubai on 11 November 2008. It is fitting that we now welcome the new *Queen Elizabeth* to Southampton for her naming ceremony and entering service when she leaves for her maiden voyage on 12 October 2010.

APPENDICES

APPENDIX A
Comparing the Eastern Docks (Old Docks) Pre-war to Today

The Eastern Docks

Before World War Two the Eastern Docks were well equipped with sheds for cargo and passengers in the Ocean Dock, Inner Dock, Outer Dock and Empress Dock.

At the western end of the Eastern Docks and within the River Test there were Berths 50 and 51, and this was where the Harland & Wolff Works was based, alongside the Trafalgar Dry Dock. Next is the Ocean Dock, where passenger and cargo sheds were situated on Berths 46–47 and Berths 43–44, and another cargo shed at Berth 45. Cargo and passenger sheds were on Berth 41 and the International Cold Store on Berth 40. Berths 38–39 had cargo and passenger sheds and a cargo shed on the dock head. Berths 34–36 in the River Itchen were also cargo and passenger sheds. Berths 34–39 were mainly used by the Union-Castle inward and outward service before they moved to the Western Docks. All the sheds on the berths in the Empress Dock were for cargo and passengers. Just inside the entrance to the Empress Dock in the River Itchen was the Prince of Wales Dry Dock. Berths 30–33, also in the River

Eastern Docks pre-war in 1939. (Courtesy of ABP)

Eastern Docks post-war in 1945. (Courtesy of ABP)

**Southampton Docks today, taken in 2009.
(Courtesy of ABP Southampton)**

Itchen, were cargo and passenger sheds, leading up to the Outer Dock where Dry Docks 1–4 were situated. Within the Outer Dock there were cargo and passenger sheds, and cargo warehouses in the Inner Dock.

During World War Two Southampton and the docks were heavily bombed and the extensive damage caused the dock company to redevelop much of the site.

The Eastern Docks Today

The UK base of Wallenius Wilhelmsen Logistics Car Carriers is based at Berth 34 and three multi-storey car parks have been built to store cars.

There is also the new addition of the purpose-built lift on/lift off facility at Berth 45 in the Ocean Dock, built in 2008 for the Huelin-Renouf weekly cargo services to the Channel Islands.

The grain terminal is at Berths 35–36, but up until 2009 there was a regular cargo shipment of wind-turbine blades to the Eastern Docks from the Vestas Wind Systems factory on the Isle of Wight. It was a regular sight to see the Vestas vessels *Blade Runner 1* and *2* bring the wind turbine blades over from the Isle of Wight. However, the factory has now closed and the facility on the Empress Dock is no longer used.

The Inner Dock has been filled in and is part of the Ocean Village Complex. The two cruise terminals, Queen Elizabeth II and the Ocean Terminal, account for the main cruise facilities within the Eastern Docks of today.

APPENDIX B
Maritime History in the Eastern Docks (Old Docks)

Southampton is renowned for its maritime heritage and the Eastern Docks, also known as the Old Docks, is where the development of Southampton Docks began in 1838.

Cruise ships that are berthed in the new Ocean Terminal are right in the middle of the maritime history and passengers on board can look around and take in some of the history.

The *Queen Mary 2* in the Ocean Terminal. (Author's Collection)

Where Are We Today in the Eastern Docks?

For any cruise ship berthed at the Ocean Terminal it is possible to look at the areas of maritime history surrounding the Ocean Dock, but it depends which side the vessel is berthed. With regards to the *Queen Mary 2*, she always berths on her portside with the bows facing north. However, sometimes vessels such as the *Queen Victoria* berth on their starboard side with their stern facing north.

What is the port side and starboard side of the ship? The port side is on the left side when facing forward, and the starboard is on the right side when facing forward.

There are areas of historical interest that can be seen from the deck of the *Queen Mary 2* while she is berthed on the port side and facing the city. First, looking west from the portside of the *Queen Mary 2*, you can see the River Test with the Town Quay, Royal Pier, and Western Dock. In the far distance the Container Terminal can be seen.

Berth 50 today, looking from deck of *QM2.* **(Author's Collection)**

New Southampton Ocean Terminal, opened in 2009.
(Author's Collection)

Trafalgar (No. 6) Dry Dock

Looking from the port side of the *Queen Mary 2* and over the
Ocean Terminal you can see the remains of the Trafalgar Dock.
Most of the Trafalgar Dry Dock has now been filled in, but
there is one section that can be seen that is near the new Ocean
Terminal at Berths 46–47.

The Trafalgar (No. 6) Dry Dock was opened in 1905 and
was so named because it was opened 100 years after the Battle
of Trafalgar. However, it had to be enlarged, first to fit in the
Olympic and later a V-shape had to be constructed at the head of
the dry dock for the *Berengaria's* bow to fit in.

The Floating Dry Dock

Due to the pressure on the Trafalgar (No. 6) Dry Dock a
floating dry dock was used between 1924 and 1934. The
floating dry dock was based near the dry dock just off Berth
50, which was later to be the site of the BOAC Flying Boat
Terminal in the late 1940s. The ocean liners would sail into the
dry dock, which had been sunk low in the water, and once the
ship was inside the dry dock would be then raised to the
surface and maintenance work on the vessel would begin.'

BOAC Flying Boat 'Airport' at Berth 50.

Looking from the portside of the *Queen Mary 2*, just past the
Trafalgar Dry Dock, there are the three brick bases that
originally linked to the floating dock, used between 1924–34,
but after World War Two they were used as the base for the
BOAC Flying Boat Terminal.

When BOAC returned to Southampton from Poole after
World War Two, the new purpose-built flying boat terminal
was opened on 14 April 1948. The terminal had its own railway
station and passengers arriving or waiting to leave could spend
time in the restaurant and bar. There were the customs and
immigration officials' areas and offices for the BOAC staff.

Trafalgar Dock when in use. The ship in the dry dock
is the troopship *Oxfordshire*. (Courtesy of ABP)

Eastern Docks. The floating dock in use in October
1932 with the *Homeric* in the dry dock. Berthed in the
Ocean Dock are the *Majestic*, *Olympic* and *Berengaria*.
Empress of Britain is in Itchen Quays. (Edwin Praine
Collection)

The old Berth 50 today. (Author's Collection)

Freight and baggage handling was undertaken to and from the flying boat. However, BOAC only operated from the Berth 50 terminal until 1950, and Aquila Airways Flying Boats started flying from there but ceased operation in September 1958.

Looking further along you can see the Town Quay from where the Hythe Ferry and Red Funnel Ferries to the Isle of Wight leave. Just past the Town Quay is the now disused Royal Pier. The Royal Pier was opened by Princess Victoria in 1833 and many of the paddle steamers would leave from there.

Just past the Royal Pier is the Mayflower Park which faces Berth 101 of the Western Docks (New Dock). It is from Berth 101 that the Royal Caribbean International *Independence of the Seas* sails from on her cruises.

The God's House

If you continue looking from the port side of the *Queen Mary 2* and to the right of the Trafalgar Dry Dock, past the car park, you can see an old stone building. That is the God's House Gate and Tower. The God's House Gate was named after a nearby hospital that was built in the 14th century. The gate was sometimes referred to as the Saltmarsh Gate because it originally opened out on to marshlands at the east side of the town.

The God's House Tower was built in the 15th century and was famous as the home of the town gunner, with guns and gunpowder also stored there. The job of the town gunner was to protect the town from attack by vessels sailing up the river. However, the gun was so powerful it had to be lashed down when fired, with the town gunner ducking for his own safety! By the 17th century the tower was used for prisoners of war and was also the town's jail. Today it is Southampton's Museum of Archaeology.

Just near the God's House Tower is the Old Bowling Green, which is claimed to be the world's oldest bowling green, dating from 1299.

South Western Hotel

Looking further right from the God's House Gate and Tower and to the north from the bows of the *Queen Mary 2* the first building near the dock is the red-bricked ABP Ocean Gate Port Office. Further back, but just to the left of the ABP Port Office and alongside the Gate 4 entrance is Admiralty House, now a block of flats. However, it was originally the dock's General Post Office, and it was from there that over 1,000 bags of mail for the *Titanic* were gathered for loading on the ship before she sailed.

Moving further right there is the old Union-Castle Line offices and just behind them is South Western House, better known as the South Western Hotel.

It was at 9.30am on 10 April 1912 that the White Star boat train left platform 12 at Waterloo Station for the Terminus Station, Southampton, with the first-class passengers for the White Star *Titanic*. The boat train crossed Canute Road, into

BOAC Flying Boat Terminal at Berth 50. (Courtesy of ABP Southampton)

God's House – looking from the deck of *QM2*. (Author's Collection)

A close-up of God's House. (Author's Collection)

Looking from the bows of the *QM2*. (Author's Collection)

the docks, and pulled up at the platform that was parallel with the White Star Dock where the *Titanic* was berthed. The first-class passengers left the boat train and entered the sheds on the quayside before boarding the *Titanic*.

Staying at the South Western Hotel before joining the Titanic was Thomas Andrews, who was the managing director of Harland & Wolff and who had been closely involved in the design of the *Titanic* with his uncle, Lord Pirrie. Also staying at the hotel was Bruce Ismay, the chairman of the White Star Line, who had driven down the day before.

Aerial view of Southampton Docks station and the South Western Hotel, now residential accommodation. (Postcard)

The White Star Dock/Ocean Dock

Moving to starboard side of the *Queen Mary 2* and looking at the quayside opposite, sometimes you will see car carriers berthed there, and the Huelin-Renouf lift on/lift off cargo facility at Berth 45. However, perhaps more interestingly, Berths 43–44, which are directly opposite the *Queen Mary 2,* are where the *Titanic* departed on 10 April 1912 for her maiden voyage.

To set the scene, here is an extract from *The Maiden Voyage* by Geoffrey Marcus in which he describes the passengers' first view of the *Titanic* as they left the quayside sheds on a bright but cold April morning: 'The new liner lay at her berth in the Ocean Dock, with three monstrous plumes of greyish smoke curling upwards from her tall funnels; her enormous hull completely dwarfing all the other shipping in the port. The Blue Peter flew at her fore yardarm. At her mainmast flew the house-flag of the White Star Line, and at her foremast the Stars and Stripes, the country of her destination; and on her bows, inscribed in letters of gold, was the name *TITANIC*.'

It is interesting to note that 'plumes of smoke' were coming out of three of the funnels, and yet the

Looking from the starboard side of the *QM2* to Berth 44, Ocean Dock, from where the *Titanic* sailed in 1912. It was then called White Star Dock. (Author's Collection)

The *Titanic* (46,000 GT) in the White Star Dock in April 1912. (© Titanic Information Center Deutschland e.V.)

Titanic had four funnels. This was because the rear fourth funnel was false and mainly used as ventilation for the engine room. However, at the time the shipping companies wanted to attract passengers and providing four funnels gave confidence to passengers that the ship was more stable and powerful. It was also thought that the *Titanic* was unsinkable, and some of the firemen had gone over to the Oriental pub, opposite Gate 4, and got quite inebriated while celebrating their forthcoming voyage to New York on 'the unsinkable'.

As the time arrived for the *Titanic* to leave, the well-known Southampton marine pilot George Bowyer took over and instructed to 'let go the stern and then the head ropes' and for the tugs to pull the *Titanic* away from the quayside. Finally he instructed 'slow ahead' and the *Titanic* was under way and moving towards the entrance to the White Star Dock. Her maiden voyage had begun.

The Art Deco-style Ocean Terminal of 1950

It was 38 years later that the quayside the *Titanic* had sailed from in 1912 was transformed with an exciting and impressive addition to Southampton Docks. This was the opening of the new Art Deco-style Ocean Terminal in 1950.

The dock sheds on Berths 43–44 that were built for the new White Star Dock in 1911 were still standing at

White Star Dock was renamed Ocean Dock in 1922. This is Berth 43–44 in the Ocean Dock in 2006. (Author's Collection)

The Ocean Terminal in Ocean Dock and Empress Dock. The *New Australia* is being fitted out in the Empress Dock. The Ocean Terminal looks very new. A paddle steamer can be seen passing the ship docked at Berth 46–7. (Courtesy of ABP)

the beginning of World War Two. However, the German bombing of the docks caused so much damage that the sheds were demolished at the end of the war and the site was cleared for a new passenger terminal to be built.

The new terminal consisted of two storeys, the lower floor for ships' stores and freight and the upper storey for passengers. The terminal was 1,297ft (389.9m) in length and was opened in 1950. It was built especially for the transatlantic service and the *Queen Elizabeth* was the first vessel to berth at the terminal.

Boat trains would bring passengers to the railway platform, where they would enter the comfortable reception halls on the first floor before boarding the ocean liner for New York. It was a time when many famous film stars, entertainers and public figures would be seen in Southampton.

The Ocean Terminal was demolished in 1983 and the only remaining part of the terminal still in existence is the electrical substation that was on the opposite side of the approach road to the Ocean Terminal. Visitors to the balcony entered by stairs at the side of the substation and a bridge across the road to join the balcony overlooking the ships.

Ocean Terminal platform and boat train. (Courtesy of ABP)

All that remains of Ocean Terminal today is the old electrical substation. (Author's Collection)

Empress Dock. (Author's Collection)

The Empress Dock

Looking past the old Ocean Terminal site you can see another dock, the Empress Dock, which was opened in 1890 by Queen Victoria and today has the National Oceanography Centre, Southampton (NOCS) based at Berths 26–27. The NOCS is on the left side of the Empress Docks, and from the exit of the dock you can see Southampton Water stretching into the distance. It is down Southampton Water that the cruise ships have to sail on their way to the Solent, around the Isle of Wight and into the English Channel.

The NOCS centre was opened in 1995 and is owned in collaboration with the Natural Environment Research Council (NERC) and the University of Southampton. It houses 520 research scientists, lecturing, support and seagoing staff, and 700 undergraduate and postgraduate students.

The *Queen Mary 2* berthed at the Ocean Terminal. (Author's Collection)

APPENDIX C
Ship Statistics in Date Order

1819 — *Savannah*: 320 GT, 98ft (29.9m) length, beam 26ft (7.9m). Built in New York of wooden construction and had side paddle wheels. Engines were later removed and she became a sailing ship from Savannah to New York. Wrecked off Long Island in 1821.

1831 — *Royal William*: 364 GT, 160ft (48.8m) length, beam 28ft (8.5m). Built in Quebec and launched in 1831. She did her transatlantic crossing from Quebec, leaving on 5 August 1833 and arriving at Cowes, Isle of Wight, on 9 September. Became a hulk in Bordeaux harbour in 1840.

1837 — *Sirius*: 700 GT, 178ft (54.3m) length, beam 25ft (7.6m), one funnel, two masts for sail. Built by Robert Menzies & Son, Leith, and launched in 1837. Wooden construction, two side paddle wheels and a speed of 8 knots. Wrecked in 1847.

1837 — *Great Western*: 1,340 GT, 212ft (64.6m) length, beam 35ft (10.7m). Built by William Patterson, Bristol, of wooden construction with one funnel, four masts for sail and two side paddle wheels. Carried 128 first-class passengers with a crew of 60 at a service speed of 8.5 knots. Sold in 1847 to Royal Mail Steam Packet Company. Scrapped in 1857.

1838 — *British Queen*: 1,863 GT, 245ft (74.7m) length, beam 41ft (12.5m). Built in 1838 by Curling & Young, London, with wooden hull and two 30ft (9.1m) diameter paddle wheels which gave her a maximum speed of 10 knots. Designed to carry 207 passengers. Sold to the Belgian government in 1841.

1840 — *Britannia*: 1,135 GT, 207ft (63m) length, beam 34ft (10.4m). Built by Robert Duncan, Greenock, with engines by Robert Napier, Glasgow, propelling two side paddle wheels at a service speed of 9 knots. One funnel, three masts and was of wood construction. Sold to the German Navy and in 1849 became the *Barbarossa*. Transferred to the Prussian Navy in 1852 and sunk in 1880 while being used for target practice.

1842 — *Hindustan*: 2,108 GT, 217.5ft length (66.3m), beam 35.7ft (1098m). Built by Thomas Wilson & Co. of Liverpool and launched in 1842. Of wooden construction, two funnels, three masts, also used for sail, side paddle wheels with a speed of 10 knots. Sunk in a cyclone in Calcutta in 1864.

1858 — *Great Eastern*: 18,914 GT, 689ft (210m) length, beam 82ft (25m), 120ft (36.6m) measuring over the paddle wheels. Built with a double iron hull, had six masts for sails which were named 'Monday to Saturday', five funnels and separate engines to power the 56ft (17m) paddles and the propeller at a speed of 13.5 knots. Sold as a cable ship in 1864 and did two transatlantic crossings in 1867. Laid cables and was scrapped in 1888.

1871 — *Adriatic* (1): 3,888 GT, 437.2ft (133m) length, beam 40.9ft (12.5m). Built by Harland & Wolff, Belfast, for the White Star Line and launched in 1871. One funnel, four masts that were rigged for sail, iron hull, single screw and a speed of 14 knots. Accommodation for 166 first-class and 1,000 third-class passengers. Scrapped in Preston in 1888.

1888 — *City of New York*: 10,499 GT 527.6ft (160.8m) length, beam 63.2ft (19.3m). Built by J.&G. Thomson, Glasgow, in steel and had three funnels. The engines were triple expansion steam engines, which powered two screws at a service speed of 20 knots. Transferred to the American Line in 1893 and renamed *New York*. Sold to the Polish Navy in 1921.

1888 — *City of Paris*: 10,499 GT, 527.6ft (160.8m) length, beam 63.2ft (19.3m). Built by J.&G. Thomson, Glasgow, in steel and had three funnels and three masts. The engines were triple-expansion steam engines, which powered two screws at a service speed of 20 knots. Transferred to the American Line in 1893 and renamed *Paris*. Renamed *Philadelphia* in 1899. Sold to New York-Naples Steamship Company in 1922.

1989 — *Teutonic*: 9,984 GT, 582ft (177.4m) length, beam 57.7ft (17.6m). Her engines were triple expansion powering two screws at 20½ knots. Became the first AMC (Armed Merchant Cruiser). Scrapped in Emden in 1923.

1889 — *Grosser Kurfürst*: 12,500 GT, 560ft (170.7m) in length, beam 62ft (18.9m). Used for New York and Australian voyages. In 1917 became US Government *Aeolus* and later *City of Los Angeles*.

1889 — *König Albert*: 10,643 GT, 499ft (152.1m) in length, beam 60ft (18.3m) Became Italian hospital ship *Ferdinando Palasciano* in 1915. Scrapped in 1926.

1897 — *Kaiser Wilhelm der Grosse*: 14,349 GT, 582ft (177.4m) in length, beam 66ft (20.1m) Accommodation for 332 first-class, 343 second-class and 1,074 third-class. Maiden voyage Bremen-Southampton-New York-Plymouth-Bremen. Was sunk by HMS *Highflyer* at Rio de Oro in 1914.

1899 — *Oceanic* (2): 17,274 GT, 606ft (184.7m) length, beam 68ft (20.7m). Two funnels, three masts and four decks, and was fitted with electric light and refrigerating machinery. Twin screws powered by triple expansion engines giving a service speed of 19½ knots. Wrecked off Foula Island, Shetlands.

1906 — *Lusitania*: 31,550 GT, 787ft (239.9m) length, beam 87ft (26.5m). Built by John Brown & Company, Clydebank, with steam turbine engines powering quadruple screw propellers at a service speed of 25 knots. Torpedoed in 1915.

1907 – *Adriatic* (2): 24,541 GT, 726ft (221.3m) length, beam 75.5ft (23m). Built by Harland & Wolff, Belfast, for the White Star Line and launched on 20 September 1906. Two funnels, four masts, and the engines were reciprocating steam powering twin screws at a service speed of 17 knots. Accommodation for 450 first-class, 500 second-class and 2,000 third-class passengers. Scrapped in Japan in 1934.

1907 – *Asturias* (1): 12,105 GT, 520ft (158.49) length, beam 62ft (18.89). Built for the Royal Mail Steam Packet Company by Harland & Wolff, Belfast, and launched on 26 September 1907 with twin screws and a service speed of 15 knots. Accommodation for 300 first-class, 40 second-class and 1,200 third-class passengers. Hospital ship from 1914–17. Torpedoed 1917 but refitted as a cruise ship and named *Arcadian* (2).

1907 – *Mauretania*: 31,938 GT, 762.2ft (232.3m) length, beam 88ft (26.8m). Built by Swan Hunter & Wigham Richardson, Wallsend-on-Tyne, of steel construction, with four funnels, two masts. Steam turbine engines powered quadruple screws at a service speed of 25 knots. Accommodation for 563 first-class, 464 second-class and 1,138 third-class passengers. Scrapped at Rosyth in 1935.

1910 – *Olympic*: 45,342 GT, 852.5ft (259.8m) length, beam 92.5ft (28.2m). Four funnels, two masts and of steel construction. Powered by eight triple-expansion reciprocating engines and a low-pressure turbine driving triple screws at a service speed of 21 knots. Scrapped at Jarrow in 1935.

1910 – *Arcadian* (1): 8,939 GT, previously *Ortona*, 7,950 GT (1899). In 1910 *Ortona* rebuilt as a cruise ship for 320 first-class passengers and renamed *Arcadian* (1). Troopship 1915–17. Torpedoed and sunk in the Mediterranean 1917.

1911 – *Albania*: 7,640 GT, 461.5ft (140.7m) length, beam 52.1ft (15.9m). Built by Swan & Hunter & Wigham Richardson, Newcastle, of steel construction, with one funnel, four masts. Twin screws powered by six-cylinder turbine giving a service speed of 11 knots. Accommodation for 50 second-class and 800 third-class passengers.

1911 – *Titanic*: 46,329 GT, 882ft (268.8m) length, beam 92ft (28m). Built by Harland & Wolff Ltd, Belfast, with triple-expansion steam engines and low pressure turbine powering triple propellers at a speed of 21 knots. Sunk in the Atlantic in 1912.

1911 – *Ausonia*: 7,907 GT, 450.6ft (137.3m) length, beam 54.2ft (16.5m). Built by Swan & Hunter, Wallsend-on-Tyne, of steel construction, with one funnel, four masts. Twin screw powered by six-cylinder turbines, giving a service speed of 12 knots. Accommodation for 90 second-class and 1,000 third-class passengers. Torpedoed in 1917, but made it to port. Torpedoed and sunk in the Atlantic in 1918.

1911 – *Ascania* (1): 9,111 GT, 466ft (142.2m) length, beam 56.1ft (17.1m). Built by Swan Hunter & Wigham Richardson, Newcastle, and launched on 3 March 1911. Two funnels, two masts, twin screwed and powered by two sets of triple-expansion steam engines by Palmers Co., Newcastle, with a service speed between 12 and 13 knots. Wrecked off Cape Ray in 1918.

1912 – *France*: 23,666 GT, 713ft (217.3m) length, beam 75ft (22.9m). Steam turbine powering quadruple screw at a service speed of 24 knots. Accommodation for 534 first-class, 442 second-class, 250 third-class and 800 steerage passengers. Sold and scrapped in Dunkirk in 1934.

1912 – *Arlanza*: 20,362 GT, 584ft (178m) long, beam of 78ft 3in (23.8m). Built by Harland & Wolff, Belfast, for the Royal Mail and completed in June 1912. Triple expansion engines with B&W turbine powering triple screws at a service speed of 18 knots. Accommodation for 107 first-class, 82 cabin-class and 275 third-class passengers. Broken up at Blyth, 1938.

1913 – *Andania*: 13,405 GT, 520.3ft (158.6m) length, beam 64ft (19.5m). Built by Scotts Shipbuilding & Engineering Company Ltd, Greenock, of steel construction, with two funnels, two masts. Twin screw powered by quadruple-expansion engines giving a service speed of 15 knots. Accommodation for 520 second-class and 1,540 third-class passengers. Torpedoed near Rathlin Light.

1913 – *Alaunia*: 13,405 GT, length 520.3ft (158.6m), beam 64ft (19.5m). Built by Scotts Shipbuilding & Engineering Company Ltd, Greenock, of steel construction, with two funnels. Twin-screw, powered by quadruple-expansion engines, giving a service speed of 15 knots. Accommodation for 500 second-class and 1,500 third-class passengers. Mined off Royal Sovereign Lightship, 1918.

1913 – *Imperator*: 52,117 GT, 919ft (280.1m) length, beam 98ft (29.9m). Steam turbine engines powering quadruple screw propellers at a service speed of 23 knots. Accomodation for 908 first-class, 972 second-class, 942 third-class and 1,772 steerage passengers. Handed over to the Cunard Line in 1921 and renamed *Berengaria*. Scrapped in 1946.

1913 – *Andes*: 15,620 GT, length 590ft (179.8) beam 65.3ft, (19.9m). Built by Harland & Wolff, Belfast, with triple screw, one funnel, two masts and a service speed of 17 knots. Accommodation for 380 first-class, 250 second-class and 700 third-class passengers. AMC 1915–19.

1914 – *Vaterland*: 54,282 GT, 950ft (289.6) length, beam 100ft (30.5). Built for Germany's Holland America Line with steam turbine engines powering quadruple-screw propellers at a service speed of 23 knots. Became *Leviathan* for United States Line in 1919. Scrapped in 1938.

1914 – *Britannic*: 48,158 GT, 852ft (259.7m) length, beam 94ft (28.7m). The third of the Olympic trio built by Harland & Wolff, Belfast, of steel construction, with four funnels and two masts. Engines were steam triple-expansion engines, powering triple screws at a service speed of 21 knots. Launched on 26 February 1914 . Accommodation was for 790 first-class, 836 second-class and 953 third-class passengers. White Star Line hospital ship. Sunk by mine or torpedo in 1916.

1914 — *Aquitania*: 45,647 GT, 901ft (274.8m) long, beam 97ft (28.6m). Built by John Brown & Company, Clydebank, with steam turbine engines powering quadruple-screw propellers at a service speed of 23 knots, slightly slower than the *Mauretania*. Maiden voyage in 1914. AMC 1914, troopship 1915, hospital ship in the Dardanelles 1920–39 Southampton to New York Service, 1939–48 troopship, 1948 transatlantic service. Scrapped in 1950.

1915 — *Almanzora*: 16,034 GT, 590ft (179.8m) length, beam 69.3ft (21.3m). Built by Harland & Wolff, Belfast, with one funnel, two masts, twin screw, speed 15 knots. Launched on 19 November 1914. Accomodation for 400 first-class, 230 second-class and 760 third-class passengers. AMC 1915, troopship 1939–45, government emigrant ship 1945–47. Scrapped 1948.

1916 — *Aurania* (2): 13,936 GT, 520.3ft (158.6m) length, beam 64ft (19.5m). Built by Swan Hunter & Wigham Richardson, Wallsend-on-Tyne, of steel construction, with two funnels and two masts. Twin screw and powered by steam turbines, single reduction engines, giving a service speed of 15 knots. Launched on 16 July 1916. Used for trooping. Torpedoed and sunk in 1918.

1921 — *Scythia* (2): 19,730 GT, 625ft (190.5m) length, beam 74ft (22.5m). Built by Vickers-Armstrong, Barrow-in-Furness. Used oil for fuel to run her turbine engines, which powered twin propellers at a service speed of 16 knots. Accommodation for 337 first-class, 331 second-class and 1,538 third-class passengers. Troopship 1939–45. Scrapped in 1958.

1922 — *Samaria* (2): 19,602 GT, 625ft (190.5m) length, beam of 73.7ft (22.5m). Built by Cammell Laird & Co. Ltd, Birkenhead, with one funnel and two masts. Double reduction steam engines powered twin screws at a service speed of 16 knots. Launched on 27 November 1920. Accommodation for 350 first-class, 350 second-class and 1,500 third-class passengers. Troopship 1948. Scrapped in 1956.

1922 — *Laconia*: 19,680 GT, was 624ft (190.2m) length, beam 73.7ft (22.5m). Built by Swan Hunter & Wigham Richardson, Wallsend-on-Tyne, in 1921, with one funnel and two masts. Twin screws gave a service speed of 16 knots. Launched on 9 April 1921. AMC 1939, troopship 1947. Torpedoed and sunk in 1942 while carrying Italian POW.

1922 — *Homeric*: 34,351 GT, 774ft (235.9m) long, beam 82ft (25m). Built for North German Lloyd in Danzig, Germany, and originally called *Columbus* but seized for war reparations and renamed in 1922. Two funnels and two masts. Engines were steam triple-expansion powering twin screws at 18 knots. Accommodation for 529 first-class, 487 second-class and 1,750 third-class passengers. Scrapped in 1936.

1923 — *Mooltan*: 20,847 GT, 600.8ft (183.1m) length, beam 73.4ft (22.4m). Two funnels and two masts, and two quadruple-expansion reciprocating steam engines powering twin screws at a service speed of 16 knots. Scrapped in Faslane in 1954.

1923 — *Ascania* (2): 14,013 GT, 520ft (158.5m) length, beam 65ft 3in (19.9m). One funnel, two masts and fitted with four steam turbines, powering twin screws at a service speed of 15 knots. One of the 'A' class intermediate steamers built in the early 1920s. Accomodation for 500 cabin-class and 1,000 third-class passengers. AMC 1939–45, landing ship for infantry 1942, troopship 1945–47. Returned to service in 1947 and scrapped in 1957.

1923 — *Arcadian* (2): 12,105 GT, formerly *Asturias* (1) (1907). Rebuilt as a cruise ship. Laid up in 1930 and scrapped in 1933.

1923 — *Athenia*: 13,465 GT, 526.3ft (160.4m) length, beam 66.4ft, (20.2m). Built by Fairfield Company Ltd, Glasgow, for the Anchor–Donaldson Line of Glasgow and chartered to Cunard. One funnel, two masts and steam turbines powering twin screws at a service speed of 15 knots. Accommodation for 516 cabin-class and 1,000 third-class passengers. Torpedoed and sunk on the first day of World War Two.

1925 — *Asturias* (2): 22,071 GT, 656ft (199.9m) length, beam of 7ft 4in (23.9m). Engines were two eight-cylinder four-stroke double-acting B&M diesel engines powering twin screws at a service speed of 17 knots. Accomodation for 410 first-class, 232 second-class and 768 third-class passengers in 1925, with a crew of 450. AMC 1939, emigrant ship 1945. Scrapped in 1957.

1927 — *Ile de France*: 43,153 GT, 791ft (214m) length, beam 92ft (28m). Built at St Nazaire for the French Line with three funnels and two masts. Steam turbine engines powered quadruple screws at a service speed of 24 knots. Launched on 14 March 1926. Accommodation for 537 first-class, 603 second-class and 646 third-class passengers. Used to take US and Canadian troops home after the war.

1927 — *Alcantara*: 22,181 GT, 630.5ft (192.2m) length, beam 78.5ft (23.9m). Built by Harland & Wolff, Belfast, with two funnels, two masts, twin screws and a speed of 16 knots. Accommodation for 432 first-class, 200 second-class and 674 third-class passengers. Launched on 23 September 1926. 1939 AMC. Scrapped in 1958.

1929 — *Atlantis*: 15,620 GT. Previously *Andes*, refitted as a cruise ship for 450 first-class passengers and became *Atlantis* in 1929. Converted from coal to oil firing and her hull painted white. Hospital ship 1939–45. Emigrant ship to Australia and New Zealand from 1948 until being scrapped in 1952.

1930 — *Britannic*: 26,943 GT, 712ft (217m) length, beam 82ft (24.9m). Built by Harland & Wolf, Belfast, for White Star Line. Diesel powering twin screws at 18 knots. Launched 1929. Accomodation for 504 cabin-class, 551 tourist-class and 506 third-class passengers. Taken over by Cunard-White Star in 1934. Scrapped in 1960.

1930 — *Georgic*: 26,943 GT, 712ft (217m) length, beam 82ft (24.9m). Built by Harland & Wolf, Belfast for White Star Line. Diesel powering twin screws at 18 knots. Launched 1931. Accomodation for 479 cabin-class, 557 tourist-class and 506 third-class passengers. Scrapped in 1956.

1930 — *Empress of Britain*: 42,348 GT, 760.6ft (231.8m) length, beam 97.6ft (29.7m). Built by John Brown & Company, Clydebank, and was the Canadian Pacific's largest passenger ship. Engines were steam turbines which powered quadruple screws at a service speed of 24 knots. Accommodation for 465 first-class, 260 tourist-class and 470 third-class passengers and carried a crew of 714. Bombed off the coast of Ireland in 1940. Largest passenger ship sunk in the war.

1930 — *Warwick Castle*: 20,445 GT, 651ft 6in (198.6m) length. The sister ship to the *Winchester Castle* and built by Harland & Wolff Ltd, Belfast, in 1930. Twin screwed giving a service speed of 17 knots. Accommodation for 260 first-class, 243 second-class and 254 third-class passengers with a crew of 350. Modernised in 1938 and re-engined, giving a service speed of 20 knots. One of her two funnels was removed and the tonnage reassessed at 20,107 GT. Torpedoed and sunk off Portugal in 1942.

1931 — *Rex*: 48,348 GT, 879.9ft (268.2m) length, beam of 97ft (29.6m). Built by G. Ansaldo & Co. of Genoa for the Italian Line. Engines were single-reduction steam turbine powering quadruple screws at a service speed of 27 knots. Launched on 31 July 1931. Accommodation for 408 first-class, 410 tourist-class and 866 third-class passengers. Took the Blue Riband in 1933. Bombed and sunk in 1944.

1931 — *Conti di Savoia*: 48,502 GT, 814.8ft (248.3m) length, beam of 96.1ft (29.3m). Built by Societa Anonima Cantieri Riuniti dell'Adriatico of Trieste. Engines were triple-expansion steam turbines powering quadruple screws at a service speed of 26.25 knots. Launched on 28 October 1931. Accommodation for 500 first-class, 366 second-class and 922 third-class passengers. Laid up in Venice in 1939, bombed and sunk in 1943, refloated in 1945 and scrapped in 1950.

1931 — *Strathnaver*: 22,547 GT, 638.7ft (194.7m) length, beam of 80.2ft (24.4m). Built by Vickers-Armstrong, Barrow-in-Furness. Engines were steam turbine powering two screws at a service speed of 21 knots. Launched on 5 February 1931. Accommodation for 498 first-class and 668 tourist-class passengers, but was changed to a one-class ship in 1954 to carry 1,252 passengers. Scrapped in Hong Kong in 1962.

1931 — *Monarch of Bermuda*: 22,424 GT, 579ft (176.5m) length, beam 76ft (23.2m). Three funnels, two masts and a cruiser stern. Engines were turboelectric, which powered four screws at a service speed of 19 knots. Accommodation for 799 first-class and 31 second-class with a crew of 456. Launched on 17 March 1931 and sailed on the Furness, Withy & Company's New York to Bermuda run from 1931–39. Troopship 1939–47. Had a serious fire in 1947 and sold to Ministry of Transport. Rebuilt as *New Australia*.

1932 — *Strathaird*: 22,568 GT, 666ft (203m) length, beam 80ft (24.4m). Built by Vickers-Armstrong, Barrow-in-Furness. Engines were steam turbine powering twin screws at a service speed of 20 knots. Accomodation for 478 first-class and 668 tourist-class passengers, but changed to a one-class ship in 1954 to carry 1,252 passengers. Scrapped in Hong Kong in 1967.

1935 — *Strathmore*: 23,428 GT, 640.3ft (195.2m) long, beam of 82.3ft (25.1m). Built by Vickers-Armstrong, Barrow-in-Furness. Engines were single reduction geared steam turbines powering twin screws at a service speed of 20 knots. Launched on 4 April 1935. Accommodation for 445 first-class and 665 tourist-class passengers with a crew of 503, but was changed to a one-class ship in 1961 to carry 1,200 passengers. Scrapped in 1969.

1935 — *Normandie*: 79,280 GT, 1,028ft (313.3m) length, beam of 117ft (35.7m). Built at St Nazaire, France. Engines were steam turbo-electric powering quadruple screws at a service speed of 29 knots. Launched on 29 October 1932. Accommodation was for 848 first-class, 670 tourist-class and 454 third-class passengers with a crew of 1,345. Was seized by USA in 1940 and renamed *Lafayette*, but as a result of a serious fire was scrapped in 1946.

1936 — *Queen Mary*: 80,773 GT (1936). Was later 81,237 GT when the engineers' quarters were added above the Verandah Grill in December 1937. Length 1,019.5ft (310.7m), beam 118ft (36m). Accommodation for 776 first (cabin) class, 784 tourist-class and 579 third-class with a crew of 1,101. Troopship 1940–46 and retired to Long Beach in 1967.

1937 — *Nieuw Amsterdam*: 36,287 GT, 758ft (231m) length, beam of 88ft (26.8m). Built for the Holland-America Line by the Rotterdam Dry Dock Company. Engines were steam turbine powering twin screws at 20.5 knots. Launched on 10 April 1937. Accomodation for 556 first-class, 455 tourist-class and 209 third-class passengers. Ocean liner service 1938–74 and scrapped in 1974.

1937 — *Wilhelm Gustloff*: 25,484 GT, 684ft (208.5m) length, beam 77ft (23.5m). Purpose-built cruise ship for the KdF programme and launched in the presence of Adolf Hitler. Diesel engines powering twin screws at 15 knots. Accommodation for 1,465 passengers.

1938 — *Stratheden*: 23,732 GT, 664ft (202.4m) length, beam 82ft (25m). Built by Vickers-Armstrong, Barrow-in-Furness. Engines were steam turbines powering twin screws at a service speed of 20 knots. Launched in 1937. Accommodation for 448 first-class and 563 tourist-class passengers, but was changed in 1961 to a one-class ship carrying 1,200 passengers. Withdrawn from Australian run in 1963 and scrapped in 1967.

1938 — *Strathallan*: 23,722 GT, 664.5ft (202.5m) length, beam 82.2 (25m). Built by Vickers-Armstrong, Barrow-in-Furness, with one funnel and two masts. Engines were steam turbines powering twin screws at 20 knots. Sunk by *U-562* (commanded by Horst Hamm) on 21 December 1942, approximately 40 miles north of Oran, while part of Operation Torch.

1938 — *Canton*: 16,033 GT, 563.3ft (171.7m) length, beam 73.3ft (22.3m). Built by Alexander Stephen & Sons Ltd, Glasgow. Engines were steam turbines powering twin screws at a service speed of 18 knots. Launched on 14 April 1938. Accommodation for 298 first-class and 244 tourist-class passengers with a crew of 319. Scrapped in Hong Kong 1962.

1939 — *Andes* (2): 26,689 GT, 669ft (203.9m) length, beam 83ft (25.3m). Built by Harland & Wolff, Belfast. Engines were steam turbines powering twin screws at a service speed of 21 knots. Accommodation for 403 first-class and 204 second-class passengers. Troopship 1939–45, cruise ship 1959 and scrapped 1971.

1939 — *Mauretania* (2): 35,738 GT, 772ft (235.3m) length, beam 89ft (27.1m). Built by Cammell Laird & Co., Birkenhead. Engine was steam turbines powering twin screw at a service speed of 23 knots. Launched on 28 July 1938 and went into service in June 1939. Accommodation for 440 cabin-class, 450 tourist-class and 470 third-class passengers. Troopship 1940–46 and scrapped in 1965.

1940 — *Queen Elizabeth*: 83,673 GT, 1,031ft (314.2m) in length, beam 118ft (36m) built by John Brown & Company, Clydebank. Accommodation for 823 first-class, 662 cabin-class, 798 tourist-class passengers with 1,318 officers and crew. Secretly sailed to New York on 3 March 1940. Used as a troopship during the war. First commercial voyage 16 October 1946, Southampton to New York.

1947 — *Caronia*: 34,183 GT, 678.5ft (209.5m) length, beam 91.4ft (27.9m). Nicknamed 'The Green Goddess'. Built by John Brown & Company, Clydebank, with one funnel and one mast. Engines were steam turbines powering twin screws at a service speed of 22 knots. Launched on 30 October 1947. Accommodation for 581 first-class and 351 cabin-class passengers. Sold in 1969 and became cruise ship *Columbia*, then *Caribia*. Sold again in 1974 but sunk in stormy weather while being towed for scrapping.

1949 — *Himalaya*: 27,955 GT, 708.7ft (216m) length, beam 90.8ft (27.7m). Built by Vickers-Armstrong, Barrow-in-Furness, and was the first post-war P&O build. Engines were steam turbines powering twin screws at 22 knots. Accommodation for 758 first-class and 401 tourist-class passengers with a crew of 572. Scrapped in 1974.

1950 — *Chusan*: 24,215 GT, 646.5ft (197.5m) length, beam 85.2ft (26m). Built by Vickers-Armstrong, Barrow-in-Furness, with one funnel and two masts. Engines were steam turbine powering twin screws at 23 knots. Launched on 28 June 1949. Accomodation for 474 first-class, 514 tourist-class passengers with a crew of 577. Scrapped in 1973.

1950 — *New Australia*: 20,256 GT, 553.2ft (168.6m) length, beam 76.7ft (23.4m). Originally *Monarch of Bermuda*. Accommodation for 1,600 as one class. Shaw Savill was asked by the Ministry of Transport to manage the vessel. Sold to Greek Line in 1958 and renamed *Arkadia*.

1952 — *United States*: 53,329 GT, 956ft (291.4m) length, beam 101.6ft (316m). Built by Newport News Ship Building, Virginia. Engines were steam turbines powering four screws at a service speed of 35 knots. Launched in 1952. Accommodation for 913 first-class, 558 cabin-class and 537 tourist-class passengers. Sold to Norwegian Cruise Line in 2003 and presently docked at Philadelphia and up for sale.

1954 — *Saxonia*: 21,637 GT, 608ft (185.3m) length, beam 80.3ft (24.5m). Built by John Brown & Company, Clydebank, with one funnel and one mast. Engines were steam turbines powering twin screws at a service speed of 21 knots. Launched on 17 February 1954. Accommodation for 110 first-class and 883 tourist-class passengers. Cruising from 1962, sold in 1973 and renamed *Leonid Sobinov*. Scrapped in 2000.

1954 — *Arcadia*: 29,734 GT, 721ft (219.8) length, beam 91ft (27.7m). Steam turbines powering twin screws at a service speed of 22 knots. Accommodation for 647 first-class and 735 tourist-class passenger. Scrapped in 1979 in Taiwan.

1954 — *Iberia*: 29,614 GT, 719ft (219.1m) length, beam 91ft (27.7m). Steam turbines powering twin screws at a service speed of 22 knots. Accommodation for 673 first-class and 733 tourist-class passengers. Scrapped in 1972 in Taiwan.

1955 — *Ivernia* (2): 17,707 GT, 598.4ft (182.4m) length, beam 79.4ft (24.2m). Built by John Brown & Company, Clydebank, and made her maiden voyage in 1955. Rebuilt for cruising in 1963 and renamed *Franconia*. Sold and renamed *Fedor Shalyapin*. Scrapped in 1999.

1960 — *Oriana*: 41,923 GT, 804ft (245.1m) length, beam 97ft (29.6m). Steam turbines powering twin screws at a service speed of 22 knots. Accommodation for 668 first-class and 1,496 tourist-class passengers. Cruising only from 1981. Scrapped in 2005 in China.

1960 — *France*: 66,348 GT, 1035.2ft (315.5m) length, beam 110.9ft (33.8m). Built by Chantiers de l'Atlantique, St Nazaire, for the French Line (Compagnie Générale Transatlantique), with two funnels and one mast. Engines were steam turbines powering four screws at a service speed of 30 knots. Launched 11 May 1960. Accommodation for 500 first-class and 1,550 tourist-class passengers. Laid up in 1974 and sold in 1977 to Swiss Company and then to Norwegian shipping magnate Lauritz Kloster. Converted as a cruise ship and renamed *Norway*. Broken up completely by 2008.

1961 — *Canberra*: 44,807 GT, 820ft (249.9m) length, beam 102ft (31.1m). Accommodation for 548 first-class and 1,600 tourist-class passengers with a crew of 960. Scrapped in 1998.

1966 — *Black Prince*: 9,499 GT (11,209 GT when refitted for cruising), 470ft (143.3m) length, beam of 66.6ft (20.3m). Built by Flender Werft, Germany, and powered by diesel engines at a service speed of 18.5 knots. Has seven passenger decks and 237 cabins for 450 passengers with a crew of 200. Was retired from being a cruise ship due to not meeting SOLAS 2010 regulations.

1967 – *Queen Elizabeth 2*: 70,327 GT, 963ft (293.5m) length, beam 105.3ft (32.1m). Built by John Brown & Company, Clydebank. Engines were two sets of geared turbines powering twin screws at a service speed of 28.5 knots. Launched on 20 September 1967. Sold to Dubai.

1995 – *Legend of the Seas*: 70,000 GT, 867ft (264.3m) length, beam 105ft (32m). Built by Chantiers de l'Atlantique, France. Has 11 passenger decks and carries 1,804 passengers with a crew of 720.

1995 – *Oriana*: 69,153 GT, 856ft (261m) length, beam 105ft (32.2m). Built by Meyer Werft, Germany, with diesel engines powering a service speed of 24 knots. Has 10 passenger decks and 914 passenger cabins for a passenger capacity of 1,818 (1,928 max) with a crew of 800.

1997 – *Dawn Princess*: 77,000 GT, 856ft (260m) length, beam 106ft (32m). Built by Fincantieri, Italy. Accommodation for 1,950 passengers with a crew of 900.

1998 – *Disney Magic*: 83,000 GT, 964ft (293.8m) length, beam 106ft (32.3m). Has 10 decks with 874 cabins for 2,400 passengers with a crew of 945. Cruising speed of 21.5 knots. Maiden voyage on 31 July 1998.

1998 – *Grand Princess*: 109,000 GT, 951ft (289.9m), length, beam 118ft (36m). Built by Fincantieri, Italy, and entered service in 1998. Has 18 passenger decks and carries 2,600 passengers with a crew of 1,200.

1998 – *Vision of the Seas*: 78.491 GT 915.3ft (279 m) length, beam 105.6ft (32.2 m). Carries 2,000 passengers with a crew of 765.

1999 – *Mistral*: 47,900 GT, 708.66ft (216m) length, beam 94.5ft (28.8m). Built by Chantiers de l'Atlantique. Service speed of 19.5 knots. Has 598 cabins for 1,200 passengers.

1999 – *Voyager of the Seas*: 138,000 GT, 1020ft (310.9m) length, beam 56ft (47.5m). Has 14 passenger decks and carries 3,114 passengers.

1999 – *Disney Wonder*: 83,000 GT, 964ft (293.8m) length, beam 106ft (32.3m). Built Fincantieri Shipyards, Venice, and has a service speed of 21.5 knots. The sister ship of the *Disney Magic* (built in 1998). Launched in 1999. Carries 2,400 passengers with a crew of 927.

2000 – *Aurora*: 76,000GT, 886ft (270m) length, beam 106ft (32.3m). Built by Mayer Werft, Germany. Engines are diesel-electric giving a service speed of 24 knots. The sister ship to the *Oriana*. Has 10 passenger decks with 935 passenger cabins (22 cabins for the disabled) and carries 1,870 (1,959 max) passengers with a crew of 850. Named by HRH The Princess Royal and entered service in 2000.

2003 – *Oceana*: 77,000 GT, 856ft (261m) length, beam 105ft (32m). Built by Fincantieri, Italy and entered service in 2000 as *Ocean Princess* (2000–02). Has a service speed of 21 knots. Has 11 decks with 1,008 cabins and carries 2,016 regular passengers (2,272 maximum) with a crew of 870. Originally *Ocean Princess*, renamed *Oceana* in 2003.

2004 – *Queen Mary 2*: 150,000 GT, 1132ft (345m) length, beam 135ft (41m). Built by ALSTOM Chantiers de l'Atlantique, France. Four diesel engines and two gas turbines propelling four pods of 21.5 MW each, (two fixed and two azimuth-see below), powering the vessel at a maximum speed of 30 knots. Carries 2,620 passengers with a crew of 1,254. Extra thick steel hull for strength and stability for Atlantic crossings and two stabilisers. Entered service in 2004 for the Cunard Line

2005 – *Arcadia*: 83,500 GT, 935ft (285m) length, beam 96ft (29.2m). Built by Fincantieri, Italy, and powered by two ABB Azipods, giving a service speed of 24 knots. Has 11 passenger decks, 14 lifts and 1,008 passenger cabins, including 30 wheelchair-accessible cabins for 2,016 regular passengers (maximum 2,388) with a crew of 880. Entered service in 2005.

2005 – *Artemis*: 45,000 GT, 754ft (230m) length, beam 106ft (32.3m). Previously *Royal Princess* (1984) and christened by the late Princess of Wales. Built by Wartsila, Finland. Has eight passenger decks with 594 passenger cabins for 1,188 passengers (maximum 1,260) and a crew of 537. Renamed as *Artemis* by Prunella Scales in June 2005, and was the first ship to feature all outside cabins. At present the smallest ship in the P&O fleet. Will be replaced in 2011 by *Royal Princess* (30,277 GT) and renamed *Adonia*.

2006 – *Crown Princess*: 113,000 GT, 951ft (289m) length, beam 118ft (36m). Built by Fincantieri, Italy with a speed of 21.5 knots. Has the capacity for 3,080 passengers and 1,200 crew.

2007 – *Queen Victoria*: 90,049 GT, 964ft (293.8m) length, beam 106ft (32.3m). Built by Fincantieri, Italy. Has 12 passenger decks and carries 2,014 passengers with a crew of 900. Entered service in 2007.

2008 – *Celebrity Solstice*: 122,000 GT, 1033ft (314.9m) length, beam 121ft (36.9m). Built by Meyer Werft, Germany, with a speed of 23 knots. Has 13 decks for 2,850 passengers 2,850 and a crew of 1,250. Entered service in 2008.

2008 – *Ventura*: 115,000 GT, 951ft (290m) length, beam 118ft (36m). Built by Fincantieri, Italy. Engines are diesel electric giving a service speed of 22 knots. Has 15 passenger decks with 1,539 passenger cabins for 3,078 passengers (maximum 3,574) and a crew of 1,226. Entered service in 2008 and was the largest cruise ship in the P&O fleet.

2009 – *Celebrity Equinox*: 122,000 GT, 1033ft (314.9m) length, beam 121ft (36.9m). Built by Meyer Werft, Germany, with a speed of 23 knots. Has 13 decks and carries 2,850 passengers with crew of 1250. Entered service 2009.

2009 – *Oasis of the Seas*: 220,000 GT, 1,184ft (360.9m) length, beam 184ft (56.1m). Cruising speed of 22 knots. Has 16 decks, 2,700 staterooms and the capacity for 5,400 passengers with a crew of 2,165.

2010 – *Azura*: 116,000GT 951.44ft (290m) length, beam 118.11m (36m). Built by Fincantieri, Italy. Speed 22 knots. Has 14 passenger decks for 3,096 passengers and a crew of 1,200. Entered service in 2010.

2010 – *Celebrity Eclipse*: 122,000 GT, 1033ft (314.9m) length, beam 121ft (36.9m). Built by Meyer Werft, Germany. Speed 23 knots. Has 13 decks for 2,850 and a crew of 1,250. Entered service in 2010.

2010 – *Queen Elizabeth*: 90,400 GT, 964ft (294m) length, beam 106ft (32m). Built by Fincantieri, Italy. Has 12 passenger decks for 2,092 passengers. Enters service in 2010.

APPENDIX D
Southampton Timeline

Date	Events
AD43–50	Roman invasion of Britain. Important trading port established on the River Itchen and named Clausentum.
407	Romans leave Britain. Anglo-Saxons use Clausentum for a time.
650–850	Anglo-Saxons suffer Viking attacks in the St Mary's area alongside the River Itchen.
980	Anglo-Saxons move due to Viking attacks from St Mary's to higher ground and new town established.
1016	Viking King Canute crowned in Southampton and later gets his feet wet!
1066	Norman Conquest. Southampton becomes an import port for trade between Normandy and England.
1338	The French raid Southampton and this leads to strengthening the town walls and other defensive structures.
1417	The town becomes a main port for the wool trade with the Continent. The Wool House built for wool storage.
1620	The Pilgrim Fathers leave Southampton in the *Mayflower* and *Speedwell*.
1700	Southampton no longer a major port due to stiff competition from London for the trade.
1750	Southampton becomes popular as a spa town.
1800	Town authorities move to create a new port to attract more sea trade to the town.
1803	New Quay, known as Town Quay, constructed. Replaced Watergate Quay.
	Southampton Harbour commissioners are authorised.
1810	West Quay jetty dilapidated. It is sold and demolished.
1833	Royal Pier is opened by Princess Victoria and her mother, the Duchess of Kent. Originally named Royal Victoria Pier but eventually shortened to Royal Pier.
1836	Formation of Southampton Dock Company. First general meeting convenes at the George and Vulture Tavern, London, 16 August.
1838	Queen Victoria's coronation.
	Foundation stone laid.
	First demonstration of telegraph.
	First regular steamship service crosses the Atlantic.
1840	Railway line between from London to Southampton completed.
1842	Outer Dock opens 29 August to accommodate two ships of the P&O Company, the 780-ton *Tagus* and the 500-ton *Liverpool*. Royal Mail Steam Packet Company's ships also use the dock from its inception.
1843	Outer Dock opens to general trade, 1 July.
1845	South Western Steam Navigation Company commence regular communication with the Channel Islands and Le Havre.
1846	No.1 Dry Dock is completed, the first ship to use it being RMSP Company's 1,939-ton *Forth* c.27 July.
1847	No.2 Dry Dock is completed.
1850	RMSP Company's 232-ton steamer *Esk* inaugurates mail and passenger service to South America in November.
1851	Inner Dock opens to shipping.
1854–56	Crimean War. Southampton is used as principal military embarkation port.
	No.3 Dry Dock opens. Union SS Company begin using docks.
1857	Union Steamship Company commence monthly mail service to South African ports with the sailing of RMS *Dane*, 530 tons. 15 September Hamburg-America Line commences calling en route from Germany to New York.
1858	Norddeutscher Lloyd vessels commence calling on the North American mail service.
1859	Extension, deepening and widening of entrance to Inner Dock. First vessel to enter is P&O Company's *Pera*, 20 May.

Date	Events
1860	Visit of the *Great Eastern* prior to her maiden voyage.
	Isle of Wight & South of England Steam Packet Company forms.
1862	London & South Western Railway take over the cross channel ferries.
1871	Rail lines to Royal Pier.
1874–1903	P&O leave Southampton for London Docks, 1874 for cargo vessels and 1881 for passenger vessels. In 1903 the mail steamers move to Tilbury.
1876	Building of Itchen Quays commences and is completed in 1895.
1877	Act of Parliament creates Southampton Harbour Board.
1879	No.4 Dry Dock is completed. Union Steamship Company start using Itchen Quays.
1880	Loss of trade and Southampton Dock Company (approved by Parliament) takes a loan for £250,000 to build a new deep-water dock.
1890	Empress Dock is opened by Queen Victoria, 26 July. At the time Southampton is the only port able to take the deepest-draught vessels at any state of tide.
1892	Southampton Docks is purchased by L&SWR on 1 November for £1,360,000. L&SWR take over running the port.
	New Royal Pier opens in 1892.
1893	American Line transfers its New York mail service from Liverpool to Southampton, the liner *New York* commencing the service on 4 March.
1894	British government choose Southampton as principal base for Indian and Colonial transport services.
	Seasonal trooping autumn to spring.
1895	No.5 Dry Dock is opened by HRH The Prince of Wales.
	Itchen Quays is completed. Work starts on South Quay and Test Quays.
1899	Boer War. Southampton is the number one principal embarkation port.
1900	Union and Castle Lines merge to form Union-Castle Line. First sailing of Union-Castle Line from Southampton by *Dunottar Castle* on 17 March. Other lines start making regular calls to the port, and Red Funnel begins day-return excursions to Cherbourg via Bournemouth with PS *Balmoral* from June to September only.
1901	International Cold Storage and Ice Company's cold store at 40 berth opens.
1902	South Quay (Berth 37) and Test Quays (Berth 38–41) open.
1904	First electric crane (50-ton at No.6 Dry Dock) is installed.
1905	No.6 Dry Dock ('Trafalgar Dock') opens 21 October. *Dunluce Castle* is the first ship to enter the Dry Dock on 17 November.
1907	White Star Line's North Atlantic express service transfers from Liverpool to Southampton. It is inaugurated by the *Adriatic*.
1908	*St Paul* collides with and sinks HMS *Gladiator* off Yarmouth on 25 August.
1911	White Star Dock opens with the sailing of White Star liner *Olympic* on her maiden voyage on 14 June.
	Cunard Line inaugurates Canadian service from Southampton with the sailing of *Albania*, on 1 May, en route from London.
1912	*Titanic* sails from Southampton on her fateful voyage. *Olympic* is her sister ship.
1913	Mayflower Memorial is unveiled by Walter Hines Page, US Ambassador.
1914–18	World War One. Docks are placed under government control and became the number one military embarkation port. Over 7,000,000 troops and nearly 4,000,000 tons of stores dealt with.
1919	Cunard Line's North Atlantic express service from Southampton is inaugurated by *Aquitania*, sailing 14 June.
1920	Canadian Pacific SS Company start their principal Canadian service from Southampton.
1922	Hythe Ferry Pier electric railway. White Star *Majestic*, formerly Hamburg–America's *Bismark*, was then the largest liner in the world.
1923	Grouping of railways – L&SWR is amalgamated with other railways in the south and the running of Southampton Docks taken over by Southern Railway.

Date	Events
1924	60,000-ton floating dock is opened by HRH The Prince of Wales on 27 June at Berth 50.
1925	P&O returns to Southampton.
1926	North German Lloyd calls at Southampton for Philadelphia–Bremen service.
1927	New docks scheme officially commences on 3 January. Land between the Royal Pier and Millbrook is reclaimed. This is called Extension Quays and consists of 400 acres of mudland reclaimed to create 1.5 miles of deep-water berths.
1929	Old *Mauretania* loses the Blue Riband after 22 years.
1931	Red Funnel's first screw vessel is the *Medina*, followed by the *Balmoral* and *Vecta*. The *Vecta* uses Voith Schneider propellers.
1932	Cunard Line's *Mauretania* is the first ship to use New Docks quays, berthed at Berth 102 on 19 October for lay-up.
1933	King George V Graving Dock opens 26 July. At the time it is the largest dry dock in the world. The planned second graving dock is never built.
1934	New Docks is completed.
	Solent Flour Mills opens.
	Holland-Africa Line commences regular monthly call on South African service.
1935	French Line transfers its New York and West Indies service from Plymouth to Southampton.
1936	*Queen Mary* sails from Southampton on her maiden voyage on 27 May.
1937	Imperial Airways inaugurates Empire flying-boat services from Southampton Docks.
1938	Southampton Dock centenary.
1939–45	World War Two. Southampton Docks deals with 4,300,000 military personnel and 3,900,000 tons of stores and equipment. The docks are bombed on the weekend of 30 November 1940. All areas of the dock are affected. Quayside sheds 103–104 are completely destroyed. In 69 air raids 226 bombs fall on the docks, and 23 sheds and warehouses are destroyed or seriously damaged.
	New *Queen Elizabeth* secretly sails from the Clyde to New York on 3 March 1940.
	International Cold Store is destroyed by bombs 1940.
	Flying Boat services are interrupted because of the war.
	The dock is particularly involved in the D-Day preparations.
1946	*Queen Elizabeth* sails from Southampton on her first commercial voyage on 16 October.
1948	Nationalisation of British Transport. The port is managed from then on by the British Transport Commission.
	Nationalisation of railways form Southern Railway to British Rail.
	Maiden voyages of *Pretoria Castle* on 22 July and *Edinburgh Castle* on 9 December.
	BOAC resumes flying boat services from Berth 50.
	New Terminal opens on 14 April.
1950	New Art Deco-style Ocean Terminal opens measuring 1,270 feet long by 120 feet wide Its railway platform has room for two full-length trains at once.
	Aquilla Airways' flying boat service is formed by Barry Aikman with services to Maderia, Lisbon, Las Palmas and Genoa.
1952	*United States* arrives at Southampton on her maiden voyage on 8 July.
	Esso Oil Refinery at Fawley opens.
1953	Coronation Year of Queen Elizabeth II.
	Union-Castle centenary.
	First cargo of bananas since the war arrives on 1 February.
1955	688,000 passengers pass through the port.
1956	Union-Castle Passenger and Cargo Terminal at Berth 102, New Docks, opens on 25 January.
1958	New cold store at Berth 108 opens.
	Port Operations service.
	World's first port radio and radar station opens at Calshot on Southampton Water (on top of Calshot Castle).

Date	Events
1959	New banana accommodation at Berth 25 is completed.
1960	First shipment of Renault cars arrives.
	P&O passenger terminal completed at Berth 106.
	Maiden voyages of *Oriana* and *Canberra*.
1963	British Transport Docks Board takes over running the docks from British Transport Commission in January.
	Port authorities start on reclamation project from King George V Dry Dock to Redbridge causeway.
1964	HM Queen Elizabeth II grants Southampton city status due to the Port of Southampton's 'importance to the nation'. It had been a county town since 1447.
	Railway steamers end service.
	British Transport Docks Board (BTDB) starts redevelopment of Inner and Outer Dock. Filling in of Inner Dock for car storage. Entrance to Outer Dock increased to 325 feet.
	Townsend-Thoresen ferry services start.
1965	National Dock Labour scheme puts an end to casual labour. Dockers now have to be registered (Jobs for Life).
	Union-Castle ships sail on Fridays. The service speeds up with the introduction of *Southampton Castle* and *Good Hope Castle*.
1966	HM Queen Elizabeth II opens the Queen Elizabeth II Passenger Cruise Terminal. Southampton Terminus Station was closed in September 1966 for passenger traffic and completely in 1968.
1967	*Queen Mary* leaves Southampton for last time in October.
	Ferry complex opened at Outer Dock on 3 July by HRH Princess Alexandra and dock renamed Princess Alexandra Dock after her.
	Normandy and P&O ferry services start. Swedish Lloyd services start.
1968	Reclamation work starts at Millbrook in October.
	Southampton Harbour Board is amalgamated with the BTDB on 1 August.
	First quay for containers opens on 28 October and the first ship to use it was the Dart Line's *Teniers*.
1969	Harbour Board and BTDB join as one in August.
	P&O ships in operation are: *Orsorva, Orcades, Oronsay, Arcadia, Iberia, Himalaya, Chusan*.
	Ro-Ro terminal is provided at Berth 201.
	Liner *United States* is withdrawn from service.
1971	Solent Containers operations start in July.
	Construction begins on the two-berth facility 204–205. Berth 205 is completed on 19 July 1978.
1972	New Port VTS (Vessel Traffic Services) facilities are built on Dock Head, Eastern Docks, replacing the one at Calshot. Up to now all vessel movement are monitored from a blacked-out room especially designed for the use of radar equipment. Solent Containers manage Berths 204–206.
1974	Liner *France* is withdrawn from service.
1977	Itchen Floating Bridge is replaced by Woolston Bridge.
1979	Royal consent is granted to name the Solent Containers' site the Prince Charles Container Terminal.
1980	Ocean Terminal closes.
1982	Associated British Ports (ABP) takes over the running of the docks as a result of the 1980 transport-privatisation of the BTDB.
	Grain terminals open at Berth 47.
	Trooping for the Falklands War begins with the liners *Canberra* and *QE2* used.
1983	Ocean Terminal is demolished.
	Second grain terminal opens on Berth 36.
	Southampton Terminus Station empty but protected from demolition.
	Dock has Freeport status.
	Townsend-Thoreson ferry services transfer to Portsmouth.

Date	Events
1984	Princess Alexandra Dock is redeveloped as Ocean Village.
	P&O Ferries transfer to Portsmouth.
1985	HRH The Prince of Wales visits the Prince Charles Container Port, now Southampton Container Terminal (SCT).
1988	150th anniversary of the founding of the Port of Southampton.
1989	National Dock Labour Scheme is abolished.
1991	The new temperature-controlled Canary Islands Fruit Terminal opens at Berth 104. Southampton is still today the sole UK port of entry for all fresh produce imported from the Canary Islands.
	New offices of ABP 'Ocean Gate' open at Berth 45.
1992	Windward Terminal opens for Geest bananas.
1995	HM Queen Elizabeth II names the new P&O cruise ship *Oriana*.
1996	Work begins to deepen the main channel to allow the increasingly deeper-draught ships to enter the port.
	University Oceanography Centre opens at Empress Dock. It later becomes National Oceanography Centre.
1997	A fourth deep-sea berth, Berth 207, is completed at Southampton Container Terminal.
1999	Fyffes' traffic transfers from Portsmouth and combines with Geest at Berth 101.
2000	ABP submits application to develop Dibden Terminal on port-owned land. This is not granted.
	The new Hapag-Lloyd cruise ship, *Europa*, makes her maiden call in August.
2001	P&O Princess Cruises' *Golden Princess*, Norwegian Cruise Line's *Norwegian Sun*, Royal Caribbean's *Adventure of the Seas* and Fred. Olsen's new third ship, *Braemar*, arrive in Southampton.
2002	Purpose-built multi-deck car terminal opens and is used by Wallenius Wilhelmsen.
	Geest and Fyffes' banana traffic transfers to Portsmouth.
2003	The port opens the improved cruise terminals and develops a third cruise facility.
	Oceania and *Adonia* joins the P&O Cruise fleet in Southampton. Also sailing from the port was Fred. Olsen Cruise Line's *Black Watch, Black Prince* and Royal Caribbean's *Jewel of the Seas*, named in Southampton.
	City Cruise Terminal is in operation. Royal Caribbean's International *Legend of the Seas* is the first to use the terminal, followed by Fred. Olsen Cruise Line, Saga Shipping and Thomson Cruises.
2004	On 12 January the world's largest liner, *Queen Mary 2*, sails from Southampton on her maiden voyage.
	Grain Terminal at Berth 47 closes.
2005	King George V Dry Dock (No.7), the last available dry dock in Southampton, is taken out of use.
	Second multi-deck car terminal opens.
2006	Royal Caribbean's *Freedom of the Seas* (160,000 GT) arrives at Southampton on 29 April. With her tonnage she becomes the world's biggest cruise ship.
	City Cruise terminal is enlarged to take Royal Caribbean's *Independence of the Seas*.
2007	*Navigator of the Seas* is in Southampton for cruise season.
	Cunard's cruise ship, *Queen Victoria*, arrives in the port.
2008	Royal Caribbean's *Independence of the Seas* is named in Southampton, sailing from Berth 101, City Cruise Terminal.
	New P&O *Ventura* arrives in the P&O home port.
	Norwegian Cruise Line's *Norwegian Jade* (93,502 GT) arrives for the cruise season, and introduces 'freestyle cruising'.
2009	New Ocean Terminal opens on Berth 46 and Celebrity's *Equinox* (122,000 GT) visits the port.
2010	P&O *Azura (116,000 GT)* and Celebrity *Eclipse* (122,000 GT) are named in April, and *Queen Elizabeth* (90,400 GT) in October.

BIBLIOGRAPHY

Booklets
150 years of Cunard 1840–1990 – Official souvenir history of the Cunard line
Cunard, Queen Victoria – limited edition, Newsquest Southern, 2007
Cunard, Queen Mary 2 – Tour guide
Cunard, Introducing Queen Mary 2, The Greatest Ocean Liner of our Time
Cunard, Triumph of a Great Tradition – Official souvenir history of the Cunard Line
Oriana – Official naming ceremony programme
Southampton Docks Booklet – British Transport Commission, 1952
Southampton Docks Booklet – Gateway to Britain, British Transport Commission
Southampton Docks Booklet – Southern Railway
Southampton Docks Centenary Booklet – 12 October 1938, Southern Railway
Southampton Docks Handbook, 1929 – Southern Railway
Southampton Docks, Official Sailing List and Shipping Guide – June 1926. S.R
Southampton Docks, Official Sailing List and Shipping Guide – June 1953. DIWE

Books
Bonsor N.R.P. *North Atlantic Seaway*, T. Stephenson & Sons Ltd, 1955
Braynard, Frank O. & Miller, William H. *Fifty Famous Liners 1*, Patrick Stephens Ltd, 1982
Braynard, Frank O. & Miller, William H. *Fifty Famous Liners 2*, Patrick Stephens Ltd, 1985
Braynard, Frank O. & Miller, William H. *Fifty Famous Liners 3*, Patrick Stephens Ltd, 1987
Cartwright, Roger & Harvey, Clive *Cruise Britannia*, The History Press, 2004.
Crabb, Brian James *In Harm's Way: HMS Kenya Second World War Cruiser*, Paul Watkins, 1998
Dawson, Philip *The Liner, Retrospective & Renaissance*, Conway, 2007
De Kerbrech, Richard P. and Williams, David *Cunard White Star Liners of the 1930s*, Conway, 1988
Deeson, A.F.L. *An Illustrated History of Steamships*, Spurbooks Ltd, 1976
Ellery, David *RMS Queen Mary: 101 Questions and Answers*, Conway, 2006
Emmons, Frederick *The Atlantic Liners 1925 to 1970*, David & Charles, Newton Abbot, 1972
Faith, Nicholas *Classic Ships*, Motorbooks International, 1996
Fox, Stephen *Transatlantic: Samuel Cunard, Isambard Brunel and the Great Atlantic Liners* Perennial, 2004
Gregor, Arthur *The SS Great Britain* The Macmillan Press, 1971
Hamilton, Keith *The Great Liners: Southampton Ships Past & Present*, Daily Echo Publications, 2009
Harris, C.J. & Inpen, Brian D. *Mailships of the Union-Castle Line*, Patrick Stephens Ltd, 1994
Hope, Bob *Don't Shoot, It's Only Me*, Macmillan London Ltd, 1990
Howard Bailey, Chris *Down the Burma Road: Work and Leisure for the Below-Deck Crew of the Queen Mary (1947–1967)*, Oral History Team, Southampton, 1994
Howarth, David and Howarth, Stephen *The Story of P&O*, Weidenfeld and Nicholson, 1986
Hutchings, David F. *QE2*, Kingfisher Railway Production, 1988
Hutchings, David F. *RMS Queen Mary*, Kingfisher Railway Production, 1986
Hyslop, Donald, Forsyth, Alistair and Jemima, Sheila *Titanic Voices*, Southampton Oral History Unit, 1994
Leonard, Alan, Barker, Rodney *A Maritime History of Southampton*, Ensign Publications 1989
Marcus, Geoffrey *The Maiden Voyage*, Unwin Hyman Limited, 1988
McCart, Neil *Atlantic Liners of the Cunard Line*, Patrick Stephens Ltd, 1990
McCart, Neil *P&O's Canberra*, Kingfisher Railway Productions, 1989
Miller, William H. *The First Great Ocean Liners*, Dover Publications, 1984
Miller, William H. *Under the Red Ensign*, The History Press, 2008
Petty Officer Price, Harry *The Royal Tour, 1901* Webb & Bower, 1980
Rabson, Stephen *P&O in the Falklands*, Published by P&O, 1982
Ransome-Wallis, P. *Merchant Ship Panorama*, Ian Allen Ltd, 1980
Robins, Nick *The Decline and Revival of the British Passenger Fleet*, Colourpoint Books, 2001
Roussel, Mike *The Story of Southampton Docks*, Breedon Books, 2009
Simpson, Colin *The Lusitania*, Little, Brown, 1973
Ward, Douglas *Complete Guide to Cruising and Cruise Ships*, Berlitz Publishing, 2010
Williams, David L. *Docks and Ports: 1 Southampton*, Ian Allen Ltd, 1984
Wills, Elspeth *The Fleet 1840–2008: Cunard*, The Open Agency, 2004 (2007 updated edition)
Wills, Elspeth *Queen Mary 2, Book of Comparisons*, The Open Agency, 2003
Woodman, Richard *The History of the Ship*, Conway Maritime Press, 1997

INDEX

INDEX OF SHIPS